# Incarnate Grace:

*Perspectives on the Ministry
of Catholic Health Care*

**EDITED BY FR. CHARLES BOUCHARD, OP, S.T.D.**

CHA.
Catholic Health Association
of the United States

Library of Congress Cataloguing-in-Publication Data
Bouchard, Charles E., Editor

1. Theology of health care
2. Catholic health care, United States
3. Catholic identity
4. Leadership formation

© Copyright 2017 The Catholic Health Association of the United States
4455 Woodson Road, St. Louis, Mo. 63134-3797

ISBN 978-0-87125-105-3

To order copies, or obtain ordering
information, please contact CHA Service
Center at (800) 230-7823.

---

The Saint John's Bible images in this publication were used with
permission from Saint John's University, Collegeville, Minnesota, USA.
All rights reserved. This handwritten illuminated Bible for the 21st
century was created to ignite the spiritual imagination of people around
the world and to give a voice to the poor and the sick. A number of
Catholic Health Association members have worked with Saint John's to
bring this work of Sacred Art to communities throughout North America
and the world.

If you are interested in learning more about the programs available
to Catholic Health Association members, contact Saint John's at
sjbheritage@csbsju.edu or call (320) 363-3209.

# CONTENTS

## FOREWORD

*Most Reverend Robert N. Lynch, D.D.*

## INTRODUCTION                                                                3

Incarnating Caritas
*M. Therese Lysaught, Ph.D.*

## I.  THEOLOGY AND HEALTH CARE                                                21

1.1  Health Care and the Response of the Triune God                          22
     *Neil Ormerod, D. Theol.*

1.2  Christology and the Essence of Catholic Health Care                      38
     *Conor M. Kelly, Ph.D.*

1.3  Interpretation of Healing Narratives in the Bible                        56
     *Fr. Sean Charles Martin, S.T.D.*

## II. THE PERSON AND HEALTH CARE                                             83

2.1  Who Counts as a Person?                                                  84
     *Daniel J. Daly, Ph.D.*

2.2  God's Presence in Our Suffering                                         102
     *Fr. Robin Ryan, CP, Ph.D.*

2.3  Catholic Health Care's Ministry to the Future                          122
     *Fr. Thomas F. O'Meara, OP, Ph.D.*

## III. SACRAMENTS AND LITURGY IN HEALTH CARE                    143

3.1  The Transformative Power of Liturgy in Catholic Health Care          144
     *Sr. Catherine Vincie, RSHM, Ph.D.*

3.2  Lessons from History on Institutional Sacramentality                 152
     *Fr. David Gentry-Akin, S.T.D.*

3.3  Eucharist as the Heart of the Ministry                               168
     *Darren M. Henson, Ph.D.*

3.4  Sacraments for the Sick and Dying                                    186
     *James M. Schellman, M.A.*

## IV. THE CHURCH AND HEALTH CARE                                195

4.1  The Meaning of Ministry in Health Care                               196
     *Fr. Charles Bouchard, OP, S.T.D.*

4.2  Canonical Dimensions of Ecclesiology:                                212
     Catholic Health Care, the Bishop and Sponsors
     *Barbara Anne Cusack, J.C.D., Fr. Francis Morrisey, OMI, Ph.D., J.C.D.,*
     *and Sr. Sharon Holland, IHM, J.C.D.*

4.3  Whose Ministry Is It?                                                230
     The Role of the Laity in the Story of Catholic Health Care
     *Zeni Fox, Ph.D.*

4.4  Theology of Institutions                                             250
     *Richard Gaillardetz, Ph.D.*

## CONCLUSION                                                     269

Formation: Catholic Theology Alive in Catholic Health Care                270
*Celeste DeSchryver Mueller, D.Min.*

## AUTHORS' BIOGRAPHIES                                           291

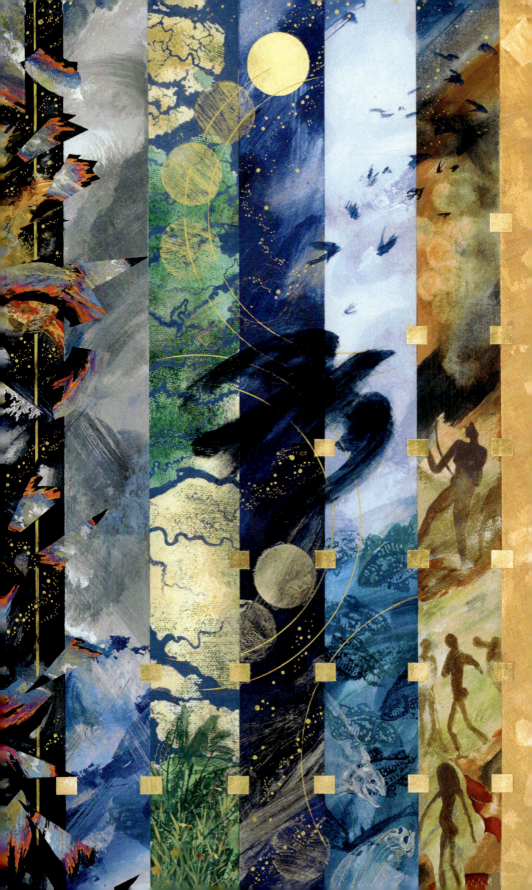

# FOREWORD

There are few intersections in church life where ecclesial polity and policy, doctrine and discussion, and practice and performance converge than in Catholic health care in the present moment. The discussion which surrounds the religious and ethical directives of the church and delivery of Gospel mandated services to those ill and suffering is ever more lively, focused and critically important. New technologies and insights hitherto both unimagined and unforeseen require theologians and medical practitioners to engage in constant dialogue.

*Incarnate Grace: Perspectives on the Ministry of Catholic Health Care*, edited by Father Charles Bouchard, OP, is both timely and very useful in assembling the insights and perspectives of those in the church's health care ministry in a format both inclusive and helpful. It can easily become the desktop reference for the deepest reflections in this present moment for all the major health care issues of concern to the church and its particular and targeted ministry to the dying and the ill. There will remain few major moments of convergence and occasional conflict left untouched by this helpful publication.

Like most Catholic bishops, I was not well prepared as a faith leader of a local diocesan community to engage in major matters surrounding both the delivery of service and the theological and biblical reasons for doing so. Had this compendium been available to me, I would have been both grateful and enlightened. I recommend it to the entire church community from its leadership through those deeply and daily involved in the ministry as more than just a starting point. I wish to thank each of its authors for their contributions and its editor(s) for assembling such helpful analyses. It may well become a ***vade mecum*** for one of the most important of the church's ministries.

## MOST REVEREND ROBERT N. LYNCH, D.D.

*Bishop Emeritus of Saint Petersburg, Florida*
*June 29, 2017, The Solemnity of SS. Peter and Paul*

# INCARNATING
# CARITAS

# INTRODUCTION:
## INCARNATING CARITAS

M. Therese Lysaught, Ph.D.
*Professor and Associate Dean, Institute of Pastoral Studies*
*Neiswanger Institute for Bioethics, Stritch School of Medicine*
*Loyola University Chicago*

I F YOU HAVE PICKED UP THIS BOOK, YOU MOST LIKELY serve as one of almost three-quarters of a million people working in Catholic health care in the U.S. It might be worth taking a moment to appreciate the scope of this shared endeavor. In January 2017, The Catholic Health Association paints a vibrant picture of this dynamic ministry:

+ 132 critical access hospitals
+ 258 trauma centers
+ 156 indigent care clinics
+ 527 hospitals providing palliative care
+ 355 hospitals with obstetrics services
+ 1,614 continuing care facilities,
    85% of which are in urban areas, and 15% in rural areas
+ 523,040 full-time employees
+ 216,487 part-time employees.

With nearly 5 million admissions annually, these facilities care for approximately 1 in 6 patients nationwide every day, including over 1 million Medicaid discharges. Catholic hospitals host more than 100 million outpatient visits, 20 million emergency room visits, and bring 527,000 babies into the world annually.

Thus, as the nation's largest group of not-for-profit health care providers, the Catholic health ministry cares for people and communities across the United States, giving special attention to those who are poor, underserved and most vulnerable, transforming "hurt into hope."[1] And you are a part of that.

Yet, the landscape of what it means to identify as a religiously affiliated institution in the 21st century is in flux. There are a number of recent legal cases that signal troubling shifts in attitudes toward the role of faith-based organizations. These include the well-known Hobby Lobby case, regarding exemption from regulations on contraception by a closely held corporation;[2] Zubik v. Burwell, brought by a number of organizations, also about the contraceptive mandate;[3] and finally, a series of class-action suits filed against Catholic and other faith-based health systems regarding long-standing religious exemptions from ERISA regulations for "church plans."[4] In addition to these cases, Catholic health care is under constant surveillance by groups such as the American Civil Liberties Union and MergerWatch who worry that religious exemptions infringe on civil rights or the quality of health care itself.[5]

1   Catholic Health Association, "U.S. Catholic Health Care — 2017." Accessed at: https://www. chausa.org/docs/default-source/default-document-library/cha_2017_miniprofile.pdf?sfvrsn=0
2   *Burwell vs. Hobby Lobby Stores, Inc.*: Accessed at: https://www.supremecourt.gov/ opinions/13pdf/13-354_olp1.pdf.
3   Timothy Jost, "Zubik v. Burwell Briefs Explore Potential Compromise (Update)," *Health Affairs Blog* (April 13, 2016). Accessed at: http://healthaffairs.org/blog/2016/04/13/zubik-v-burwell-briefs-explore-potential-compromise/.
4   Julie Minda, "Dozens of Faith-Based Providers Targeted in Pension Law Suits," *Catholic Health World*, October 1, 2016. Accessed at: https://www.chausa.org/publications/catholic-health-world/article/october-1-2016/dozens-of-faith-based-providers-targeted-in-pension-lawsuits and Emma Green, "The Supreme Court Case that Could Bankrupt Religious Schools and Hospitals," *The Atlantic* (December 12, 2016). Accessed at: https://www.theatlantic.com/ politics/archive/2016/12/advocate-health-care-erisa/510218/. This case was decided in favor of religiously affiliated hospitals by a Supreme Court ruling on June 5, 2015. See *Advocate Health Care Network v. Stapleton*, U.S., Nos. 16 – 74; 16 – 86; 16 – 258, 6/5/17.
5   American Civil Liberties Union, "Health Care Denied." Accessed at: https://www.aclu.org/ feature/health-care-denied. See response from Catholic Health Association: https://www. chausa.org/newsroom/news-releases/2016/05/09/catholic-health-association-responds-to-aclu-merger-watch-report.

These developments reflect what Richard Gaillardetz identifies in his chapter in this volume as "the contemporary anti-institutionalist impulse," "a sweeping cultural distrust of public institutions" rooted in an increasingly atomized individualism (252). They also reflect increased animosities toward the public practice of religious identity. On one side, there appears to be a campaign to eliminate the *practice* of religious identity in any venue that interfaces with government, professional, or public spheres. On the other side, strident claims about the violation of religious liberty are made by those committed to practicing religious identity in aggressively visible ways but who reduce religious identity to what amounts to a few issues almost exclusively related to sexuality and reproduction while for all appearances ignoring broad swaths of Christian religious convictions and commitments. Ironically, driving these conflicts is a shared commitment to the severing of any relationship between religion and government. Both sides seek a purity — whether purely secularist or purely religious — that requires faith to be completely siloed or privatized. Both sides create difficulties for those with more traditional understandings of the collaboration for the common good and who seek to advance the vision of the Second Vatican Council of the church *in* the world.

Yet questions of public policy are only one side of the coin. These developments also raise familiar questions for Catholic organizations: What does it mean for us to be a *Catholic* health care institution? What does it mean to be a part of the *ministry* of Catholic health care? What are the differences between a secular, non-profit health system and a Catholic health system? As these cases and the public posture of many religious leaders suggest, is religious identity simply about a few discrete practices that we *do not* do (e.g., contraception, abortion, physician-assisted suicide, and certain reproductive technologies)? Or does our Catholic identity bring anything distinctive to *how* we approach end-of-life care, population health, emergency health services, and behavioral health — perhaps even the entire way we think about promoting health and caring for the sick?

*Incarnate Grace: Perspectives on the Ministry of Catholic Health Care*, clearly argues the latter. What is more, it pushes the conversation deeper. It seeks to plumb not only what *actions* make (or should make) Catholic health care distinctive; it seeks to lift up what drives, empowers, and gives shape to those actions, to help us to understand the *why* as well as the *what*. It suggests, following the heart of the Christian tradition, that *action* is rooted in *identity*, that *what we do* should flow from *who we are*. Only once we understand who we are — individually and corporately — can we authentically discern how to respond to the evolving landscape in which we work and whether we are living our identity consistently across all our actions.

As such, it continues the work begun in *Caritas in Communion: Theological Foundations of Catholic Health Care*.[6] *Caritas in Communion* (hereafter CIC) drew deeply from the lived wisdom of those who work in Catholic health care to sound out key theological convictions that shape, sustain, and motivate the ministry. It is humbling and a great honor to find such an esteemed group of Catholic theologians expanding on the components of the vision outlined there, bringing additional dimensions of the tradition into the conversation, and raising as-yet-unanswered questions.

In doing so, *Incarnate Grace* provides three important resources for people who work in Catholic health care — whether they are Catholic or not — as they embark on the journey of exploring Catholic identity. First, it provides new *resources for deeper reflection* on the theological convictions named in *Caritas in Communion*. Christology, sacramentality, church, sponsorship and more are each fleshed out here in chapter length. These chapters are but introductions to deep wells of theological scholarship, but they bring each topic to life in accessible ways, drawing connections between these theological convictions and the day-to-day realities of Catholic health care. Hopefully, they will pique your interest and draw you to delve further into the topics discussed here.

Second, as I suggested in CIC and as Robin Ryan notes explicitly in his chapter, we all work with *implicit theologies*. We all have implicit understandings of what we mean when we hear the terms Jesus, church, ministry, suffering, God, and more. CIC and *Incarnate Grace* provide

---

6   M. Therese Lysaught, *Caritas in Communion: Theological Foundations of Catholic Health Care*. Catholic Health Association, 2014. Available at: https://www.chausa.org/store/products/ product?id=2828.

companions for those in Catholic health who ask themselves: What is my implicit theology? Where does it come from? How does it play out in my day-to-day life, especially in ways that I have not heretofore recognized? What are its limitations and how might I enhance it through greater reflection and shared conversation with my colleagues?

Finally, from the *Ethical and Religious Directives for Catholic Health Care Services* to the mission statements of most health systems, we know that those who work in Catholic health care continue to advance Jesus' healing ministry. A repeated theme echoes throughout *Incarnate Grace*: that the heart of Catholic identity is, in Sean Martin's phrase, "*the imitation of the divine.*" To incarnate grace is to embody in our actions the work of God in the world.

This is no small task. But if undertaken by three-quarters of a million people — that alone would change health care in the U.S.! As a starting point for reflecting on this mission, allow me to outline the ways in which *Incarnate Grace* elaborates on the introduction to the theological foundations of Catholic health care identified in *Caritas in Communion*. I also hope to identify ways in which it expands that vision to incorporate additional theological convictions, and close with further questions elicited by this study and the ongoing ministry of Catholic health care. Along the way, a refrain will be: What is your implicit theology? How are we called to imitate the divine as individuals and, more strangely, as health care *institutions*?

## ELABORATING CARITAS IN COMMUNION

CIC was the outcome of a year-long collaborative listening session designed to hear the theology at the heart of the Catholic health care ministry. At the heart of this foundation, it noted, is *caritas*, God's essential nature as love and grace. God's *caritas* is manifest in, with and through Jesus and the Holy Spirit — the Trinitarian communion. From this communion emerges a sacramental *caritas*-shaped church, a communion from which baptized Christians bring *caritas* into the world through institutional ministry and witness to the faith. To reprise:

At the outermost level — the level of visible behaviors — we find
the stories of the founders of Catholic health care and the principles
of Catholic social thought. These are the tangible manifestations —
the mountain ranges, if you will — of the topography of Catholic
identity. Immediately undergirding these are the theological concepts
of ministry and evangelization, the grounding for both Catholic
social thought and the work of religious communities. Undergirding
ministry and evangelization, we find the fundamental doctrines of
sacramentality and ecclesiology, both of which are necessarily rooted
in Christology — the person and work of Christ. And at the center
of it all, at the heart of Catholic identity in Catholic health care, is
charity or caritas — the fundamental theological reality: that God is
love, that God so loved the world…. God's essence — revealed in the
Trinity, in every action of God toward humanity and the world —
is caritas in communion. (CIC 45)

In painting the overview of this framework, CIC offered brief snapshots
of key theological convictions, noting that they are dynamically
interrelated. Each component mutually shapes our understanding
of the others. *Incarnate Grace* delves more deeply into many of these
components, illuminating these interconnections, and addressing a number
of the "questions for further exploration" named in CIC. Specifically,
*Incarnate Grace* deepens the conversation on God, Jesus, ministry, church,
sacramentality, and sponsorship.

## God

Neil Ormerod elaborates on God's Trinitarian nature, building on the
notion of *caritas* or grace-experienced-as-love-and-gift as the starting point
for the Christian life. Through a Trinitarian spirituality of the theological
virtues — love (charity, *caritas*), faith, and hope — he fleshes out the
interrelationships among the Persons of the Trinity, Father, Son and Spirit.
In so doing, he suggests practical ways in which understanding God as
Trinity shapes the work of Catholic health care. It calls us to *see* God's
grace as potentially present at each and every moment of our journey with
patients and families, no matter how dark or difficult those moments might

be. It calls us to *say* "Yes" to this gift of God's *caritas* when we encounter it. And it calls us to *embody* or imitate God's *caritas* and a countercultural hope in our encounters with others. Each reader should stop and reflect: "how does this understanding of God articulated in CIC and *Incarnate Grace* interface with my own implicit understanding of who God is?"

## Jesus

The Second Person of this Trinitarian God is the Son, God Incarnate as Jesus Christ. CIC noted that Catholic health care explicitly draws its identity from Christology, seeing its reason-for-being as continuing the healing ministry of Jesus represented in the Gospels. CIC made clear that Catholic health care needs to articulate a more balanced Christology, one that understands Jesus both "from below" — the work of the fully human Jesus depicted in the Gospels — but also "from above" — attending to Jesus' divine nature (CIC 25). Ormerod provides a more in-depth account of Christology from above.

Conor Kelly's study complements Ormerod's by enriching the traditional understanding of Christology from below. Gesturing toward the social, political and economic dimensions of Jesus' context, he shifts standard understandings of Jesus as healer — one who physically touched those considered religious and social outcasts and one who attended primarily to those who were poor — into language drawn from liberation theology. Liberation theology helps us to understand more clearly the *how* of Jesus' healing — that this work was rooted first in the practice of *accompaniment* that reflects the deeper theological reality of God's solidarity with us, especially in our suffering and brokenness, incarnated in Jesus. As such, Christology provides a non-negotiable model for the practice of Catholic health care that we are called to imitate and embody.

## Ministry and Church

CIC drew on important work done by Fr. Charles Bouchard and Zeni Fox to begin to clarify the question: What does it mean to refer to Catholic health care as a ministry? In *Incarnate Grace*, we hear directly from

Bouchard and Fox, as they reprise that material and take it to the next step. Bouchard takes up a question posed in CIC: In what sense can *institutions* be considered as ministries? This is not just a hypothetical question — it is at the heart of the legal cases outlined earlier. But as Bouchard makes clear, the answer is still evolving, complicated by ecclesiastical reservations about lay ministry and pragmatic aspects of Catholic health care, from financing to collaborative endeavors.

Fox looks at this issue from the angle of history. She highlights the stories of St. Vincent's Hospital in New York City and St. Michael's Hospital in Newark, New Jersey. Her history demonstrates what the richness of an ecclesial, institutional ministry looked like in an earlier era — a ministry that comprised a rich collaboration of religious, lay persons, and non-Catholic collaborators. These stories, read through the lens of the Second Vatican Council, provide a framework for self-reflection for both bishops and leaders of health systems to enrich their own vision of Catholic health care as a ministry.

Fox's inductive description of the church-in-action is nicely complemented by Richard Gaillardetz's nuanced discussion of what comprises an institution or organization and the complex attitudes toward institutions in the U.S. context, even among Catholics. He challenges those in leadership to ask themselves: What do we visualize when we hear the word institution or organization? What are the "interlocking systems" that structure our organizations? Which systems are invisible to us? Where do they come from? Who do they benefit and who do they exclude or oppress? What fundamental visions or narratives do they embody?

## Sacramentality

Catholic institutions ought to differ from other institutions in a key way. Using a historical narrative similar to Fox's, but focusing on the Sisters of Charity of the Incarnate Word, David Gentry-Akin shows how the work of these sisters is sacramental. According to Gaillardetz, sacramentality is the foundational "interlocking system" for Catholic institutions. The church itself, he notes, is understood to be a sacrament, the ongoing embodiment in the world of the Body, presence and work of Jesus Christ. Catholic health care, as a ministry of the church, shares in that sacramental identity. As I noted in CIC:

> Daily, the sacraments renew the church. They ground the ministerial vocations of the faithful, seeking to transform us into the likeness of Christ so we can bear that likeness into the world. Both Catholic persons and Catholic institutions — specifically Catholic health care — have a vocation to embody this incarnational and participatory sacramentality. Catholics hold that the sacraments truly make Christ present. Therefore, Catholic persons and institutions are called to incarnate, embody, truly make Christ present in the world, enabled by the grace that comes through their participation in the sacramental life of the church. (CIC 40)

*Incarnate Grace* immerses readers in this dimension of Catholic health care in three essays. The chapters by Catherine Vincie, Darren Henson, and Jim Schellman, together with Gaillardetz, elaborate the recursive relationship between Eucharist, Viaticum, liturgy, and the church's sacramental nature. These chapters outline the theoretical and theological vision behind the understandings of ministry discussed by Fox and Bouchard. And they make clear why Christology (our understanding of who Jesus is) matters. For in the transformative power of the liturgy we meet the foundation of the claim that our work is to imitate the divine.

## Sponsorship

This responsibility is personal and corporate, exercised in communion as church. What are some of the parameters of this communion? *Incarnate Grace* provides a helpful primer on the complicated and evolving canonical notion of sponsorship. Starting from the Second Vatican Council's re-grounding of lay ministry in Baptism, Barbara Anne Cusack, Fr. Francis Morrisey and Sr. Sharon Holland complement the chapters by Bouchard, Fox, and Gaillardetz, tracing the ministry of the laity from its individual starting point through public (or ministerial) juridic persons, in communion with diocesan bishops. They also distill for readers the essential components of canon law for Catholic health care.

## EXPANDING THE THEOLOGICAL VISION

In these ways, *Incarnate Grace* elaborates on the theological foundations of Catholic *identity* outlined in *Caritas in Communion*. But it goes beyond that framework, introducing additional theological topics relevant to the *work* of Catholic health care — Scripture, the human person, suffering, and death.

*Scripture*

One of these is the foundational role of Scripture which infuses the day-to-day work of Catholic health care — a reflection on a lectionary reading opening a meeting, a psalm being read by a chaplain at a patient's bedside, a scripture passage artistically gracing a visitor waiting room. What is more, historically, Catholic health care has been catalyzed and shaped by the Scriptures, either in the way it formed the sisters and other religious who cared for the sick via their daily prayer of the Liturgy of the Hours or by the way the Gospel witness of Jesus' life and ministry informed their mission.

Although prayerful engagement with scripture is necessary, Fr. Sean Martin reminds us that more is required, that "the hard work of exegesis is...essential to the task of constructing a theology of health care." He demonstrates how exegesis — going deeper into the texts using the tools of scripture scholars — illuminates deeper meanings of foundational narratives of healing from the Hebrew Scriptures and the New Testament. He lifts up key scriptural themes from across the entire corpus that should help shape our understanding what it means to imitate the divine in Catholic health care. His addendum on "Varieties of Biblical Interpretation" is a helpful aid for a more critical and constructive engagement with the Word of God. It will help both Catholic and non-Catholic leaders understand how their approaches to Scripture differ and complement one another.

## *The Human Person*

*Incarnate Grace* also extends the CIC framework with a rich theological reflection on the human person. The triad of essays by Daniel Daly, Fr. Robin Ryan, and Fr. Thomas O'Meara introduces the topic of *theological anthropology* which is jargon for "the understanding of the human person." Daly shows how our understanding of the human person is informed by our prior understandings of who God is, who Jesus is, and what the church is. Consequently, a Catholic or Christian understanding of the human person differs in important ways from the anthropology that shapes much of U.S. culture, particularly around issues in medicine. Those who serve on ethics committees should reflect on the extent to which their thinking is shaped by these culturally dominant anthropologies and how a theological understanding of the human person might change how we think about clinical ethics. It might change how clinical staff think about and deliver patient care, e.g., am I treating a body or a person? For senior leaders, it might change how we think about our various "markets": Are they only customers, a payer mix or a revenue source, or human persons in need? Daly also demonstrates how Christian thinking about the human person evolves over time, as the work and life of Christians in the world encounters new ideas, philosophies and cultures, bringing these into conversation with central theological convictions. Yet in the end, we find that at the heart of our understanding of the human person is *caritas*. Made in the image and likeness of God, we are called to honor that in others and to embody it ourselves.

## *Suffering*

A central challenge to the whole theological edifice, though, is the pain, loss and suffering that bring people into our health care facilities. How can this God of *caritas* and solidarity also be the God of so much tragedy, diminishment and death? In these situations, Fr. Robin Ryan asks how we should speak about God in light of suffering and evil. He notes that we all carry around implicit theologies of suffering — some helpful, some unhelpful, some inconsistent or muddled. A key task for those of us who work in health care is to reflect on our own implicit theologies, to make them explicit, to understand where they come from and how they are informed by other theological commitments. Ryan opens a conversation about that process — a process which is not easy and cannot be completed in a single session but rather must extend over time. The scriptural witness points to a God of compassion who accompanies us in our suffering. As such, we find a model for those who work in Catholic health care — a response of compassionate accompaniment.

## Death

The companion of much of the pain, illness, and suffering encountered in Catholic health care is death. But while it is a constant in our work, it often becomes a reality which-shall-not-be-named in our culture, parish congregations and even our hospitals. Fr. Thomas O'Meara provides an *eschatological* perspective as a way to help us explore our implicit theologies of death and the afterlife. Such reflection is crucial for those who work in Catholic health care because too often our care for the patient ends abruptly the moment life ceases. All our patients will die — not necessarily while immediately in our care, but they will. As will we. We accompany many who suffer into the mystery that lies beyond the moment of death. What then? What happens to the human person? What happens to the care provider? How do we carry out our task of compassionate accompaniment in light of the ultimate reality of eternal life?

## ELICITING FURTHER QUESTIONS

*Incarnate Grace* also elicits several questions for further exploration around spiritual formation, evolving ecclesiology, and Catholic social thought.

## Spiritual Formation

How does Catholic health care as church attend to the spiritual formation of all of its associates, both Catholic and non-Catholic? As noted in CIC, "The Christian life is understood as a pilgrimage, a journey in which we grow in virtue and holiness. Such growth necessarily emerges in response to particular persons and situations" (CIC 21). How does Catholic health care nurture growth in holiness?

The sisters and brothers who founded and grew Catholic health care were not, for the most part, trained theologians. They were activists and practitioners. They did not necessarily bring to Catholic health care a robust, explicit and carefully detailed understanding of the theological foundations of the work as articulated above. But they did bring a deep immersion in ongoing practices of spiritual formation, practices in which they continued to engage while they worked in Catholic health care. Practices such as daily prayer, regular worship (perhaps even daily), retreats and spiritual direction informed their day-to-day lives and work. They sought to live the Gospel, to care for the poorest and most marginalized, to witness to the work of Jesus and the church in the world.

The workforce and leadership in Catholic health care have shifted from those in religious life to lay persons — both Catholic and non-Catholic. They often come to the work of Catholic health care with much passion but with little experience of spiritual formation. As Celeste Mueller notes in her chapter, this has given rise to a variety of approaches to ministry leadership formation over the past 20 years. She provides a helpful overview from her experience with one such program, demonstrating how it incorporates many of the topics detailed in *Incarnate Grace* — how "theology" becomes practical. How do we extend formation beyond the limited number of persons in formal programs? How do we blend spiritual formation with effective business leadership? How do we share our theological tradition and our spirituality with associates who do not share our religious beliefs?

A key question to ask within our systems is this: In what ways do Catholic hospitals and systems encourage, nurture and reward the *daily, ongoing, spiritual* formation of its members *as part of the work of health care*? Is this something recommended for associates but on their own time? What would it look like to encourage, nurture and incentivize associates to attend to their own spiritual formation *on work time* — given that it's not something that is directly reimbursable? I am confident that that question gives many readers of this book pause. Does it reveal the ways we prioritize finances over faith or the ways in which we share a discomfort with the public practice of faith beyond carefully circumscribed houses of worship? Surely our founders did not see it that way.

*Evolving Ecclesiology*

It has often been said that praxis precedes theory or, in our case, theology. Historically, the lived realities and experience of the faithful (what some refer to as "first order practice") provide the material upon which theologians reflect. Theology, therefore, is a "second order" activity, reflectively bringing the resources of the tradition to bear on practice of the church in the world, providing insight and guidance to that practice but also gleaning new insights about God and theological realities based on the activity of God among God's people. Practice, then, is the leading edge. It might be true, as Bouchard notes, that "practice and language [have] gotten ahead of theology" (201).

My work in and study of Catholic health care suggests that Catholic health care is — or could be — leading the development of new insights into ecclesiology. Those in the ministry of Catholic health care, catalyzed by the Second Vatican Council, have boldly lived the reality of this mission, identifying problems in our practice of the faith and creating new ecclesiological questions, many of which have yet to be answered.

For example, if we understand Catholic health care as part of a communion as church, we are led to ask: How do our health care institutions interface with other components of the church, particularly parishes? When we speak of "the church," do we mean only the bishops? There seems to be little substantive structural interaction between hospitals and parishes, save sacramental or pastoral visits by priests or a few commissioned parishioners who bring communion to the sick. This has not always been the case, as Zeni Fox makes clear in her history.

As we move toward population health models, strengthening the relationships between hospitals and parishes seems a natural move. It is here that many of our associates receive their spiritual formation and sustenance. Equally, parishes and local congregations include many who will find their ways into our emergency rooms, outpatient clinics, physician's offices, and in-patient beds. As such, parishes can and should serve as key partners for education around ethical issues that plague so many hospitals, especially end-of-life care. And, as systems begin to re-envisage community transformation in ways informed by findings on the social determinants of health, parishes will again be necessary partners in implementing structural social changes designed to promote the wellness and flourishing of all in our communities.

The realities of Catholic health care institutions themselves raises new ecclesiological questions. Unlike parishes and even many other Catholic ministries, health care institutions are religiously pluralistic — in staff, in leadership, in clientele. Many who work in Catholic health care are not baptized, though they may be deeply committed to the mission. Many within health care do understand their work as a ministry, yet they have no official ecclesial standing (CIC 33). Or, as Gaillardetz asks, "How can Catholic health care institutions participate in the sacramentality of the church when they are both led and staffed by many who are themselves not Catholic?" (264). How do we think theologically about non-Catholic — and perhaps, non-baptized — members of sponsor boards, as also discussed in this volume by Bouchard and Cusack, Morrisey and Holland? Such practices raise for the church new and important questions that might push us to come to see new dimensions of the church and to expand our theological understanding of what it means to be involved in this ministry.

## Catholic Social Thought

Catholic health care is deeply committed to the principles of Catholic social thought and has been a major force in helping the church articulate the principles and put them into practice. Threads of this run through the essays in *Incarnate Grace*, and Conor Kelly helpfully brings into the conversation insights from liberation theology.

Important questions remain, however, about how thoroughly Catholic health care is willing to recognize the powerful economic critique voiced in liberation theology. Jesus did not simply accompany the poor; reading the Gospels in the light of liberation theology would also recognize the political and economic context of Jesus' healing practices and reveal the Gospels' critique of these structures. If we read the Gospels through 21st century eyes, we can miss important subtleties that would have been obvious to the original readers. Exegesis is crucially important for unleashing the powerful critique that permeates the Judeo-Christian Scriptures. Scripture scholar Ched Meyers offers such a reading in his book *Binding the Strong Man: A Political Reading of Mark's Story of Jesus* (Orbis, 2008). Myers makes clear that much of the illness experienced by those in Mark's Gospel results from what we could call today the social determinants of health or what liberation theologians and St. John Paul II would call the structures of sin.

Accompanying patients — especially the poor and marginalized — is an important embodiment of the Gospel and Catholic social thought. But liberation theology also presses us to ask: In what ways does the contemporary infrastructure of Catholic health care participate in the structures of sin, the structures of oppression, and invisible structures of violence? Are there ways in which business ventures and market models — with economies of scale, efficiencies, outsourcing, financing and more — are informed more by economic theories that exacerbate racism and income inequality than by the Gospel? What would it look like for Catholic health care to drink deeply from the well of liberation theology? Is Catholic social teaching practiced equally in our system offices as well as in our community clinics?

## GO FORTH TO LOVE AND SERVE THE LORD

I hope this roadmap highlights connections between the chapters that follow and gives you a sense of the dynamic and progressive interplay between theology, Catholic health care and the life of the church. I hope it launches you on a powerful and grace-filled journey of personal and communal reflection and conversation in which you wrestle with yourselves and colleagues about your understandings of who God is, what it means to be engaged in the 2,000-year-long healing ministry of Jesus, and to witness to the presence of God in our world of brokenness and hope. Whether that witness calls you to be a prophetic voice in the public sphere, a sacramental presence at the bedside, or a liberating companion for the poor, our solidarity is empowered by the God who is in solidarity with us and who we are called to imitate as we sojourn in communion as church in the 21st century.

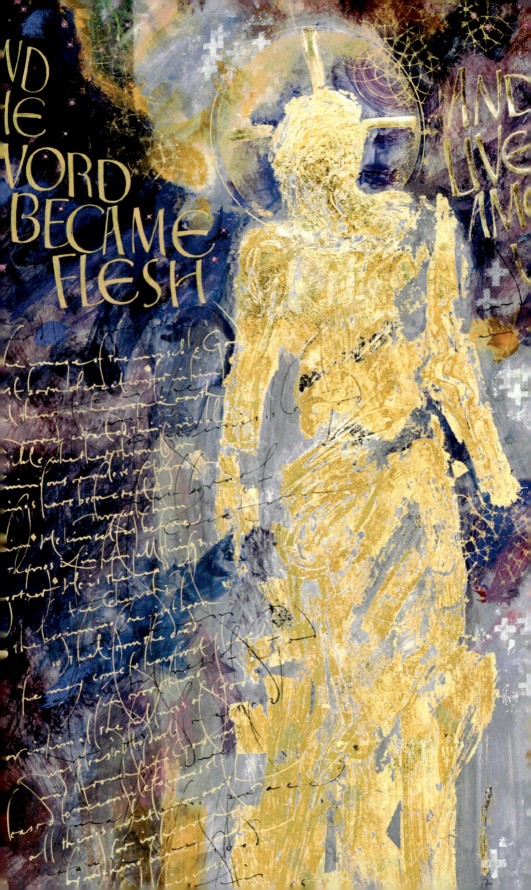

# I

# THEOLOGY AND HEALTH CARE

## CHAPTER SUMMARY

Health care workers are constantly exposed to the problem of
human suffering in their patients and in themselves as they seek
to alleviate suffering and work towards renewed health. The
question is: "Where is God in this suffering?" This chapter argues
that sanctifying grace and the theological virtues of faith, hope
and charity are participations in the four Trinitarian relations.
Through grace, which we live out in faith, hope and charity, God
responds to our human condition in such a way that we manifest
the Trinitarian life. The chapter explores how each of these
elements contributes to God's response to suffering.

# 1.1 HEALTH CARE AND
# THE RESPONSE OF THE TRIUNE GOD

Neil Ormerod, D.Theol.
*Professor of Theology*
*Australian Catholic University*

HEALTH CARE WORKERS ENCOUNTER THEIR fellow human beings in some of the most difficult and life-changing circumstances imaginable, facing life and death decisions, at times of great sadness and sometimes of great joy. For suffering patients, medical staff can be a source of both hope and anxiety on their human journey. No one can avoid the cycle of birth and death with its attendant sufferings and illnesses. We know that life has a beginning, middle, and an end, but when we are confronted with the realities of suffering and death it often comes as something of a surprise. We ask: Why me? Why now? What's happening to my body, to me?

Catholic health organizations are called on to reflect the mission of the church, to be the presence of Christ to a suffering person. Since we know He came "that we may have life, and have it to the full" (Jn 10:10), there is a challenge and difficulty for those who work in health care: How and where do we find the fullness of life in this time of anxiety, suffering and doubt? Where is God for us in the here and now of this person's life? These questions arise not just for the patients in need of care, but also for the physicians, nurses and other caregivers who journey with their patients and witness the sufferings of others.

## A TRINITARIAN SPIRITUALITY

The Trinity is central and mysterious to most Christians. As Christians
we may be familiar with a range of biblical quotations that make some
reference to the three divine persons in one way or another, for example,
2 Cor 13:13 "May the grace of the Lord Jesus Christ, and the love of God,
and the fellowship of the Holy Spirit be with you all." Or we may have
heard the Nicene Creed proclaimed, "I believe in one God, the Father
almighty ..." and wondered what it is all about. In the last 50 years or so
there has been an explosion of interest in the theology of the Trinity, much
of it focusing on the notion of the Trinity as a community of love.[1] One
approach seeks to relate our experience of God as Trinitarian with the
practice of theological virtues of faith, hope and charity, grounded in the
life of grace.[2] I believe these virtues are central to a Trinitarian response
to the context of Catholic health care.

## GROUNDED IN GRACE

The starting point for the Christian life is found in God's grace. God
is the one who takes the initiative, entering into our human condition
and revealing Himself to be a God of profound and unending love.
To experience that grace is to experience God's love. As St. Paul puts it:
"God's love has been poured into our hearts through the Holy Spirit that
has been given to us" (Rom 5:5). St. John further clarifies the nature
of this experience: "In this is love, not that we loved God but that he
loved us" (1 Jn 4:10).

The experience of grace is first and foremost an experience of love through
the gift of the Holy Spirit poured into our hearts. This personal presence
of the Holy Spirit represents our first encounter with God as triune. This

---

1   A seminal work here is John Zizioulas, *Being as Communion: Studies in Personhood and the
    Church* (Crestwood, N.Y.: St. Vladimir's Seminary Press, 1985).

2   In arguing this I am following in particular the lead of the work of Robert M. Doran, *The
    Trinity in History: Missions and Processions* (University of Toronto Press, 2012). For a more
    approachable account, see Neil Ormerod, "The Metaphysics of Holiness: Created Participation
    in the Divine Nature," *Irish Theological Quarterly* 79, no. 1 (2014): 68 – 82.; "A (Non
    Communio) Trinitarian Ecclesiology: Grounded in Grace: Lived in Faith, Hope and Charity,"
    *Theological Studies* 76, no. 3 (2015): 448 – 67.

presence may be accompanied by powerful emotions in us, as witnessed in various charismatic and Pentecostal communities, or as a continuous undercurrent in life like the gentle breeze that Elijah encountered on the mountain (1 Kgs 19:11-13). God gives us the gift of the divine Spirit which makes us loveable and the recipient of love. Grace is not something we earn from God, nor something we can manipulate out of God; it is pure gift, unearned, undeserved, unjustified except as a sign of divine generosity.

Theologically, this gift of the Spirit relates us to the divine procession of the Spirit. As we say in the Creed, the Spirit "proceeds from the Father and the Son."[3] In the life of grace the Father and Son together breathe the Spirit into our hearts. This is the personal identity of the Spirit whose very being is this relationship to Father and Son.[4] Theologically, we hold that while we feel this presence of the Spirit in our hearts, it is normally mediated to us through the signs and symbols of the sacraments and liturgy. As St. Augustine noted, sacraments are visible signs of invisible grace. In addition to the seven sacraments identified by the church, genuine sacramentality is possible in our human encounters through expressions of care and concern shared between us. As Blessed John Henry Newman reflected in his personal motto, "Heart speaks to heart."

## CHARITY — DOING THE WORK OF THE FATHER AND SON IN BUILDING THE KINGDOM

In addition to the profound insights St. Augustine and St. Thomas Aquinas gave us in their writings, there is something else to consider. If the Spirit dwells in our hearts through grace, and the Spirit is a relation to the Father and Son who together pour the Spirit out for us, then in a certain sense, not only the Spirit, but the Father and Son also dwell in our hearts. As St. Thomas Aquinas notes, the whole Trinity is present in grace.[5] As Jesus

---

3   This is the classical Western formulation, originating in Augustine but incorporated into the Nicene Creed in the West in about the 8th century. While it is not accepted in the Eastern Orthodox tradition, it is firmly within the Catholic tradition, through its creedal incorporation.

4   Technically, Aquinas describes the persons as subsistent relations. The persons are their relationships to the other persons. These relations are captured in the two processions, of the Son from the Father, and the Spirit from the Father and the Son.

5   Aquinas, *Summa Theologica*, Ia Q. 43, Art. 5.

states, "Those who love me will keep my word, and my Father will love them, and *we will come to them and make our home with them*" (Jn 14:23), significantly spoken in the context of "Holy Spirit, whom the Father will send in my name" (Jn 14: 26). How then might we think of the presence together of Father and Son as those who breathe the Spirit into our hearts?[6]

Following the suggestion of Robert Doran, we may think of this in what the tradition called the habit or virtue of charity. Here we can take a lead from John's Gospel where he speaks of the "work" of the Father and the Son. For example: "Jesus said to them, 'My food is to do the will of him who sent me and to complete his work.'" (Jn 4:34); "But if I do them, even though you do not believe me, believe the works, so that you may know and understand that the Father is in me and I am in the Father." (Jn 10:38). While the language of the Synoptic Gospels is quite different, we can identify this notion of the work of the Father and Son as equivalent to the ways in which Jesus talks about the Kingdom of God as constituting his mission here with us.

Our ability to contribute to the building of God's kingdom is grounded in grace. When we know ourselves to be profoundly loved, we in our turn are able to "love God with all our heart, mind, and strength and your neighbor as yourself" (Lk 10:27). This insight is captured by Benedictine monk Sebastian Moore who loved playing with words such as desirable and desire-able. Moore claims that we are desire-able (that is, able to desire) to the extent that we are desirable: "This sense of myself as desirable is the basis of all my relating. For it is the heart of desiring. It is because I am desirable that I am desire-able."[7] This liberation of our desire though grace opens our hearts to love as God loves. Through the Father and Son dwelling in us, we become sources of the divine Spirit for the world. Without this grounding in grace our actions become activism, and we burn ourselves out. On the other hand, without our engagement for others in charity, the gift of grace turns inward and festers in *self*-fulfillment. Grace and charity are linked as the Holy Spirit is linked to the Father and Son.

---

6   For both Augustine and Aquinas, the Spirit proceeds from the Father and the Son as from a single principle.

7   Sebastian Moore, *Let This Mind Be in You: The Quest for Identity through Oedipus to Christ* (London: Darton, Longman and Todd, 1985): 14.

Thus far we have spoken about the Trinitarian presence of the Spirit as our experience of grace, of being loved profoundly by God, and the presence of the Father and Son together, whereby we share their common work of building God's kingdom. These are not remote or rare experiences for us, but part of our common life as Christians, given a Trinitarian explanation. Can we push this further to find ways in which we relate to the Father and Son individually as Father and Son?

## FAITH — CHRIST LIVING IN ME

In the Nicene Creed we recall what is said of the Son, "God *from* God, Light *from* Light, true God *from* true God, *begotten*, not made." Just as the Spirit proceeds from the Father and Son, so too the Son proceeds from (or is begotten of) the Father. And just as the Spirit is present to us as the grace of the love of God poured into our hearts, so too we know that the Son is present to us in Jesus through the incarnation:

> For us and for our salvation he came down from heaven: by the power of the Holy Spirit he became incarnate from the Virgin Mary, and was made human.

A traditional theology spoke of these two presences as the Spirit and the Son; the invisible mission of the Spirit in grace and the visible mission of the Son through the incarnation. Jesus truly is God's Word made flesh, God from God, incarnate in human history.

How then might the Son be present within us, much as the Spirit is present within us, what Aquinas calls the invisible mission of the Son?[8] Here we can reflect on Jesus as God's Word. Although John's Gospel refers to the Son as the Word who was with God from the beginning, we rarely ask what that "word" might be. St. Paul does to some extent tell us what God's word is to us:

---

8   Aquinas, Summa *Theologica* Ia. Q. 43, Art. 5 ad1, "Some gifts nevertheless, by reason of their own particular nature, are appropriated in a certain way to the Son, those, namely, which belong to the intellect, and in respect of which we speak of the mission of the Son."

> As surely as God is faithful, our word to you has not been "Yes and
> No." For the Son of God, Jesus Christ, whom we proclaimed among
> you, Silvanus and Timothy and I, was not "Yes and No"; but in him
> it is always "Yes." For in him every one of God's promises is a "Yes."
> For this reason it is through him that we say the "Amen," to the glory
> of God. (2 Cor 1:18-20)

The Word is God's "Yes" to all that God is and does. We see this as the
faithful obedience of Jesus, who never stops saying "yes" to God because he
is the incarnation of God's own "Yes" to us. St. Paul also tells us that this
same Jesus lives in those of us who believe: "It is no longer I who live, but it
is Christ who lives in me. And the life I now live in the flesh I live by faith
in the Son of God" (Gal 2:20). For us this obedience is manifest in the
obedience of faith.

Inasmuch as we say "yes" to the gift of God's love poured into our hearts,
Christ lives in us and we manifest a divine faith. Sometimes this is explicit
and deliberate as when we make a confession of Christian faith, and at other
times it can be implicit and anonymous. We find this more anonymous
aspect in the experience of Dag Hammarskjöld, former secretary general of
the United Nations, who kept a personal diary of his spiritual experiences
which was only published after his untimely death in a plane crash:

> I do not remember who or what put the question. I do not even
> remember when it was put. I only know that at some moment I did
> answer yes [to something or someone] and from that moment on my
> life in surrender has a goal, a meaning! [9]

This is the nature of faith, saying "yes" to God in trust and obedience within
the concrete circumstances of our lives. Through living a life of faith we can
truly say that God's Word, his eternal "Yes", lives in our hearts, just as the
Holy Spirit dwells in us as divine love.

---

9    Dag Hammarskjold, *Markings*, ed. L. Sjoberg, trans. W.H. Auden (Knopf, 1978).

## HOPE — LONGING TO SEE THE FACE OF THE FATHER

Jesus experienced a sacred intimacy with the Father. A traditional teaching of the church held that Jesus enjoyed the beatific vision throughout his life. The *Catechism of the Catholic Church* speaks of Jesus' special knowledge thus: "Such is first of all the cases with the intimate and immediate knowledge that the Son of God made man has of his Father." It is exemplified in the "divine penetration he had into the secret thoughts of human hearts."[10] This special intimacy is part of Jesus' identity as the only begotten Son of the Father, and is not something we all share in this life.

Jesus taught us the Lord's Prayer so that we are able to pray, "Our Father, ...", praying with hope for the coming of God's kingdom. Through our faith we become adopted sons and daughters of the Father (Rom 8:12-17) and we can say that Christ dwells in us. However, while we may not have the special intimacy that Jesus has of his Father in this life (though we may share in this in our death), there is in us a hope that orients us to that special relationship with the Father. We can long for the day when we see God face-to-face: "For now we see in a mirror, dimly, but then we will see face to face. Now I know only in part; then I will know fully, even as I have been fully known" (1 Cor 13:12).

In the New Testament we often find the virtue of hope linked with endurance and suffering. We have referred to the verse of Rom 5:5 on God's love poured into our hearts. It is worthwhile considering the entire context of the quote:

> ...we boast in our *hope* of sharing the glory of God. And not only that, but we also boast in our sufferings, knowing that suffering produces endurance, and endurance produces character, and character produces *hope*, and *hope* does not disappoint us, because God's love has been poured into our hearts through the Holy Spirit that has been given to us. (Rom 5:2-5)

---

10 *Catechism of the Catholic Church*, #43.

This is perhaps why St. Paul speaks of "hoping against hope" (Rom 4:18), for when our common human optimism about the future hits a brick wall we need a more powerful source of hope, one that transcends the limits of our present existence.

As Pope Benedict XVI reminds us in his encyclical *Spe Salvi*, hope is intimately linked with faith. "'Hope', in fact, is a key word in Biblical faith — so much so that in several passages the words "faith" and "hope" seem interchangeable"[11] Without hope, in times of suffering and hardship our faith may falter; without faith, our hope has no clear grasp of what its ultimate goal is. As St. Peter notes, "Through him you have come to trust in God, who raised him from the dead and gave him glory, so that your faith and hope are set on God" (1 Pt 1:21). From our Trinitarian perspective, just as grace and charity are linked through the relationship of the Spirit to the Father and Son, so too faith and hope are linked through the relationship of the Son to the Father.

In summary we may say:

+ Through grace we enjoy the indwelling of the Holy Spirit as love;
+ Through charity we join in the work of the Father and Son in building God's kingdom;
+ Though faith Christ lives in us and we become adopted sons and daughters of God;
+ Through hope we long to see the Father face-to-face.

Grounded in grace and exercised in faith, hope and charity, we live out a Trinitarian spirituality.

## TRINITARIAN SPIRITUALITY AND HEALTH CARE

We can now turn our attention to how this relates to the specific context of health care, a mission of service that has been part of the church's life since Jesus' own healing work in Palestine. Health care provides a privileged place to share the church's mission.

---

11   Benedict, XVI, *Spe Salvi*, n.2.

## RESPECTING THE MYSTERY OF GRACE:
## THE SPIRIT BLOWS WHERE IT WILLS

There is something fundamentally mysterious about the operation of divine grace. The scholastics had a technical term, "operative grace," whose clinical precision obscures the depth of the mystery: God acts in us through the Holy Spirit. This is a matter of God's choosing, in time, place and circumstance, an act of sovereign freedom on God's part whereby the Father and Son breathe the Spirit into our hearts. The Spirit blows where it wills. It is not for us to question the timing and location of such a sovereign act, but we can be confident that in the benevolence of divine providence, God intends the salvation of all people.

What this means is that each and every moment in health care, no matter how dark or difficult, has the potential to be a moment of grace — counselling grieving parents; passing on the bad news of test results; performing an emergency surgery; or washing bedpans. There are untold moments of grace for staff and patients, moments when God's love can touch a heart in ways that radically change a situation, from one of resentment to joy, anger to forgiveness, fear and anxiety to acceptance and peace.

Two moments stand out for me as moments that have particular potential for divine grace: the imminence of birth and the threat of death. These are times of great stress, physically and emotionally. They are situations that are difficult to control, and the process and outcomes can be unpredictable. They are times of waiting for physical processes to take their course in their own time, according to their own rhythms. This lack of control is anxiety-provoking and is particularly stressful as there are so many situations in contemporary life where we are able to control our environment and the outcomes of our decisions. God's gracious initiative at such times is a further reminder that while we cannot be in control for some of the most important things in our lives, we remain loved and cared for. As Jesus reminded his listeners: "Can any of you by worrying add a single hour to your span of life?" (Mt 6:27).

If grace is the heart of our spiritual life, the chapel may be the heart of the mystery of grace in a Catholic hospital. The chapel is a constant reminder of God's presence and God's willingness to touch our lives, a persistent invitation to grace. When we enter a chapel we enter into a different space, more silent and serene, as the space itself offers a summons to open our hearts to God's presence. The presence of the Blessed Sacrament reminds us of the depths of divine love demonstrated by Jesus' death for our sake, the death of a divine friend offering us friendship through the gift of his own life. The chapel conveys a constant message: "You are precious in my sight and I love you" (Is 43:4). A hospital can build a community of grace through the regular creation of a sacred space (reflection times, liturgies, staff retreats) in which God's gift of the Spirit may be drawn into our hearts and assure us of God's love.

## CALLED TO LOVE AS WE HAVE BEEN LOVED

The pouring of the Spirit into our hearts is a gift and an invitation. The gift lets us know that we are loved. The invitation calls us to share in the work of the Father and Son to build God's kingdom, pouring out the Spirit to others, to love them as God loves and to share God's love with others. In Catholic health care settings this means that the staff are called to be a sacrament of God's presence to one another and to the patients in their care.

If the gift of the Spirit can occur in any situation, no matter how dark or difficult, the readiness to respond to that gift also cannot be contained or controlled. It is not always easy to respond to an ever present invitation to act with an open heart. People who are suffering and whose lives have been turned upside down through trauma or loss are not always going to be sweetness and light. Overwhelmed with sadness and hurt, they can sometimes lash out in anger, with hospital staff bearing the brunt of their pain. These situations take us into the heart of the paschal mystery, of suffering and sin, self-sacrifice and redemption.[12] Jesus taught his followers to turn the other cheek when struck, to walk the extra mile, to return curses with blessings, to love our enemies. Jesus on the cross spoke of forgiveness

---

12 For an excellent account of the "law of the cross," see William P. Loewe, *Lex Crucis: Soteriology and the Stages of Meaning* (Minneapolis: Fortress, 2016).

towards his executioners. When love, forgiveness and mercy are present, even the hardest of hearts can soften and be touched by God.

At the same time, health care staff have a right to be safe at work, free from abuse and threats and not be afraid of doing their jobs. But if one's existence is grounded in God's love and in the grace of the Spirit, there are times when a higher law intervenes, a law of mercy, forgiveness and self-sacrifice. Often anger can be alleviated by a kind word; violence averted by accepting risk to protect another and pain assuaged by tenderness. These approaches do not guarantee positive outcomes or safety for staff. Without a grounding in grace, such situations can lead to resentment and burn-out from staff who feel unrealistic expectations have been placed on them.

Just as we can patiently await — but not demand — the gift of God's grace, so too we cannot demand that people respond with self-sacrificing love, but when it does happen we can give thanks to God for its occurrence.

## FAITH: SAYING "YES" TO THE MYSTERIOUS PROVIDENCE OF GOD

We often think of faith in terms of an explicit affirmation of beliefs, such as "Jesus is my lord and savior." This can indeed be an important element of what faith means. However, there are times when we seem to think our faith functions as a kind of divine talisman that will ward off harm and danger. When we experience a serious illness or physical disability, we have something of a "faith crisis": "Why is this happening to me? I believe in God. I do the right things." We believe in God so God should protect us. But the New Testament is very clear that this is not how God and faith work. Those who believe can expect to suffer and bear witness to God in that suffering. While faith may involve some explicit affirmations of belief, more fundamentally it is saying "yes" to the mysterious unfolding of divine providence in our lives.

It is worth recalling again the quote from Dag Hammarskjöld: "I do not remember who or what put the question. I do not even remember when it was put. I only know that at some moment I did answer yes [to something or someone] and from that moment on my life in surrender has a goal, a meaning!" This quote expresses what I think St. Paul was getting at with his term, "the obedience of faith" (Rom 1:5, 16:26). Hammarskjöld uses the term "surrender," which captures the same sense. We give ourselves over to a higher mystery, trusting, surrendering, obeying, wherever it might take us.

If this is the heart of faith, we can find it apart from any explicit religious beliefs or affiliations. Many people who work in Catholic health care settings are from diverse religious affiliations or none at all. Part of the mission of a Catholic hospital, however, is to support a peaceful acceptance of the journey of suffering, which may end in death or healing or arduous rehabilitation. This is equally true for the staff who are also on a faith journey, dealing with their own issues in relation to suffering and death, and learning the limits of what modern medicine can achieve. Their ability to "let go and let God" can contribute to an atmosphere of acceptance that enables patients to respond in faith as well.

## NEVER LOSING HOPE IN THE DARKEST OF TIMES

Over the last century we have witnessed stunning advances in diagnostic means that can pinpoint our problems, drugs that cure diseases, surgical techniques that restore wholeness and rehabilitation methods that get us back on our feet. As a young adult in 1979, I remember hearing about a by-pass operation performed on the tennis great Arthur Ashe.[13] It made international headlines. Back then it was major surgery; now it is almost routine, with people coming out of hospital in under a week. People come to doctors with the hope, indeed the expectation, that modern medicine will provide a cure.

At times, healing is made possible, almost miraculously, at the hands of skilled doctors and surgeons. But there are also times when all the skill, techniques and technological advances of modern medicine, cannot cure. At such times we can speak about a "hope against hope", a hope not in human ingenuity and skill, but in the power of the God who loves us

---

13  It made a deep impression because my father had died of a heart attack some five years earlier, and I wondered whether such surgery, which was not common in Australia at the time, would have prolonged his life.

and wants to bring us to salvation. This is not necessarily hope for some miraculous cure — though this can happen — but a more fundamental hope and question: Shall we see the face of God?

> As a deer longs for flowing streams, so my soul longs for you, O God. My soul thirsts for God, for the living God. When shall I come and behold the face of God? (Ps 42:1-2)

As St. Paul claimed, "suffering produces endurance, and endurance produces character, and character produces *hope*, and *hope* does not disappoint" (Rom 5:3-5) because our final destiny lies not in this temporal realm but in seeing the face of the Father, in sharing the same intimacy with the Father that the Son experienced during his earthly life.

A Catholic hospital must bear witness to this hope. The mystery of death is not to be met with despair and hopelessness, but with a sure confidence that each and every death is an encounter with the Father who wills all people to be saved (1 Tm 2:4).

## CONCLUSION

The Trinity — God as Father, Son and Spirit — is central to Christian understanding and identity. Yet the mystery of the Trinity at work in human hearts cannot be confined to the church and those committed to Christian faith. We know that God wills all people to be saved and that God is at work in and through the lives of every person. Grounded in the reality of grace (Spirit) we live our lives in building God's kingdom of love (the work of Father and Son), saying "Yes" to God's call in our life in joyful hope of union with the Father. Each of these distinctive Trinitarian elements plays itself out in the context of Catholic health care as hospital workers and patients experience healing and hope, even in the context of suffering, illness and death.

## DISCUSSION QUESTIONS

1. Can there still be room for the life of grace in institutions
   such as hospitals which are dominated by demands for efficiency?
   Can there be room for the Spirit to blow where he wills?

2. In what ways can the institutional settings of a hospital impede or
   foster the virtues of faith, hope and love in staff and patients?

3. How might one speak of a message of faith and hope in situations
   of terminal illness?

CHAPTER SUMMARY

Christology, the theological explanation of the person and
the significance of Jesus Christ, is an important foundation
for Catholic health care that speaks directly to the distinctive
aspects that set this ministry of the church apart from its non-
Catholic peers. This chapter discusses two images — Christ the
healer and the Christ of solidarity — showing how both can
define and defend unique Catholic commitments to holistic
healing and accompaniment, giving a robust theological basis for
the essence of Catholic health care in today's world.

## 1.2 CHRISTOLOGY AND THE ESSENCE
## OF CATHOLIC HEALTH CARE

Conor M. Kelly, Ph.D.

*Assistant Professor, Theological Ethics*
*Marquette University*

I N HIS INSPIRING MEMOIR, *TATTOOS ON THE HEART*, the Jesuit priest Gregory Boyle reflects on his ministry to gang members in Los Angeles and repeatedly acknowledges that virtually every aspect of his work defies conventional wisdom. His parish's willingness to welcome gang members, no questions asked, strikes most people as an invitation to violence; his relentless efforts to hire formerly incarcerated men from rival gangs to work at Homeboy Industries seems like a recipe for disaster; and his managerial penchant for second, and third, and fourteenth chances would get him laughed out of any self-respecting business competition. Noting the juxtaposition with most definitions of common sense, Boyle simply admits, "Not much in my life makes any sense outside of God."[1] It is a profound and moving confession, and I love sharing it with my students because I think Boyle's statement captures something of the essence of what it means to be a follower of Christ in this world. I bring it up here because I also think it says something significant about the essence of Catholic health care — a point Boyle himself suggested in his keynote address at the Catholic Health Association's 2016 Catholic Health Assembly.

---

1   Gregory Boyle, *Tattoos on the Heart: The Power of Boundless Compassion* (New York: Free Press, 2010): 21.

Now, I am fully aware of the economic and social pressures affecting Catholic health care, and I know there are many ways in which Catholic health care institutions meet the traditional expectations of the health care industry. After all, they are judged by the same standards of efficiency and patient satisfaction as their non-Catholic peers. But that is not the essence of Catholic health care. These characteristics are incidental attributes, not the core identity. The heart of Catholic health care lies in the little things and major commitments that make this ministry unique, such as charity care, outreach to vulnerable populations, a focused attention on the common good and the prioritization of Catholic ethical guidelines that permeates all manner of health care services. At this essential level, there really is not much that makes sense outside of God.

In order to understand Catholic health care, then, we need to understand something about God. In the Catholic tradition, the most complete understanding of God is available only in Christ, whom the Second Vatican Council identified as "the fullness of revelation."[2] Consequently, Jesus Christ is the key to a true appreciation of the essence of Catholic health care. This is as it should be, especially in light of the sacramental understanding of Catholic health care institutions that Richard Gaillardetz has articulated elsewhere in this volume. As Gaillardetz explains, church institutions (including Catholic health care institutions) share in the mission of the church, which is to witness to "the practices and values associated with the reign of God."[3] Since those practices and values are expressed in the person of Christ, the primordial minister of the reign of God, we can fairly say that Catholic health care institutions embody this mission whenever they make Christ present in the world. Christology — the study and interpretation of Jesus Christ — is therefore one of the most important theological foundations for Catholic health care because one's understanding of Christ directly influences one's interpretation of what it means to make

---

2    *Dignitatis Humanae* (Nov. 18, 1965), 2. Available online at: http://www.vatican.va/
      archive/hist_councils/ii_vatican_council/documents/vat-ii_const_19651118_dei-verbum_
      en.htmlhttp://www.vatican.va/archive/hist_councils/ii_vatican_council/documents/vat-
      ii_const_19651118_dei-verbum_en.html.
3    Richard Gaillardetz, "Theology of Institutions," 263 – 264 .

Christ present in health care settings. Yet because God is a mystery, there is no single exhaustive account of Christ, and there are, instead, multiple Christologies.

In light of these realities, the purpose of this chapter is to explore how different Christological models can help explain the essence of Catholic health care so that we might better defend those distinctive features of the Catholic health care mission and identity that, much like Fr. Gregory Boyle's choices, do not make sense apart from God. To this end, I would like to suggest that we can go a long way toward reaching a fuller understanding of our essential task if we augment our typical "Christ-the-healer" model of Christology with the "Christ of solidarity" model found in contemporary liberation theologies.

## CHRIST THE HEALER: A VISION FOR HOLISTIC HEALING

In many ways, the most obvious parallel for linking contemporary Catholic health care with the person of Jesus Christ is found in the healing miracles of Jesus recounted in the Gospels. There is no question that this was a central feature of Jesus' life, especially as the early Christian community commemorated that life in their initial accounts. Across all four Gospels, there are vivid stories of Jesus healing men, women and children from all manner of afflictions, including deadly fever (Jn 4:46-54), paralysis (Mk 2:1-12), blindness (Lk 18:35-43), hemorrhaging (Mt 9:20-22), leprosy (Mk 1:40-45), demonic possessions (Lk 26-39), and even death itself (Jn 11:38-44). Judging by the number of times the Gospels inform us that people came to see Jesus expressly to be cured (see Mt 4:23-25; Mk 1:32-34; Lk 6:17-19), we can surmise that Jesus had quite the reputation as a healer. As a result, it is entirely legitimate to speak of a Christ-the-healer Christology that emphasizes the healing work of God incarnate in Jesus Christ. Indeed, Matthew's Gospel uses one of his unique "fulfillment quotations" to suggest that Jesus' impressive work as a healer partially confirmed his identity as the Christ, for in accordance with Isaiah's prophecy about the suffering servant, "He took our infirmities and bore our diseases" (Mt 8:17; cf. Is

53:4).[4] For all these reasons, the account of Christ the healer offers a viable Christological model for articulating the essence of Catholic health care, and we ought to take it seriously. I will, therefore, discuss the ways that this Christology might help explain those features of Catholic health care that are incomprehensible without reference to God. I will also describe the limitations of this approach because, in the end, this model needs a complement if we wish to capture the fullness of Catholic health care today.

In my view, a Christ-the-healer Christology has two key benefits for those who wish to define and defend the unique approach of Catholic health care as a ministry of the church: its logical simplicity and its description of a distinctive way of healing. The first of these advantages is fairly straightforward. The image of Christ the healer is immediately recognizable to those who have heard about Christ in almost any context. In fact, Jesus is described as a miraculous healer in other religious traditions, most notably Islam.[5] Christ the healer therefore provides a readily accessible link between Christology and Catholic health care, allowing one to say simply that Catholic health care makes Christ present by healing, just as he did while on earth. The equation requires no mental gymnastics because it unites one of the most familiar features of Jesus Christ with one of the most obvious aspects of health care ministry. In addition, this Christological link presents a no-nonsense response for the elements of Catholic health care that would seem to defy common sense. Like the "just say no" campaign, this Christology allows one to change the terms of the conversation and refute would-be critics with a nice statement of one's convictions — in this case: He healed, so we heal. Given the clarity of that reasoning, not much more would need to be said.

Yet other things can be said, because a Christ-the-healer Christology reveals more than just the basic fact *that* Jesus healed; it also tells us something about the *way* Jesus healed. This leads to the second key benefit of this Christology as a theological foundation for Catholic health care, because Catholic health care does not merely make Christ present by engaging in a

---

4    On Matthew's use of fulfillment quotations, see Daniel J. Harrington, *The Gospel of Matthew* (Collegeville, MN: Liturgical Press, 1991): 38 – 39, 116 – 17.

5    Warren Larson, "Jesus in Islam and Christianity: Discussing the Similarities and the Differences," *Missiology* 36, no. 3 (July 2008): 327 – 341, at 331.

healing ministry in general. Instead, it truly makes Christ present by trying
to heal in the particular way that Jesus healed. By building on
the Christology of Christ the healer, then, we can define and strengthen
the distinctive approach to healing that sets Catholic health care apart
from its secular counterparts. We can do this most effectively by attending
to the implications that Jesus' healing miracles would have had in his
historical context.

The first thing to note about Jesus' historical context is that most of his
ministry occurred in Galilee at a time when the ruling political authorities
were demanding higher payments from the area's rural workers in order
to fund ambitious growth for urban areas.[6] As a result, "there were no
medical 'safety nets'.... Debilitating illness, or disability resulting from
an accident while working, could mean descent into poverty and an
untimely death."[7] Illness therefore brought stress and fear along with its
somatic symptoms, as most victims had to worry about the long-term
consequences of their poor health. Furthermore, illnesses in Jesus' time also
included social consequences. A number of biblical scholars have noted the
distinction in medical anthropology between disease (as a biological reality
with pathological causes) and illness (as a psychosocial reality with cultural
causes) in order to insist that the illnesses Jesus confronted in his healing
miracles were not merely biological problems but also inherently social ones
as well.[8] John J. Pilch explains how leprosy serves as a paradigmatic example
because the actual (biological) disease of leprosy does not seem to have
been present in Galilee at the time Jesus lived, yet Jesus' contemporaries
certainly identified a certain kind of skin condition as the illness of leprosy,
imposing specific social sanctions on those who exhibited symptoms of
this condition.[9] Most of these sanctions resulted from the "purity system"
that associated certain illnesses, including leprosy, with impurity, with the
implication that other healthy people should avoid those who were sick and

---

6   Eric Eve, *The Healer from Nazareth: Jesus' Miracles in Historical Context* (London: SPCK, 2009),
    125 – 27.

7   Harold Remus, *Jesus as Healer* (Cambridge: Cambridge University Press, 1997), 2.

8   See, for example, John Dominic Crossan, *The Birth of Christianity: Discovering What Happened
    in the Years Immediately after the Execution of Jesus* (San Francisco: HarperOne, 1999), 293 –
    94; Pilch, *Healing in the New Testament: Insights from Medical and Mediterranean
    Anthropology* (Minneapolis, MN: Fortress Press, 2000): 13 – 14, 24 – 25.

9   Pilch, *Healing in the New Testament*, 39 – 54, 142.

impure lest they also become impure by contact and association.[10] Thus, in Jesus' day, illness meant not only physical affliction but also social isolation.

Given this context, Jesus' healing was both a transformation of physical symptoms and a response to social rejection. According to Pilch, this is the significance of the fact that Jesus so often healed by touch, for "in these instances…Jesus' touching is a concrete way of demonstrating that the individual is a full member of the community as Jesus understands it."[11] The distinctive value of his healing miracles — at least from the perspective of the ones healed — was the remarkable combination of physical restoration alongside the possibility of returning to social life without any stigma. Consequently, we might say that Jesus healed in a way that restored and reintegrated people, both individually and communally.[12] Frankly, this effect of Jesus' healing should not be surprising, because "Jesus insisted that his message of the kingdom of God was acted out in his miracles and exorcisms."[13] Since the reign of God is defined, in the words of John Dominic Crossan, as "a divinely mandated and nonviolent resistance to the normalcy of discrimination, exploitation, oppression, and persecution," it makes sense that we would see in the Gospel healings a reversal of social marginalization.[14] The model of Jesus' ministry, therefore, amounts to a distinctive way of healing, because his commitment to the reign of God points to a more holistic form of healing than simply curing sickness and disease.

In light of the historical implications of Jesus' healing miracles, we can imagine how a Christ-the-healer Christology might helpfully legitimate a similarly distinctive way of healing in contemporary Catholic health care. Wendy Cotter explains that Jesus' healings indicate the concerns that should

---

10  Eve, *The Healer from Nazareth*, 139.

11  Pilch, *Healing in the New Testament*, 52.

12  For more on the social impacts of Jesus' healing miracles, see Keith Warrington, *Jesus the Healer: Paradigm or Unique Phenomenon?* (Waynesboro, GA: Paternoster Press, 2000): 3 – 6.

13  Graham Stanton, "Message and Miracles," in *The Cambridge Companion to Jesus*, ed. Markus Bockmuehl (Cambridge: Cambridge University Press, 2001): 56 – 71, at 57.

14  Crossan, *The Birth of Christianity*, 317. For a more comprehensive overview of the scholarly understanding of the reign of God and its significance in Jesus' ministry, see Lisa Sowle Cahill, "Kingdom of God," in *Global Justice, Christology, and Christian Ethics* (Cambridge: Cambridge University Press, 2013): 76 – 121.

animate his disciples, who, she contends, "must be ready to abandon a cautious cultivation of public honor by conformity to social strictures and obedience to social norms in their outreach to others… [so that all] petitioners are received with the same equanimity, respect, and concern, no matter their background or status."[15] Thus, a dedication to imitating Christ the healer would certainly justify the common commitment to caring for the poorest and most vulnerable populations despite the obvious business challenges accompanying this decision. At the same time, this Christological model would also helpfully orient Catholic health care to the importance of holistic healing. Just as Jesus responded to physical symptoms and social consequences, Catholic health care can make Christ the healer present by attending to all aspects of a patient's holistic well-being, not just his or her physical maladies. In a context where "modern professional health care tends to treat disease but not illness,"[16] this attention to both phenomena would definitely qualify as a distinctive element of Catholic health care that does not fully make sense according to conventional standards. With the Christology just described, however, it would certainly be reasonable in light of Christ.

We can now see the advantages of describing Catholic health care with reference to a Christ-the-healer Christology. First, the visibility of this aspect of Jesus' ministry offers an easy explanation for the fact that Catholic health care exists at all. Second, the specifics of Jesus' work as a healer justify Catholic health care's distinctive commitments to underserved populations and to holistic care. While these benefits are significant, there are also important limitations that accompany this Christological model, which undermines its potential as an exclusive theological basis for mission and identity in contemporary Catholic health care. Consider what I called the most obvious advantage of a Christ-the-healer Christology: its emphasis on healing. This does provide a clear link between the work of Jesus and the work of Catholic health care, but, for all its clarity, this connection is dangerously narrow. Yes, healing is an important aspect of Catholic health care, and a focus on holistic healing is even more essential, but responding

---

15  Wendy J. Cotter, *The Christ of the Miracle Stories: Portrait through Encounter* (Grand Rapids, MI: Baker Academic, 2010): 255.

16  Arthur Kleinman and Lilias H. Sung, "Why Do Indigenous Practitioners Successfully Heal?," *Social Science and Medicine* 13B, no. 1 (1979): 7 – 26, at 8.

to symptoms — even when those symptoms are defined broadly — is not all that Catholic health care does. Preventive care is another major component of Catholic health care that is increasingly vital in today's context, and yet this aspect of the mission is not easily captured by an emphasis on healing. Granted, if we expand Jesus' healing to include not only diseases and illnesses but also sicknesses (i.e., the social conditions that increase risk factors for diseases), then there might be an argument for some elements of preventive care, especially when that care is directed to vulnerable populations.[17] Even this does not go far enough though, because preventive care is a requirement for all and population health must address the concerns of everyone in a given community, so this Christological model can only justify a portion of Catholic health care's essential tasks.

Another potential shortcoming in the Christ-the-healer Christological model is its inability to account for the finite nature of human health care. Christ healed by the power of God, and so the Gospels attest to an utterly successful healing ministry. There were no illnesses that Jesus could not overcome. As we know all too well, though, this is not the case for us today. Even when we set aside preventive care and focus exclusively on those patients who do come to Catholic health care seeking help with symptoms, there are conditions, diseases, and even illnesses we are powerless to cure or improve. While this is not an insignificant problem for medicine in general, it is an even bigger concern for Catholic health care, where long-term care facilities greatly outnumber hospitals, meaning that much of our health care ministry is directed at those patients who are unlikely to find medical healing.[18] When we attempt to justify the work of Catholic health care primarily on the basis of a Christ-the-healer Christology, we also leave this significant portion of Catholic health care mission unaddressed.

For all these reasons, a Christ-the-healer Christology is a natural and beneficial model for Catholic health care, but it is not comprehensive

---

17  For the distinctions between disease, illness, and sickness, and their connections to healing ministry, see Crossan, *The Birth of Christianity*, 293 – 95, 302.

18  According to the Catholic Health Association, there are approximately 600 Catholic hospitals in the United States versus 1,400 "long-term care and other health facilities." Catholic Health Association of the United States, "Catholic Health Care in the United States: Facts and Figures," last modified January 2016, accessed August 11, 2016, https://www.chausa.org/about/about/facts-statistics.

enough to stand on its own. Certainly, its simplicity and its focus on holistic healing are undeniable assets, but the gaps surrounding preventive and long-term care are too important to ignore. As some of the most prominent components of Catholic health care today, preventive care and long-term care both demand an adequate Christological foundation. Fortunately, the Christ-the-healer model does not have to operate in isolation. There are other Christological options, and the Christ-of-solidarity model developed by liberation theologians is particularly well suited to expand our understanding of the theological rationale for the essence of Catholic health care in these areas as well as others. Alongside Christ the healer, this solidarity Christology translates to a particular way of responding to patients in need, helpfully offering an additional image of Christ that can define and defend all aspects of Catholic health care ministry, not just healing.

## CHRIST OF SOLIDARITY: A MISSION OF ACCOMPANIMENT AND A COMPLEMENT TO CHRIST AS HEALER

The central message of a Christ-of-solidarity Christology is that God is with us in a profound way through the person of Jesus Christ, the Word made flesh. Proponents of this Christological model insist that, in Christ, God's presence with humanity is radical and exhaustive, such that there is no element of human existence that is left untouched by God. While the argument for this closeness often focuses on the experience of suffering, the implications of this Christology for Catholic health care extend beyond the immediate parallels one might see in the many ways Catholic health care institutions respond to suffering. Ultimately, this Christological model offers the theological foundation for a distinctive mission of accompaniment that Catholic health care institutions can embody in all the human interactions that they sponsor, from surgeons working to address the pain of acute wounds to primary care providers developing wellness plans for healthy young adults to hospice nurses preparing patients and their families for the end of life. In this way, a Christ-of-solidarity Christology has the power to explain all aspects of Catholic health care with reference to the Catholic understanding of God as revealed in Christ.

The primary basis of the Christ-of-solidarity model is experiential more than theoretical. Thus, we should not be surprised that liberation theologians have contributed much to this Christology, because liberation theology is emphatically attentive to the historical implications of Christian faith commitments.[19] The roots of this Christology predate the birth of liberation theology, though. Most observers point to the Second World War when the atrocities of the Holocaust prompted Dietrich Bonhoeffer, a German Lutheran pastor and captive of the Nazi regime, to declare, "only the suffering God can help."[20] Jürgen Moltmann, a fellow German and theologian, took this claim to heart as he grappled with the horrors of the war and its aftermath, prompting him to search for the suffering God. He found the answer he needed in the cross of Christ, who died "'for us,' so that he could be the Brother of all forsaken people and could bring them to God."[21] In Moltmann's interpretation, the point of the death of Christ was not only to free us from sin, but also to show us "that God could be *beside us* in our suffering and with us in our pain. That means: God's *solidarity with us.*"[22] Through the work of the Spanish-born Jesuit Jon Sobrino, who spent considerable time living with the poor in Latin America, this conviction has become a staple of liberation theologies because it provides hope to the oppressed, "who rejoice in having a God who comes close to them through his suffering."[23] Today, liberation theologians writing from a variety of contexts take this claim seriously and insist that the saving message of the cross is not just the victory over sin and death found in the resurrection, but also the complete solidarity of God with all those who suffer found in the cross itself.

---

19  For a good overview of the methodological commitments that distinguish liberation theology, including an emphasis on history, see Francis Schüssler Fiorenza, "Liberation Theology," in *New Catholic Encyclopedia*, 2nd ed. (Washington, DC: Catholic University of America Press, 2003) 8:554 – 56.

20  Dietrich Bonhoeffer, *Letters and Papers from Prison*, enlarged ed., ed. Eberhard Bethge, trans. Reginald Fuller, Frank Clarke, John Bowden, et al. (London: SCM Press, 1971), 361 (letter from July 16, 1944).

21  Jürgen Moltmann, *Jesus Christ for Today's World*, trans. Margaret Kohl (Minneapolis, MN: Fortress Press, 1994): 36.

22  Moltmann, 38 (original emphasis).

23  Jon Sobrino, *Christ the Liberator: A View from the Victims*, trans. Paul Burns (Maryknoll, NY: Orbis Books, 2001): 272.

Obviously, the Christ-of-solidarity model says something specific about the problem of suffering, but it also reveals a more general point about the significance of Jesus Christ. As Sobrino's discussion of solidarity Christology makes clear, the true importance of saying that Jesus is God, even as he suffers and dies on the cross, is that this creates an unqualified "affinity" between God and humanity, which "reach[es] down to the deepest levels in human beings, to where the expectation of salvation is most necessary and, at the same time, seems most difficult to achieve — in suffering."[24] From a Christ-of-solidarity perspective, then, Jesus' passion and death are the paradigmatic proof of a conviction that the Gospel of Matthew attaches to the birth of Christ, namely that Jesus is "'Emmanuel,' which means 'God is with us'" (Mt 1:23). It is therefore fitting that Sobrino would insist, "The cross should not be seen as an arbitrary plan of God's or as a cruel punishment inflicted on Jesus, but as a consequence of God's original choice, incarnation, a radical drawing near for love and in love, wherever it leads, without escaping from history or manipulating it from the outside."[25] Thus, the central message of this solidarity Christology is not that God is with us in our suffering — although that is true — but that God is with us in *everything*, in a way that is so deep and all-encompassing that it does not exclude the most trying elements of the human condition. This is the fundamental insight that the discussion of Christ's suffering reveals, and this is the reason that the Christ-of-solidarity model represents a helpful addition to the Christological explanation of the essence of Catholic health care.

In terms of practical implications for Catholic health care, the Christ-of-solidarity model provides the basis for articulating and defending a distinctive mission of accompaniment. Since the key claim of this Christology is that God is always with us, professionals working in Catholic health care can make the Christ of solidarity present whenever they are present to the people in a deep way that imitates Jesus as Emmanuel. Consistent with the emphases of the theologians who have developed this Christological model, health care workers can embody this form of

---

24  Jon Sobrino, *Christ the Liberator*, 266.
25  Jon Sobrino, *Jesus the Liberator: A Historical-Theological Reading of Jesus of Nazareth*, trans. Paul Burns and Francis McDonagh (Maryknoll, NY: Orbis Books, 1993): 244.

compassionate presence most directly in their interactions with those
who suffer in some way. This solidarity Christology also implies a holistic
approach to health care in Catholic settings, encouraging every professional
to move beyond symptoms in order to treat persons. Specifically, the
Christ-of-solidarity model promotes an openness to the other that seeks
genuine understanding, so that health care professionals might truly be
with their patients, working and walking alongside them in every aspect
of their treatment, sharing the human and not just the medical experience.
The point of this interaction is not healing, which is already presumed by
the health care setting, but accompaniment, which is the distinctive feature
added by placing this interaction in a *Catholic* health care context.

As we can see, the Christ-of-solidarity Christology illuminates a particular
way of healing in Catholic health care, but it does so in a fashion that shifts
the focus away from healing. As a result, this Christology has the advantage
of explaining additional aspects of Catholic health care, adding to the
explanation of the essence of Catholic health care that a Christ-the-healer
model provides. After all, the vision of accompaniment derived from the
Christ-of-solidarity model is both appropriate and effective in the context
of healing, but it is hardly restricted to the response to suffering. Sobrino's
description of God's solidarity with us in Christ applies just as well in other
contexts, including the two significant contexts left under-analyzed in the
previous Christological model: preventive care and long-term care.

Certainly Sobrino's account of "a radical drawing near for love and in love,
wherever it leads," suggests a rationale for Catholic health care's concern
with preventive care, which requires a full picture of the patient's life and
lifestyle, and which seeks to build a non-judgmental relationship of care
"wherever it leads." Significantly, this rationale is relevant in all cases, not
just in efforts to provide preventive care for underserved populations. At
the same time, the image of God's solidarity on the cross also justifies a
preferential option for otherwise abandoned populations in Catholic health
care. Hence, this Christology provides a balanced defense of preventive
care in Catholic settings. Similarly, because Christ's accompaniment in
solidarity is based on God's decision to join with our shared humanity, a
solidarity Christology can also inform and defend the growing commitment

to population health that places Catholic health care workers in solidarity with the broader communities in which they are located. When guided by the Christ of solidarity, these activities will be undertaken as a form of institutional accompaniment alongside a corporate people, reflecting a willingness to share the burdens of the community as a whole for the long haul and a readiness to work with the community to empower its members to find solutions from within, rather than imposing them from without.

In addition, this Christological model also offers a theological foundation for the Catholic commitment to long-term care. Insofar as Catholic health care makes the Christ of solidarity present, it will be faithful to its patients, even when medical solutions are either not viable or no longer desirable. In these moments, the vision of a God who accompanies us "without escaping from history or manipulating it from the outside" is exactly what drives the readiness to be at the bedside, sharing in the frustrations of medical futility and human finitude. As one can imagine, this is especially pertinent in the context of care for the elderly as well. Often we cannot cure those who are aging, but we can always accompany them. Quality senior care, like quality long-term care, will require us to deepen our understanding of God's solidarity with us in Christ especially as we accompany those preparing for death.

To give one practical example, this vision for solidarity through accompaniment is beautifully embodied in the reflections of Mary Lee Freeman, a palliative care nurse practitioner who relayed in an issue of *Commonweal* that her work is driven by the realization that she is "the last new person to get to know them," which means that she is always attentive to the ways that she can afford "the dying person…a last chance to be better than he [or she] really was." Her words in that essay show a level of familiarity with her patients as unique human persons with individual histories and deeply human needs that can only come from a true accompaniment.[26] If Freeman's experience is any indication — and I believe it is — then Catholic health care already embodies the mission of accompaniment that emerges from a solidarity Christology, especially

---

26  Mary Lee Freeman, "Caring for the Dying: My Patients, My Work, My Faith," *Commonweal* 131, no. 2 (Jan. 30, 2004): 11 – 15.

in long-term care settings. This means that the solidarity Christology of liberation theologies can indeed speak to the essence of Catholic health care, because it offers a clear rationale for the kind of distinctive work that already sets Catholic health care apart. Hence, the Christ of solidarity model can extend the insights of its Christ the healer counterpart, helping us to explain with greater precision why long-term care is such a major component of Catholic health care today.

For all these reasons, the Christ of solidarity provides a strong and encompassing Christological foundation for Catholic health care, helping us to expand our horizon and deepen our explanations beyond the convictions that naturally emerge from a Christ-the-healer model. Of course, Christ the healer is and likely will remain the more obvious image for Catholic health care, but this is not a bad thing because a Christ-the-healer model reinforces the Catholic commitment to holistic care. By appealing to the Christ of solidarity as well, we can then develop a comprehensive explanation of all the aspects of Catholic health care that set this work of the church apart from other, non-Catholic approaches. Significantly, the Christ-of-solidarity Christology justifies a mission of accompaniment that can imbue every interaction in a Catholic health care setting with a profound sense of Catholic identity. Of particular importance in today's context, this embodiment of Catholic identity does not presume any particular faith commitments from the parties involved. The Catholic nature of this mission comes from the link to the person of Christ, whose Incarnation, ministry and death all attested to a way of being in solidarity with us. Catholic health care institutions embrace this decidedly theological mission and identity whenever they insist that compassionate solidarity and accompaniment constitute the distinctive essence of health care in a Catholic setting. By asserting that the rationale for this essence is Christ himself, Catholic health care institutions ensure that they are fulfilling their sacramental mission as an institution of the Catholic Church. The Christ-of-solidarity Christology therefore provides a rich theological foundation for Catholic health care that applies to all aspects of this ministry and is accessible to all those who wish to contribute to this mission, even in a pluralistic context. Ultimately, if that is not enough to defend my claim that we should look to extend our Christological reflections beyond Christ the healer to also include the Christ of solidarity, then I do not know what is!

## CONCLUSION

I think that everyone involved in Catholic health care would agree that there is something distinctive about this approach to health care, and (I hope) everyone would also agree that we ought to keep it that way. Preserving this distinctiveness is no easy task, especially in an increasingly complex and competitive health care marketplace. We will have a better chance of success, though, if we are able to identify and defend the essence of the Catholic approach to health care, for the essence is that which is most at risk to market pressures because the essence makes the least amount of sense in light of conventional reasoning. Indeed, much like Fr. Gregory Boyle's work with gang members in Los Angeles, not much about that essence makes sense outside of God. This is especially true when we define that essence with reference both to Christ the healer and to the Christ of solidarity, for as the Episcopal priest Samuel Wells has persuasively argued, "Our culture's operational assumption has long been that the central problem of human existence is mortality," so most institutions are oriented to fixing the problems caused by finitude. In contrast, there is not a lot of sympathy for those who would suggest that isolation is the real problem that must be countered with a shared presence of accompaniment before we introduce action.[27] Yet the latter approach is the essence of Catholic health care, which spends resources and energy on accompanying everyone, even when the prospects for overcoming human finitude are long gone. By most conventional standards, this would be a foolish choice, but when we ground Catholic health care in the dual Christologies of Christ the healer and the Christ of solidarity, this becomes the only choice, and that makes perfect sense.

---

27  Samuel Wells, "Rethinking Service," *The Cresset* 76, No. 4 (Easter 2013): 6 – 14, available online at http://thecresset.org/2013/Easter/Wells_E2013.html.

## DISCUSSION QUESTIONS

1. What Christological image holds the most relevance for your work in Catholic health care: Christ the healer, the Christ of solidarity or some other image? Why?

2. How would you define the essence of Catholic health care? In what ways, if any, would you connect or relate this essence to one of the two Christological models mentioned above?

3. To what extent does the essence of Catholic health care require an explicit reference to theological commitments such as Christology?

### CHAPTER SUMMARY

As an anthology of sacred literature, the Bible took shape over the course of millennia. Despite the variety of literary forms contained in the Bible, and the disparate circumstances in which these texts originated, several unifying themes emerge in the Scriptures. One theme that united this collection of sacred texts is the conviction believers should imitate God in the way they conduct their lives. In the Bible, the divine is the paradigm for the human, and is the object not just of praise and thanksgiving, but of imitation.

In the course of reading the Bible, one encounters various characters — Elijah and Elisha in the Old Testament, for instance, and Jesus of Nazareth in the New Testament — whose lives and healings serve as models for believers as they seek to imitate the goodness, mercy and healing power of God. The biblical narratives move from "is" to "ought" by presenting figures who in their imitation of God, serve in turn as models to imitate.

# 1.3 INTERPRETATION OF HEALING NARRATIVES IN THE BIBLE

Fr. Sean Charles Martin, S.T.D.
*President*
*Aquinas Institute of Theology*

T VATICAN II, THE COUNCIL FATHERS EXPRESSED the hope that "the study of the sacred page should be the very soul of sacred theology," (*Dei Verbum 24*). Despite their somewhat archaic terminology — *sacra pagina* or "sacred page" is a term used by medieval theologians to refer to the Bible — the bishops expressed a very contemporary desire that Catholic theology should be "powerfully strengthened and constantly rejuvenated" when theologians engage the Scriptures in bringing the light of faith to the questions of the day. It is fair to say that the hope of the bishops at Vatican II has largely been realized, at least in the traditional theological disciplines of Christology, Mariology, ecclesiology and ethics, which all routinely refer to in the Scriptures. But as new needs emerge, as in the theology of Catholic health care, it is important to take care that these developing fields also find a way to ground themselves in the witness of the Scriptures.

This is no easy task. The healing arts, as practiced in ancient Israel or Greco-Roman Judaea, differ considerably from those of today. When the Bible speaks of physicians, for instance, it sometimes does so disparagingly: King Asa is criticized for seeking the help of physicians, rather than relying upon God (2 Chr 16:12), and Job denounces his would-be comforters as

"worthless physicians" (Jb 13:4). But the third century BCE Jewish
scribe Jesus ben Sira who wrote the Book of Sirach praised physicians
as creations of God by means of whom the healing power of God is
mediated to humanity (Sir 38:1-8). It is clear that healing is strongly
associated with religious leaders in the Bible. In the Torah, for example,
anyone who believes he or she has been cured of leprosy is required to
go to a priest to certify the cure (Lev 14:1-9; see also Lk 17:14). Healing
was one of the primary signs that a prophet was authentic (1 Kgs 17:17-24).
In the early church, James exhorted Christians to call upon the elders
of the church to pray for healing (Jas 5:14). How does one reconcile
these seemingly conflicting positions in the Scriptures with respect to
the ministry of health care?

What must be stressed time and again is that the sacred literature which
Christians call the Bible is not a systematic compendium of concepts and
theses about the God of Abraham, Isaac, and Jacob, whom Christians
understand to be God and Father of Jesus Christ. In actuality, the Bible
is an anthology of narratives, poetry, legislation, musical texts, oratory,
memories, ritual texts, and the like. Indeed, the Greek word *biblia*, whence
the English word "Bible" is derived, is a plural noun meaning "scrolls,"
thereby indicating how ancient Greek-speaking Jews and Christians
understood the pluriform character of their sacred literature. Furthermore,
this anthology of sacred literature was formed over a long period of time.
The oldest poetic fragment preserved in the Hebrew Scriptures, the Song of
Miriam (Ex 15:21) may date to about 1200 BCE, while the latest texts of
the New Testament were probably composed in the last decade of the first
century CE, if not the first decades of the second century CE.

Since 1943, with the promulgation of the ground-breaking papal encyclical
*Divino Afflante Spiritu* by Pope Pius XII, the Catholic Church has approved
of an interpretative approach to the Scriptures commonly referred to as the
historical-critical method. Reading the Scriptures by means of the historical-
critical method involves two steps: (1) determining the literary form of the
passage in question so that the reader understands whether the passage is
poetry, chronicle, legislation, or some other genre; and (2) understanding
the historical circumstances out of which the passage emerged and the
readership to which it was addressed. *Divino Afflante Spiritu* has had

an enormous influence over succeeding generations of Catholic biblical scholars. *Dei Verbum*, the Dogmatic Constitution on Divine Revelation promulgated at Vatican II, incorporated much of the teaching of Pope Pius XII. It reminded Catholics that readers of the Scriptures "must look for that meaning which the sacred author, in a determined situation and given the circumstances of his time and culture, intended to express and did in fact express, through the medium of a contemporary literary form" (*Dei Verbum*, 12). It is not too much to say that, thanks to the official approbation of the historical-critical method by Pope Pius XII and the Council Fathers at Vatican II, Catholic biblical scholarship has flourished over the past 75 years. In addition to the historical-critical method, biblical scholars have developed a number of other complementary methods and approaches that help shed light on the meaning of the Scriptures. In 1993, fifty years after *Divino Afflante Spiritu*, the Pontifical Biblical Commission released *The Interpretation of the Bible in the Church*, a document which reviewed developments within the field of biblical interpretation over the previous 50 years, and affirmed that the historical-critical method remains "indispensable … for the scientific study of the meaning of ancient texts." For a review of additional methods in common use among biblical scholars, see the addendum to this article.

Consequently, any attempt to ground a theology of health care in the witness of the Scriptures must take due consideration of the disparate circumstances in which these texts were both formed and preserved, the multiple intentions embodied in their literary forms, their capacities to simultaneously persuade and subvert, as well as the multiple ways in which these texts were re-read and reinterpreted over the course of their long history. The hard work of exegesis is therefore essential to the task of constructing a theology of health care.

What follows here is not an attempt to formulate **the** definitive biblical theology of health care. Rather, it aims to provide a series of reflections about certain foundational narratives in both the Hebrew Scriptures and the Christian Scriptures and to analyze the ramifications these narratives can have for those who seek to minister in Catholic health care.

## IMITATION OF THE DIVINE

Even if we understand the complex character of the Bible in its origins, various literary forms and multiple ways in which it has been interpreted several unifying themes emerge in the Scriptures. One theme that unites this disparate collection of sacred texts is the conviction that God is wont to intervene into human history in order to end injustice, bring about the divine plan for humanity and inaugurate what Jesus called the "reign of God." In addition, both the Hebrew Scriptures and the New Testament insist that believers should imitate God in the way in which they conduct their lives. "Be holy, for I the Lord your God am holy" (Lev 19:2). "Be perfect, therefore, as your heavenly Father is perfect" (Mt 5:48). In the Bible, the divine is the paradigm for the human. The divine is the object not just of praise and thanksgiving, but of imitation.

This insistence on imitation of God is thus at the heart of biblical spirituality. If God is presented as generous in the narratives, songs and ritual texts of Israel, as well as in the example of Jesus, then those who believe in God are called to be generous. If God is portrayed as merciful in these texts, then those who believe in God are called to be merciful. And if God is depicted as the one who heals humanity of its ills, then those who believe in God are called to heal the sick. The idea of imitation also appears in Conor Kelly's article, "Christology and the Essence of Catholic Health Care" elsewhere in this publication where he proposes imitating the Christ of Solidarity.

## GOD AS HEALER

One of the titles by which God is known in the Torah is *YHWH Raphah*, "the Lord who heals" (Ex 15:26). This title is inextricably tied to the narrative within which it appears. In this section of Exodus, the Hebrew people have just escaped from slavery in Egypt by crossing the Sea of Reeds. After a three-day journey without water through the wilderness, they have come to a place called Marah. The water there is undrinkable because it is bitter (Hebrew, *marah*), so Moses throws a log into the water, whereupon it becomes sweet. God then urges the people to listen to the divine voice and obey the divine commandments. It is at this point that God is revealed as "the Lord who heals." The title for God links healing and liberation here, thanks to the narrative context of the Exodus event. The divine title *YHWH Raphah*, "the Lord who heals," thereby suggests that liberation from slavery amounts to a kind of healing, and healing from disease amounts to a kind of liberation from servitude.

Theologically, this range of meaning in the divine title has some interesting implications for those who minister within Catholic health care. From this point of view, the work of restoring people to health is an act of liberation, and one by which those who are healed benefit from the primordial liberating act of God that is recounted in the Book of Exodus. And if the patient who is restored to health is the beneficiary of a divine act of liberation, all those who make that recovery possible — physicians, nurses, therapists, pharmacists, technicians, and the like — stand in the place of God and serve as agents through whom the healing and liberating power of God is bestowed upon those who need it. Whether they are conscious of it or not, they imitate the God who frees and heals.

## HEALING AND RELATIONSHIP WITH GOD

This notion of imitation is set forth in the Scriptures not as a principle or precept, but by means of example or paradigm. In the course of reading both the Old Testament and the New Testament, one encounters various characters — the prophets Elijah and Elisha in the Hebrew Scriptures, for instance, and Jesus of Nazareth in the New Testament. The pattern of their lives, and their actions serve as models for believers as they seek to imitate the goodness, mercy and healing power of God.

A story about the Israelite prophet Elijah in 1 Kings 17:17-24, illustrates this point. It is important to note Elijah's name means "Yahweh is my God," signifying a close identification between the prophet and the God in whose name he ministers. Elijah has gone into exile in the land of Sidon, probably because of his acrimonious relationship with Ahab and Jezebel, king and queen of Israel. While in Zarephath, a village near Sidon, he encounters a widow and her son, both of whom Elijah saves from starvation (1 Kgs 17:8-16). Subsequently, the boy becomes seriously ill and dies (1 Kgs 17:17-18). But Elijah takes the youngster and calls upon the Lord in the classic rhythm of lament, first in complaint — "O Lord, my God, have you brought calamity even upon the widow with whom I am staying, by killing her son?" And then in petition, "O Lord, my God, let this child's life come into him again." (1 Kgs 17:20-21). The child is restored to health, and the widow recognizes Elijah's privileged relationship with God: "Now I know that you are a man of God, and that the word of the Lord in your mouth is truth" (1 Kgs 17:24).

This narrative operates on a number of different levels. In considering the perspective of the participants in the narrative, it is important to note that the woman is a widow whose only son is in danger of death. As a result, she represents a particularly vulnerable class of individuals for whom the legal systems of the ancient Near East, including Israel, made special provision (Ex 22:22-23; see also Dt 10:18). That Elijah intervenes on her behalf with God indicates that the healing power of God should be made available especially to the most vulnerable persons in society. The fact that neither she nor her son belong to the Chosen People makes the prophet's intervention all the more remarkable, since it suggests that the healing power of God should be broadly dispensed, without regard to ethnicity, nationality or religious affiliation.

From a thematic perspective, the widow's recognition of Elijah's privileged relationship with God ascribes the healing of her son not to the person of the prophet, but to the God whom he serves. Similarly, Elijah's prayer over the boy invokes divine power, not his own (1 Kgs 17:21). This understanding of healing as a manifestation of divine compassion and power runs counter to a scientific understanding of healing as the result of the application of certain medical technologies and pharmaceuticals, the outcome of which is both measurable and predictable. In this story, the favorable outcome is the result of the prophet's relationship with God, not the specific actions that he takes.

A similar story about Elijah's protégé, Elisha, is preserved in 2 Kings 4:8-37. Elisha has become friends with a childless Shunammite woman and her husband. Because the couple were extraordinarily hospitable to the prophet, Elisha promises that they will soon have a child. In due course, the woman conceives and gives birth to a son (2 Kgs 4:17). Years passed, and the youngster develops a headache while working in the fields and subsequently dies in the arms of his mother (2 Kgs 4:20). The woman hurries to Elisha, insisting he follow her back to her village. There, he, performs a strange ritual on the boy:

> When Elisha came into the house, he saw the child lying dead in his bed. So he went in and closed the door on the two of them, and prayed to the Lord. Then he got up on the bed, and laid upon the child, putting his mouth upon his mouth, his eyes upon his eyes, and his hands upon his hand; and while he lay bent over him, the flesh of the child became warm. He got down, walked to and fro in the room, then got up and bent over him; the child sneezed seven times, and the child opened his eyes (2 Kgs 4:32-35).

It is tempting to see the actions of the prophet as an attempt to administer mouth-to-mouth resuscitation. But it would be anachronistic to ascribe current first aid procedures to ancient narratives. As in the case of Elijah and the widow of Zarephath, the point is not the specific actions that the prophet takes, but the reasons he does them. The infertile couple is granted a son, thanks to the word of the prophet, and the son's life is subsequently saved, thanks to the actions of the prophet, precisely so that this Shunammite couple can participate in the blessings of the covenant made with Abraham. This covenant promised another infertile couple (Abraham and Sarah) that they would be the ancestors of a people more numerous than the stars in the sky (Gn 15:1-6). To bear and raise children, in this view, is the most concrete way in which descendants of Abraham were able to appropriate the promises of the covenant. Elisha's words and actions in this story helped the Shunammite couple realize their human and their religious aspirations.

Precisely because Elijah and Elisha serve as paradigms of prophetic action in the Scriptures, the stories told about them not only preserve memories of colorful and compassionate men of God but also establish a kind of mandate for believers. What Elijah and Elisha are, believers should strive to be. In other words, biblical narratives move from "is" to "ought" by presenting figures who, in their imitation of God, serve in turn as models to imitate.

It is not hard to see the implications of these narratives of Elijah and Elisha. First, for Catholic health care to be authentic to its identity, it must be founded on a deep and abiding relationship with God, akin to that of the two prophets. Second, the most vulnerable members of society must be the beneficiaries of the prophetic ministry that is Catholic health care, like the widow of Zarephath and her son. Third, the ministry that is Catholic health care should be offered to anyone who is in need, regardless of race, color, creed or social location. In addition, Catholic health care must address the needs of the entire person — physical, social and spiritual needs alike.

## RITUALS OF HEALING IN ANCIENT ISRAEL

The rhythm of lament that is found in the story of Elijah and the widow of Zarephath — complaint, petition, and recognition of divine activity — is also found in a number of psalms that were used in rituals of healing in ancient Israel. The Book of Psalms is, of course, the hymnbook of Israel, and like other hymnbooks, the psalms were meant to be sung within the context of liturgical rites. Of course, what have survived are only the lyrics to these ancient hymns and not the melodies to which those lyrics were set.

Of the 150 canonical psalms that are contained in the Book of Psalms, there are approximately 40 individual laments and around a dozen communal laments, though, admittedly, it is not always easy to distinguish between an individual lament and a communal one. Typically, however, communal laments use the first person plural (Ps 44), and individual laments use the first person singular (Ps 51). These laments were sung whenever an individual or a community encountered a situation that prompted them to turn to God in complaint and petition and raise their voices to sing their laments. So, a lament could be sung in time of war (Pss 2, 3, 80, 137), or when one has become the object of persecution (Pss 10, 56), or when one is conscious of an offense which has harmed one's relationship with God (Pss 32, 51, 102, 130, and 143). In addition, a number of psalms address the phenomenon of illness and the desire that God swiftly come to the aid of the individual who has become sick (Pss 6, 22, 38, 41, 102, 116, and perhaps Ps 130).

What is important to note about this last category of laments is the imagery that is used to depict illness. At times, the images look like the physical description of illness. For instance, Psalm 38 describes wounds that have become infected (v. 5) and constant pain (v. 17). Psalm 102 appears to describe muscular atrophy and weight loss (vv. 5, 11; see also Ps 22:16-17). More frequently, however, distress is presented metaphorically: Psalm 22 depicts illness as though one is surrounded by bulls, lions, or dogs (vv. 12-13; 16); Psalm 102 speaks of illness in terms of exile and loneliness (vv. 6-7); Psalm 116 describes sickness as being caught up in a snare (v. 3), and Psalm 130 deploys the image of deep water in which one is in danger of drowning ("the depths," v. 1) to communicate the dangers of illness. The use of metaphor in these psalms permits an almost infinite adaptability in their use, so that deep water, for instance, can be used to characterize the dangers associated with childbirth, or the wounds that result from battle, or the onset of life-threatening illness, or even the aches and pains that come with aging.

Furthermore, it is important to note these laments were composed long before the age of antibiotics, antihistamines and analgesics. Illness in our time is often experienced as a mere inconvenience — you awaken with a stuffy head and a fever, so you take an aspirin and a decongestant, call in sick and spend the day napping on the couch. In the age of the psalmists, today's fever could lead to tomorrow's life-threatening illness, and the next day's funeral. Hence, the note of urgency and terror in so many of these laments.

An astute reader of these psalms of lament will note a recurring pattern that indicates the ritual setting in which the psalms were sung, probably the temple or shrine to which the individual requesting divine assistance would go on pilgrimage. The psalms typically invoke God by name and then present the complaint. Whether plainly put, or metaphoric, the complaint is consistent — I am sick, I may be dying and I need the help that only God can give. Then the psalm presents the reasons why God should send help, which vary from psalm to psalm. Sometimes the reason is the faithfulness of the one who prays (Ps 41:12); sometimes the reason is the faithfulness of God, either to the petitioner (Ps 22:9-10), or the petitioner's forebears (Ps 22:4-5), or even the essential nature of God to be faithful (Ps 102:12-13;

Ps 130:7B-8). The next element is an abrupt change of tone, in which the petitioner then expresses his or her gratitude to God in words of praise and thanksgiving (Ps 6:8-10; Ps 22:21B-31; Ps 41:11-13; Ps 102:18-22; Ps 116:4-19). It is possible that what accounts for the abrupt change of tone from pleading to praise and thanksgiving is that the petitioner has been assured by the temple personnel that the animal sacrifice offered on behalf of the petitioner has been accepted and that the petitioner's prayer has been heard.

From one point of view, the setting implied by these psalms of lament in time of sickness seems very foreign from the contemporary American experience of health care. We do not often think of going to the doctor as a ritualized experience, much less a plaintive cry for help. And yet the sequence of events implied by these psalms of lament — pilgrimage, complaint, waiting and relief — is familiar enough to any sick person who has struggled to the clinic or doctor's office, presented the symptoms, had tests run, waited for the results, and then been prescribed some medication. The sense of well-being that comes, even before the prescription has been filled, echoes the praise and thanksgiving that concludes these psalms of lament.

## JESUS AND HEALING

Jesus was, of course, well-known as a healer during the course of his ministry. All four Gospels attest to his power to restore health and life to those who were afflicted with illness or disability (e.g., Mt 8:1-4; Mk 2:1-12; Lk 4:38-39; Jn 4:46-54). The Synoptic Gospels (Mt, Mk and Lk) recount stories in which Jesus brought health to lepers (Mk 1:40-45 || Mt 8:1-4 || Lk 5:12-16; and Lk 17:11-19); restored sight to the blind (Mk 8:22-26; Mk 10:46-52 || Mt 20:29-34 || Lk 18:35-43); and gave strength and mobility to the paralyzed (Mt 9:1-8 || Mk 2:1-12 || Lk 5:17-26, and Jn 5:1-18). Such stories about Jesus typically follow a familiar pattern:

1. Someone is sick or disabled;
2. Jesus either says or does something, or both which cures the individual's illness;
3. The individual demonstrates his or her return to well-being;
4. The bystanders who witness the cure express praise and thanksgiving.

In the Synoptic Gospels, the cures performed by Jesus point to some facet of the reign of God about which Jesus has been preaching. When emissaries from John the Baptist come to Jesus to inquire about his identity and mission (Mt 11:2-6 || Lk 7:18-23), Jesus does not answer them directly; rather, he alludes to a series of prophecies found in Isaiah (29:18; 35:5-6; and 61:1) which were believed to describe what the reign of God would resemble — the one who is deaf will hear; the one who is blind will see; the one who is lame will leap like a deer; those who are captive will be set free. What is noteworthy about these prophecies is the extent to which the elimination of disability and illness are presented as signs of the power and the presence of God. Thus John the Baptist and his emissaries, and presumably the readers of the Gospel, can draw their own conclusions about the identity and mission of Jesus.

Furthermore, Jesus' answer to questions about his identity and mission links the recovery of health to the liberation of those who have been enslaved. That link between health and freedom, already established in the Hebrew Scriptures by the divine title *YHWH Raphah* ("the Lord who heals," Ex 15:26) takes concrete shape in these stories in which people, isolated by illness and disability, are restored to the fullness of life, thanks to the intervention of Jesus of Nazareth.

This is particularly apparent in the stories which depict Jesus' willingness to heal those suffering from leprosy. Leprosy in the Scriptures is not the contemporary condition known as Hansen's disease, but appeared to be some sort of skin ailment, identified by the appearance of scales or rashes on the skin of the individual who was afflicted (see Lev 13:1-44). The social consequences of being diagnosed with leprosy in Israel and Judaea were enormous: the individual was expected to wear torn clothing, and cry out "Unclean! Unclean!" should anyone come near. Perhaps worst of all, a leper was expected to leave home and go into internal exile, probably as a form of quarantine that was meant to protect the leper's family and fellow villagers (Lev 13:45-46). The anguish of leprosy was comprehensive, affecting all aspects of life.

So when Jesus heals lepers (Mt 8:1-4 || Mk 1:40-45 || Lk 5:12-16; Lk 17:11-19), he is not only restoring them to health, he is restoring them to human community. They will be permitted to return home and rejoin their families, once they demonstrate their recovery to the priests, whose function in first century Judaea included certifying that recovery had, in fact, taken place (see Lev 14:1-9). Thus, Jesus' acts of healing in these stories address the needs of the entire person — physical, social and religious.

There is another important aspect to the stories of Jesus and the lepers. Even before they are restored to good health, Jesus typically flouts the established norms of no contact with lepers and touches them (Mt 8:3 || Mk 1:41 || Lk 5:13). In effect, Jesus rejects the stigma attached to leprosy and enters into an authentic human encounter with the leper, one in which the person is more than the disease. Mark's version of this story accentuates the humanity of this encounter between Jesus and the leper by noting that Jesus is "moved with compassion" by the leper's request for healing (Mk 1:41).

The Gospel of John, so different in both plot and theme from the three Synoptic Gospels, nevertheless includes stories in which Jesus restores health to those who have been ill. Like the stories in the Synoptics, the Johannine narratives of healing also are characterized by a sequence of four events in which (1) someone is sick or disabled; (2) Jesus performs an act that cures them; (3) they demonstrate recovery by doing something they were previously unable to do; and (4) people who witnessed the cure react to it.

In the Gospel of John, Jesus heals a royal official's son in Capernaum (Jn 4:46-54); he heals a paralytic at the pool near the Sheep Gate in Jerusalem (Jn 5:1-15); he restores sight to the man born blind (Jn 9:1-41); and he raises Lazarus from the dead (Jn 11:1-44). While some of these episodes bear some resemblance to stories about Jesus in the Synoptic accounts — John 4:46-54 bears some resemblance to Mt 8:5-13 || Lk 7:1-10 and Jn 5:1-15 has some parallels in Mk 2:1-12 — the Johannine Gospel also preserves narratives of healing that do not appear in the Synoptic Gospels, like the cure of the man born blind.

The story begins with a question from the disciples whether the blind man's disability is the consequence of his sin or that of his parents (Jn 9:2). Implicit in the disciples' question is the assumption that disability is a punishment for wrong-doing but Jesus' reply rejects their assumption:

"It was not that this man sinned, or his parents, but that the works of God might be made manifest in him" (Jn 9:3). Suffering, in Jesus' view, is not the occasion to assign blame, but the reason to imitate the goodness of the God who heals: "We must work the works of him who sent me" (Jn 9:4).

Ancient writers knew the difference between an acute illness, a chronic illness, and a congenital disability, even if they would not have used that precise terminology. This man's blindness was congenital and was considered to be the hardest case to cure, which is why the otherwise unidentified man who sees for the first time exclaims, "Never since the world began has it been heard that anyone opened the eyes of a man born blind" (Jn 9:32). That Jesus is able to perform this cure speaks to his compassion, but also to his power.

The actual cure is related very briefly. Jesus anoints the man's eyes with mud and spittle and sends him off to wash in the pool of Siloam. The man returns, able to see (Jn 9:6-7). The rest of this very lengthy episode deals with the ambivalent reactions of the bystanders — some admire Jesus for what he has done, but others criticize him for having violated Sabbath restrictions on work (Jn 9:13-16). Through it all, the man himself becomes increasingly insightful about Jesus' identity. Initially, he identifies him only by name (Jn 9:11), then as a prophet (Jn 9:17), then as one who is "from God," (Jn 9:33), and finally, as "Lord," (Jn 9:38). The experience of being healed has brought this man to faith in God. This dynamic in the story runs counter to the common conviction that faith in God will bring about one's healing.

All these stories about Jesus have repercussions for Catholic health care. In taking Jesus as its model, Catholic health care must also comprehensively address all the needs — physical, spiritual and psycho-social — of those who seek healing and relief. Second, Catholic health care should reject the social stigmas attached to disease and disability and welcome to the healing ministry anyone with that human touch that acknowledges the essential humanity of each person and sees the patient as more than a constellation of symptoms. Thirdly, the compassion which is so characteristic of Jesus — literally, his "suffering-with" or sympathy for those to whom he ministered — must be the underlying motivation for anyone who seeks to minister in the name of Jesus. And finally, it must be acknowledged that, in many places, the healing compassion that so many people experience when they encounter Catholic health care at its best can be a means by which they are led to encounter "the Lord who heals." This reflects the sacramental nature of health care which is discussed in several other chapters in this volume.

## CONCLUSION

To develop a theology of health care that is grounded in the Scriptures, one must develop an appreciation for sacred literature and the indirect, even leisurely, way in which such sacred stories and songs seek to communicate their themes. The stories in both the Hebrew Scriptures and the New Testament are not *Aesop's Fables* — tidy little tales that can be summed up by the maxim that concludes them. The narratives that are found in places like 1 Kings, 2 Kings, and the Gospels of Matthew, Mark, Luke and John require a kind of extended meditation in order for them to release their wisdom. Similarly, the laments found in the Book of Psalms give voice to the deepest longings — and deepest frustrations — of the human spirit. This religious poetry demands of those who read it a commitment that is commensurate with the anger found therein, the anguish, and the faith in the "Lord who heals." This reflects the sacramental nature of health care which is discussed in several other chapters of this publication.

In the end, any biblical theology of health care must move beyond meditation to action, precisely because these texts and tales demand that one imitate the Lord who heals. In the model of Elijah, Elisha, and Jesus of Nazareth, those who are in the service of this healing God today seek to bring health to a waiting world.

## DISCUSSION QUESTIONS

**1.** How does your work in Catholic health care imitate the "God who heals?"

**2.** How does your work in Catholic health care reach out to include anyone who has been relegated to the periphery of society?

**3.** How does your work in Catholic health care address all the needs — physical, social, psychological, spiritual — of those who seek healing and relief?

## ADDENDUM

*To provide readers with additional background and context for biblical interpretation, we present a brief summary of the most important points in The Interpretation of the Bible in the Church (available online at* http://catholic-resources.org/ChurchDocs/PBC_Interp.htm*)*

### KEY PRINCIPLES FROM *THE INTERPRETATION OF THE BIBLE IN THE CHURCH*

(Pontifical Biblical Commission, 1994)

In the history of interpretation, the rise of the historical-critical method opened a new era. With it, new possibilities for understanding the biblical word in its originality opened up. Just as with all human endeavor, though, so also this method contained hidden dangers along with its positive possibilities. The search for the original can lead to putting the word back into the past completely so that it is no longer taken in its actuality. It can result that only the human dimension of the word appears as real, while the genuine author, God, is removed from the reach of a method which was established for understanding human reality.

The application of a "profane" method to the Bible necessarily led to
discussion. Everything that helps us better understand the truth and
appropriate its representations is helpful and worthwhile for theology.
It is in this sense that we must seek how to use this method in theological
research. Everything that shrinks our horizon and hinders us from seeing
and hearing beyond that which is merely human must be opened up.
Thus the emergence of the historical-critical method set in motion at the
same time a struggle over its scope and its proper configuration, which
is by no means finished as yet.

The problem is therefore quite old. But it has been accentuated with the
passage of time. Readers today, in order to appropriate the words and deeds
of which the Bible speaks, have to project themselves back almost 20 or 30
centuries — a process which always creates difficulty.

Furthermore, because of the progress made in the human sciences,
questions of interpretation have become more complex in modern times.
Scientific methods have been adopted for the study of the texts of the
ancient world. To what extent can these methods be considered appropriate
for the interpretation of Holy Scripture? For a long period the church in
her pastoral prudence showed herself very reticent in responding to this
question, for often the methods, despite their positive elements, have
shown themselves to be wedded to positions hostile to the Christian faith.
But a more positive attitude has also evolved, signaled by a whole series of
pontifical documents.

## A. HISTORICAL-CRITICAL METHOD

The historical-critical method is the indispensable method for the scientific
study of the meaning of ancient texts. Holy Scripture, inasmuch as it is the
"word of God in human language," has been composed by human authors
in all its various parts and in all the sources that lie behind them. Because
of this, its proper understanding not only admits the use of this method but
actually requires it. The historical-critical method is:

+ A historical method, not only because it is applied to ancient texts —
   in this case, those of the Bible — and studies their significance from

a historical point of view, but also and above all because it seeks to shed light upon the historical processes which gave rise to biblical texts, diachronic processes that were often complex and involved a long period of time. At the different stages of their production, the texts of the Bible were addressed to various categories of hearers or readers living in different places and different times.

+ A critical method, because in each of its steps (from textual criticism to redaction criticism) it operates with the help of scientific criteria that seek to be as objective as possible. In this way, it aims to make accessible to the modern reader the meaning of biblical texts, which often are very difficult to comprehend.

+ An analytical method, because it studies the biblical text in the same fashion as it would study any other ancient text and comments upon it as an expression of human discourse. However, above all in the area of redaction criticism, it does allow the exegete to gain a better grasp of the content of divine revelation.

## B. NEW METHODS OF LITERARY ANALYSIS

No scientific method for the study of the Bible is fully adequate to comprehend the biblical texts in all their richness. For all its overall validity, the historical-critical method cannot claim to be totally sufficient in this respect. It necessarily has to leave aside many aspects of the writings which it studies. It is not surprising, then, that at the present time other methods and approaches are proposed which serve to explore more profoundly other aspects worthy of attention.

In Section B, we will present certain methods of literary analysis which have been developed recently. In the following sections (C, D, E), we will examine briefly different approaches, some of which relate to the study of the tradition, others to the "human sciences," others still to particular situations of the present time. Finally (F), we will consider the fundamentalist reading of the Bible, a reading which does not accept any systematic approach to interpretation.

Taking advantage of the progress made in our day by linguistic and literary studies, biblical exegesis makes use more and more of new methods of literary analysis, in particular rhetorical analysis and narrative analysis.

## 1. Rhetorical Analysis

Rhetorical analysis in itself is not, in fact, a new method. What is new is the use of it in a systematic way for the interpretation of the Bible and also the start and development of a "new rhetoric."

Rhetoric is the art of composing discourse aimed at persuasion. The fact that all biblical texts are in some measure persuasive in character means that some knowledge of rhetoric should be part of the normal scholarly equipment of all exegetes. Rhetorical analysis must be carried out in a critical way, since scientific exegesis is an undertaking which necessarily submits itself to the demands of the critical mind.

## 2. Narrative Analysis

Narrative analysis offers a method of understanding and communicating the biblical message which corresponds to the form of story and personal testimony, something characteristic of holy Scripture and, of course, a fundamental modality of communication between human persons. The Old Testament in fact presents a story of salvation, the powerful recital of which provides the substance of the profession of faith, liturgy and catechesis (cf. Ps 78:3-4; Ex 12:24-27; Dt 6:20-25; 26:5-11). For its own part, the proclamation of the Christian kerygma amounts in essentials to a sequence telling the story of the life, death and resurrection of Jesus Christ, events of which the Gospels offer us a detailed account. Catechesis itself also appears in narrative form (cf. 1 Cor 11:23-25).

# C. APPROACHES BASED ON TRADITION

The literary methods which we have just reviewed, although they differ from the historical-critical method in that they pay greater attention to the internal unity of the texts studied, remain nonetheless insufficient for the interpretation of the Bible because they consider each of its writings in isolation. But the Bible is not a compilation of texts unrelated to each other; rather, it is a gathering together of a whole array of witnesses from one great tradition. To be fully adequate to the object of its study, biblical exegesis must keep this truth firmly in mind. Such in fact is the perspective adopted by a number of approaches which are being developed at present.

## 1. Canonical Approach

The "canonical" approach, which originated in the United States some 20 years ago, proceeds from the perception that the historical-critical method experiences at times considerable difficulty in arriving, in its conclusions, at a truly theological level. It aims to carry out the theological task of interpretation more successfully by beginning from within an explicit framework of faith: the Bible as a whole.

To achieve this, it interprets each biblical text in the light of the canon of Scriptures, that is to say, of the Bible as received as the norm of faith by a community of believers. It seeks to situate each text within the single plan of God, the goal being to arrive at a presentation of Scripture truly valid for our time. The method does not claim to be a substitute for the historical-critical method; the hope is, rather, to complete it.

## 2. Approach Through Recourse to Jewish Traditions of Interpretation

The Old Testament reached its final form in the Jewish world of the four or five centuries preceding the Christian era. Judaism of this time also provided the matrix for the origin of the New Testament and the infant church. Numerous studies of the history of ancient Judaism and notably the manifold research stimulated by the discoveries at Qumran have highlighted the complexity of the Jewish world, both in the land of Israel and in the Diaspora, throughout this period.

### 3. Approach by the History of the Influence of the Text (<Wirkungsgeschichte>)

This approach rests upon two principles: a) a text only becomes a literary work insofar as it encounters readers who give life to it by appropriating it to themselves; b) the appropriation of the text, which can occur either on the individual or community level and can take shape in various spheres (literary, artistic, theological, ascetical and mystical), contributes to a better understanding of the text itself.

## D. APPROACHES THAT USE THE HUMAN SCIENCES

In order to communicate itself, the word of God has taken root in the life of human communities (cf. Sir 24:12), and it has been through the psychological dispositions of the various persons who composed the biblical writings that it has pursued its path. It follows, then, that the human sciences — in particular sociology, anthropology and psychology — can contribute toward a better understanding of certain aspects of biblical texts. It should be noted, however, that in this area there are several schools of thought with notable disagreement among them on the very nature of these sciences. That said, a good number of exegetes have drawn considerable profit in recent years from research of this kind.

### 1. Sociological Approach

Religious texts are bound in reciprocal relationship to the societies in which they originate. This is clearly the case as regards biblical texts. Consequently, the scientific study of the Bible requires as exact a knowledge as is possible of the social conditions distinctive of the various milieus in which the traditions recorded in the Bible took shape. This kind of socio-historical information needs then to be completed by an accurate sociological explanation, which will provide a scientific interpretation of the implications for each case of the prevailing social conditions.

The sociological point of view has had a role in the history of exegesis for quite some time. The attention which Form-criticism devoted to the social

circumstances in which various texts arose (<sitz im leben>) is already
an indication of this: It recognized that biblical traditions bore the mark
of the socio-cultural milieu which transmitted them. In the first third
of the 20th century, the Chicago School studied the socio-historical
situation of early Christianity, thereby giving historical criticism a
notable impulse in this direction.

## 2. Psychological and Psychoanalytical Approaches

Psychology and theology continue their mutual dialogue. The modern
extension of psychological research to the study of the dynamic structures
of the subconscious has given rise to fresh attempts at interpreting
ancient texts, including the Bible. Whole works have been devoted to the
psychoanalytic interpretation of biblical texts, which has led to vigorous
discussion: In what measure and under what conditions can psychological
and psychoanalytical research contribute to a deeper understanding of
sacred Scripture?

## E. CONTEXTUAL APPROACHES

The interpretation of a text is always dependent on the mindset and
concerns of its readers. Readers give privileged attention to certain aspects
and, without even being aware of it, neglect others. Thus it is inevitable
that some exegetes bring to their work points of view that are new and
responsive to contemporary currents of thought which have not up till
now been taken sufficiently into consideration. It is important that they do
so with critical discernment. The movements in this regard which claim
particular attention today are those of liberation theology and feminism.

## 1. The Liberationist Approach

The theology of liberation is a complex phenomenon, which ought not
be oversimplified. It began to establish itself as a theological movement
in the early 1970s. Over and beyond the economic, social and political
circumstances of Latin America, its starting point is to be found in two great
events in the recent life of the church: the Second Vatican Council, with its

declared intention of "aggiornamento" and of orienting the pastoral work of the church toward the needs of the contemporary world, and the Second General Conference of the Episcopate of Latin America held at Medellin in 1968, which applied the teachings of the council to the needs of Latin America. The movement has since spread also to other parts of the world.

Liberation theology is not content with an objectifying interpretation which concentrates on what the text said in its original context. It seeks a reading drawn from the situation of people as it is lived here and now. If people live in circumstances of oppression, one must go to the Bible to find nourishment capable of sustaining the people in its struggles and its hopes. The reality of the present time should not be ignored but, on the contrary, met head on, with a view to shedding upon it the light of the word. From this light will come authentic Christian praxis, leading to the transformation of society through works of justice and love. Within the vision of faith Scripture is transformed into a dynamic impulse for full liberation.

The main principles guiding this approach are the following:

+ God is present in the history of his people, bringing them salvation. He is the God of the poor and cannot tolerate oppression or injustice.

+ It follows that exegesis cannot be neutral, but must, in imitation of God, take sides on behalf of the poor and be engaged in the struggle to liberate the oppressed.

+ It is precisely participation in this struggle that allows those interpretations to surface which are discovered only when the biblical texts are read in a context of solidarity with the oppressed.

## 2. The Feminist Approach

The feminist biblical hermeneutic had its origin in the United States toward the end of the 19th century. In the socio-cultural context of the struggle for the rights of women, the editorial board of a committee charged with the revision of the Bible produced "The Woman's Bible" in two volumes (New York 1885, 1898).

This movement took on fresh life in the 1970s and has since undergone an enormous development in connection with the movement for the liberation of women, especially in North America. To be precise, several forms of feminist biblical hermeneutics have to be distinguished, for the approaches taken are very diverse. All unite around a common theme, woman, and a common goal: the liberation of women and the acquisition on their part of rights equal to those enjoyed by men.

## F. FUNDAMENTALIST INTERPRETATION

Fundamentalist interpretation starts from the principle that the Bible, being the Word of God, inspired and free from error, should be read and interpreted literally in all its details. But by "literal interpretation" it understands a naively literalist interpretation, one, that is to say, which excludes every effort at understanding the Bible that takes account of its historical origins and development. It is opposed, therefore, to the use of the historical-critical method, as indeed to the use of any other scientific method for the interpretation of Scripture.

The fundamentalist interpretation had its origin at the time of the Reformation, arising out of a concern for fidelity to the literal meaning of Scripture. After the century of the Enlightenment it emerged in Protestantism as a bulwark against liberal exegesis.

## 1. Characteristics of Catholic Interpretation

Catholic exegesis does not claim any particular scientific method as its own. It recognizes that one of the aspects of biblical texts is that they are the work of human authors, who employed both their own capacities for expression and the means which their age and social context put at their disposal. Consequently, Catholic exegesis freely makes use of the scientific methods and approaches which allow a better grasp of the meaning of texts in their linguistic, literary, socio-cultural, religious and historical contexts, while explaining them as well through studying their sources and attending to the personality of each author. Catholic exegesis actively contributes to the development of new methods and to the progress of research.

What characterizes Catholic exegesis is that it deliberately places itself within the living tradition of the church, whose first concern is fidelity to the revelation attested by the Bible. Modern hermeneutics has made clear, as we have noted, the impossibility of interpreting a text without starting from a "pre-understanding" of one type or another.

Catholic exegetes approach the biblical text with a pre-understanding which holds closely together modern scientific culture and the religious tradition emanating from Israel and from the early Christian community. Their interpretation stands thereby in continuity with a dynamic pattern of interpretation that is found within the Bible itself and continues in the life of the church. This dynamic pattern corresponds to the requirement that there be a lived affinity between the interpreter and the object, an affinity which constitutes, in fact, one of the conditions that makes the entire exegetical enterprise possible.

All pre-understanding, however, brings dangers with it. As regards Catholic exegesis, the risk is that of attributing to biblical texts a meaning which they do not contain but which is the product of a later development within the tradition. The exegete must beware of such a danger.

## CONCLUDING OBSERVATIONS

+ Sacred Scripture has come into existence on the basis of a consensus in the believing communities recognizing in the texts the expression of revealed faith. This means that, for the living faith of the ecclesial communities, the interpretation of Scripture should itself be a source of consensus on essential matters.

+ Granted that the expression of faith, such as it is found in the sacred Scripture acknowledged by all, has had to renew itself continually in order to meet new situations, which explains the "re-readings" of many of the biblical texts, the interpretation of the Bible should likewise involve an aspect of creativity; it ought also to confront new questions so as to respond to them out of the Bible.

+ Granted that tensions can exist in the relationship between various texts of sacred Scripture, interpretation must necessarily show a certain pluralism. No single interpretation can exhaust the meaning of the whole, which is a symphony of many voices. Thus the interpretation of one particular text has to avoid seeking to dominate at the expense of others.

+ Sacred Scripture is in dialogue with communities of believers: It has come from their traditions of faith. Its texts have been developed in relation to these traditions and have contributed, reciprocally, to the development of the traditions. It follows that interpretation of Scripture takes place in the heart of the church: in its plurality and its unity, and within its tradition of faith.

+ Faith traditions formed the living context for the literary activity of the authors of sacred Scripture. Their insertion into this context also involved a sharing in both the liturgical and external life of the communities, in their intellectual world, in their culture and in the ups and downs of their shared history. In like manner, the interpretation of sacred Scripture requires full participation on the part of exegetes in the life and faith of the believing community of their own time.

+ Dialogue with Scripture in its entirety, which means dialogue with the understanding of the faith prevailing in earlier times, must be matched by a dialogue with the generation of today. Such dialogue will mean establishing a relationship of continuity. It will also involve acknowledging differences. Hence the interpretation of Scripture involves a work of sifting and setting aside; it stands in continuity with earlier exegetical traditions, many elements of which it preserves and makes its own; but in other matters it will go its own way, seeking to make further progress.

A PRIEST PASSED BY ON THE OTHER SIDE

A LEVITE PASSED BY ON THE OTHER SIDE

BUT A SAMARITAN WAS MOVED TO PITY

AND BANDAGED HIS WOUNDS

WHICH ONE OF THESE WAS A NEIGHBOR TO THE MAN WHO FELL INTO THE HANDS OF ROBBERS?

# II

# THE PERSON AND HEALTH CARE

CHAPTER SUMMARY

This chapter contrasts the Catholic understanding of personhood
with a widely accepted colloquial usage of the term. While the
Catholic account emphasizes that all human beings should be
treated as persons and have transcendent value, the colloquial
approach ascribes personhood to those who have certain
abilities and capacities. The Catholic and colloquial approaches
to personhood influence moral positions on important issues
in health care ethics such as abortion, physician-assisted
suicide and euthanasia, care and treatment of the poor and the
intellectually disabled. Asking "Who is a person?" is not an "ivory
tower exercise;" it has real-world effects.

## 2.1 WHO COUNTS AS A PERSON?

———

Daniel J. Daly, Ph.D.
*Associate Professor, Theology*
*Saint Anselm College*

A S THE FATHER OF TWO YOUNG BOYS I NOTICED that when each child reached around six months of age many family and friends would say: "What a little person he is now!" These statements always coincided with some new activity that one of the boys was doing: intentionally reaching for a favorite toy or interacting and laughing with someone. The descriptor "person" seemed to be reserved for babies who could perform certain tasks. As a professor of theological ethics I realized that this colloquial definition of "person" mapped somewhat with philosopher Mary Anne Warren's approach. Warren argued that a human being is also a person if he can perform certain tasks, such as communicate with others, self-reflect and execute self-motivated activity.[1] According to this account, fetuses, the intellectually disabled, and those lacking cognition are human beings, but not persons.

The Catholic tradition takes a different approach. The purpose of this chapter is to present the Catholic understanding of personhood, with an eye to how such a position influences Catholic health care ethics. The first part of the chapter presents Warren's influential "performance based"

---

1    Mary Anne Warren, "On the Moral and Legal Status of Abortion," *Monist* 57 (1973).

notion of personhood. This view presents an important and influential contemporary approach to personhood and provides important points of contrast which make the Catholic position clearer. The second part focuses on the Catholic tradition on personhood, including the development of the concept of personhood and the current state of the question. Part three shows how the Catholic and colloquial approaches to personhood influence moral positions on important issues in health care ethics, such as abortion; physician-assisted suicide and euthanasia; care and treatment of the poor; and the status of people who are intellectually disabled. How one answers the question, "Who is a person?" is not an "ivory tower" exercise; it has real-world effects.

## I.  THE COLLOQUIAL VIEW

In her widely read and cited 1973 article entitled "On the Moral and Legal Status of Abortion," Mary Anne Warren articulated a notion of the person that is quite similar to the one I introduced at the beginning of the chapter. Warren's notion of the person is important because it provides a rigorous philosophical explanation of the underlying reasons why many people hold the colloquial view of personhood. Warren began her argument for the pro-choice position by framing a distinction between the categories of "human being" and "person." According to Warren, human beings who are not persons simply possess a human genome. These beings, she later argued, are not members of the "moral community" and do not possess human rights. A being possesses personhood if it possesses at least one of the following traits: consciousness of self and the world, a developed ability to reason, self-motivated activity, the ability to communicate about an indefinite variety of topics, and has "self-concepts" and self-awareness. As I noted in the introduction, this roughly maps with how many people use the concept in everyday speech. This is the colloquial view of personhood, which is largely about personal presence and activity.

Warren's definition of the person was not, however, an exercise in purely speculative philosophy. Her definition was at the service of an argument for abortion rights. Warren argues that the fetus does not possess any of the traits that, she claims, constitute personhood. Because it does not possess even one of the traits, the fetus is a not a person. Her argument continues by noting that only persons have rights, such as the right to life. Because the fetus is not a person, it follows that the fetus does not have the right to life. The mother, however, possesses the right to "protect her health, happiness, and freedom." In the exercise of her rights she may find it necessary to terminate the pregnancy, which would be morally permissible according to Warren because no other persons' rights would have been violated by the abortion.[2]

But her argument does not stop there. Her article also implies that euthanasia is permissible for those with no "appreciable mental capacity," such as patients in a permanent vegetative state, or those with intellectual disabilities. Those human beings do not meet the criteria for personhood and thus do not possess the right to life. The same is true for infants. So, nine years after her original article was published Warren appended a "Postscript on Infanticide." Therein she argued that "infanticide....does not constitute the killing of a person," and can be morally justified in certain situations.[3] While many people who hold the colloquial view of personhood would disagree with her conclusions regarding euthanasia and infanticide, she argues that those positions are the logical extension of such a portrait of the human person.

While Warren corroborates and lends intellectual depth to the colloquial notion of personhood, her approach also fits with two pervasive contemporary medical ethical notions of personhood. First, in clinical practice personhood is often reduced to an activity of the person such as the capacity to make decisions for oneself. That is, the key aspect of personhood is a human being's capacity to exercise autonomy. This is the approach taken in the most important text in contemporary secular medical ethics, Tom Beauchamp's and James Childress's *The Principles of Biomedical Ethics*. The authors offer autonomy as the principle that medical professionals should follow in order to respect the patient as a person. But, while virtually no medical ethicist would argue against the importance of

---

2    Warren maintained that abortion was immoral only when it involved "wantonly destroying a potential person, when doing so isn't necessary to protect anyone's rights," 59.

3    Warren, "On the Moral and Legal Status of Abortion: Postscript on Infanticide" in *Biomedical Ethics*, 7th ed., eds. T.A. Mappes and D. DeGrazia (New York: McGraw-Hill, Inc. 1996): 474.

autonomy, many object to the reduction of a person to his or her capacity to make autonomous requests. Instead, bioethicist Robert Veatch calls for the "respect of persons" to replace the focus on patient autonomy.

> Respect for autonomy may sound like a synonym for "respect for persons," but the former, the Beauchamp-Childress term, implies that it is only a person's autonomy that is to be respected, which raises the question of whether other aspects of a person also should command respect and whether nonautonomous persons also command respect.[4]

As in Warren's understanding of personhood, the Beauchamp and Childress approach implies that the essential personal characteristic is the ability to exercise reason, self-motivated activity and communication. If a patient has these traits then his autonomy is to be respected. If a patient does not have these traits, then what of the patient is to be respected? Is the incapacitated patient worthy of respect? If so, on what grounds? On this matter the *Principles of Biomedical Ethics* takes a pass.[5]

Second, Warren's notion of the person also fits with the contemporary conflation of the quality and value of a human life. Warren argued that personhood is based on a set of capabilities which would enable the person to live "a reasonably satisfactory life."[6] The implication is that a life without such capabilities is neither satisfactory nor valuable. A December 2016 op-ed in the *Boston Globe*, which supported late-term abortion rights, included a similar moral sentiment. The article quoted a couple whose fetus was diagnosed in utero with spina bifida and would be likely permanently wheelchair bound. The couple asked, "The question for us is, what her quality of life would have been?"[7] The couple decided to abort the fetus.

---

4    Robert Veatch, *Hippocratic, Religious, and Secular Medical Ethics: The Points of Conflict* (Washington D.C.: Georgetown University Press, 2012), 166.

5    See Tom Beauchamp and James Childress, *The Principles of Biomedical Ethics*, 7th ed. (New York: Oxford, 2012), chapter 5. There they write, "The concept of personhood is so inherently contestable that we avoid it in this book insofar as possible. This language is too unclear regarding what is to be respected and how it is to be respected."

6    Warren, "On the Moral and Legal Status of Abortion," 473.

7    Michael Cohen, "The Unimaginable Cruelty of 20-week Abortion Bans," *Boston Globe*, December 15, 2016, accessed January 11, 2017. https://www.bostonglobe.com/opinion/2016/12/15/wife-and-grappled-with-possible-abortion/vr6Ft3yRaU57SKeZRBEBvI/story.html.

The overriding question for Warren and this couple is about the quality of life. For Warren, at least, the quality of life is seen as interchangeable with the value of life. Human beings who have low-quality lives are not as valuable as those who have high-quality lives.

Thus, it is clear that one's notion of personhood matters a great deal. It informs the moral positions that one takes on issues from abortion and infanticide, to end-of-life ethics and the treatment of the disabled. Getting personhood right will make a great deal of difference. Quite possibly, it will make all the difference.

## II. PERSONHOOD IN THE CATHOLIC TRADITION

The Catholic attitude toward personhood is different. It developed over many centuries and deserves a brief recapitulation. The Roman philosopher Boethius offered the first philosophical treatment of the person, in which he asserted that "a person is an individual substance of a rational nature."[8] The great medieval scholar St. Thomas Aquinas appropriated Boethius' definition and expanded the concept in two ways. He argued that persons have free will,[9] and that they are undivided wholes.[10] While persons have powers or aspects of their personhood, they are not an aggregate of their individual powers. Persons are one being, simply. These explanations of personhood are largely philosophical and ontological. One hundred years before Aquinas, Richard of St. Victor's interpretation was a more existential and theological pass at human personhood. He wrote that a person is an "incommunicably proper existence of a spiritual nature."[11] Josef Ratzinger (the future Pope Benedict XVI) noted that Richard's definition of the person rightly emphasized that the person is a uniquely existing being whose existence is spiritual and relational.[12] It also illumined that no one person can be interchanged with another. Unlike things, persons are

---

8   Boethius, *De Duabus Naturis*, 3.

9   Aquinas, *Summa Theologiae*. Trans. Fathers of the English Dominican Province (Allen, TX: Christian Classics, 1981), I 29.1.

10  Aquinas, 29.4.

11  Richard of St. Victor, as quoted in Josef Ratzinger, "Concerning the Notion of Person in Theology" *Communio* 17 (1990): 448.

12  Richard of St. Victor, 449 – 52.

irreplaceable.[13] Both the ontological and existential approaches remain in the tradition today.

The contemporary theological consensus on personhood is best summarized by Norris Clarke's notion that the person is "substance in relation."[14] Clarke argued that the person is "bi-polar," as he is present in himself and oriented toward others. Here human relations and relationships are not "add-ons," but are constitutive of the person himself. For instance, the best definition of me must include the fact that I am Brendan's and Daniel's father, Kate's husband, a child of God, a professor of students, and so on. My relations are my substance. It is not as if I exist and then I enter into relations.

Clarke's treatment marries the ontological approach of Aquinas to the existentialist and relational approach of Richard. It is just such an approach that one finds in the *Catechism of the Catholic Church*. In its treatment of personhood the *Catechism* moves from statements about the uniqueness and importance of human relationality to articulations of the nature of personal substance and identity. The *Catechism's* section on "Man" begins by stating that the "human person is the 'only creature capable of knowing and loving God.'"[15] The person's relationality with God and others is presented as the primary characteristic.

The *Catechism* then turns to the substantial self. The emphasis throughout this treatment is the singularity and unity of personal being. Following Aquinas, the church maintains that the person is a single whole. The human person is a unity that emerges from within the relation of the body and the soul.[16] For this reason, the person cannot be reduced to either body or soul. Persons do not have bodies, and do not have souls; they are embodied souls, or ensouled bodies.[17] There is a strand of contemporary Christian thinking which has, mistakenly, appropriated a Platonic approach to the body-soul

---

13  Karl Rahner, *Sacramentum Mundi* (New York: Herder and Herder, 1968): 405.

14  Norris Clarke, "Person, Being, and St. Thomas," *Communio* 19 (1992): 607.

15  *Catechism of the Catholic Church*, 1703, accessed January 11, 2017, http://www.vatican.va/ archive/ENG0015/_INDEX.HTM

16  *Catechism*, 365.

17  Margaret Farley, *Just Love: A Framework for Christian Sexual Ethics* (New York: Continuum, 2006): 116. Farley uses the language of embodied spirits and enspirited bodies, which I take to be synonymous with embodied souls, and ensouled bodies.

question. In this account the body is viewed as tending toward sin, and needs to be "overcome" by the soul, which is the person's true identity and is oriented toward God. However, the Catholic tradition has maintained that the person is identified with his body to point that the body, and not just the soul, is resurrected.[18] Thus, if death is the end of the relation of body and soul, resurrection is the reconstitution of the person through the body/soul relationship. The substantial self is also constitutively relational. The spiritual soul is infused by God, into the person. Further, the person's body is relational, composed of the mother and father, formed in the mother's womb, and nourished and sustained by the created world.

## When Does Personhood Begin?

In the medieval period scholars not only debated what personhood is, but also when personhood begins.[19] The theory of delayed animation, or delayed ensoulment, emerged from this era and is chiefly credited to the two theological heavyweights of the Christian tradition: Sts. Augustine and Thomas Aquinas.[20] Augustine argued that the spiritual soul is infused by God when the human body is formed. Because the human body is not substantially formed at conception, the spiritual soul is not infused at that moment. Gratian and Pope Innocent III codified Augustine's theology of ensoulment, and noted that abortion before ensoulment was not homicide, but was still a wrongful action. Following the embryology of Aristotle, Aquinas maintained that the human soul was infused, by God, into the embryo at 40 days gestation for males, and 90 days for females. Thus, for Aquinas the killing of an embryo pre-ensoulment was a serious sin, but was not equivalent to murder. The teachings of Augustine, Gratian, Innocent and Aquinas solidified the church's commitment to the distinction between unensouled and ensouled human life.

---

18   Brian Robinette, *Grammars of Resurrection* (New York: Herder and Herder, 2009), 121.

19   For further reading on this topic see D.A. Jones, "Thomas Aquinas and Augustine on Delayed Animation," *Thomist* 76 (2012).

20   The theological tradition of delayed animation is acknowledged in The Congregation for the Doctrine of the Faith's "The Declaration on Procured Abortion," 7, accessed January 11, 2017, http://www.vatican.va/roman_curia/congregations/cfaith/documents/rc_con_cfaith_doc_19741118_declaration-abortion_en.html.

While the distinction between ensouled and unensouled life was removed from canon law in 1869, questions about the moment of ensoulment have yet to be resolved. In 1974 the Congregation for the Doctrine of the Faith promulgated the "Declaration on Procured Abortion." The document hesitated to make a definitive ontological claim about the embryo. "From a moral point of view this is certain: even if a doubt existed concerning whether the fruit of conception is already a human person, it is objectively a grave sin to dare to risk murder."[21] Note that this is a moral claim, and is not a definitive claim about what the conceptus is. This approach continued in the 1987 document on assisted reproductive technologies, *Donum Vitae*.

> …the conclusions of science regarding the human embryo provide
> a valuable indication for discerning by the use of reason a personal
> presence at the moment of this first appearance of a human life: how
> could a human individual not be a human person? The Magisterium
> has not expressly committed itself to an affirmation of a philosophical
> nature, but it constantly reaffirms the moral condemnation of any
> kind of procured abortion.[22]

Here the Magisterium, teaching office of the Catholic Church, explicitly admitted that it had no official position on the personhood of the embryo. Like the "Declaration," *Donum Vitae* offered a moral norm: "the human being is to be respected and treated as a person from the moment of conception…" Again, the Magisterium did not claim that the human being (i.e., the embryo) is a person, instead, it states that the human being should be treated *as if* it was a person. Finally, Pope John Paul II's 1995 encyclical *Evangelium Vitae* constituted the most authoritative document to directly address the issue of ensoulment. Regarding ensoulment and the ethics of abortion John Paul II wrote that

> …what is at stake is so important that, from the standpoint of
> moral obligation, the mere probability that a human person is
> involved would suffice to justify an absolutely clear prohibition of

---

21  Congregation for the Doctrine of the Faith, "Declaration on Procured Abortion," 13.

22  Congregation for the Doctrine of the Faith, *Donum Vitae*, I.1, accessed January 11, 2017, http://www.vatican.va/roman_curia/congregations/cfaith/documents/rc_con_cfaith_doc_19870222_respect-for-human-life_en.html.

any intervention aimed at killing a human embryo…."The human being is to be respected and treated as a person from the moment of conception; and therefore from that same moment his rights as a person must be recognized, among which in the first place is the inviolable right of every innocent human being to life."[23]

In concert with previous magisterial teaching, John Paul II admitted that the question of the precise moment of the infusion of the soul into the human conceptus remained open. It remains so today. But the possibility that the soul could be infused at conception means that the conceptus should be treated *as if* it were a person.

## Personhood and Human Dignity

All that has been said thus far about the person is, in reality, a reflection on the fact that each person is created in the image of God. This faith commitment emerges from the first chapter of the book of Genesis (1:27), which teaches that "God created mankind in his image; in the image of God he created them; male and female he created them." The image of God is principally in persons in two ways. First, the Triune God is pure relationality. God's very being is a relationship among the Father, Son and Spirit. Each human person images God as a relational being.[24] Second, God is the Good. That is, God is the fullness of goodness, and all things are "good" by participation in God's goodness. Human persons are good in an ontological, not necessarily moral, sense. Thus, while people have the capacity to do evil, they still possess a value because they image God. The value that each and every person possesses is conceptualized in the phrase "human dignity." For Aquinas this meant that each person is "more valuable than all the galaxies."[25]

---

23  John Paul, *Evangelium Vitae*, 60, accessed January 11, 2017, http://w2.vatican.va/content/john-paul-ii/en/encyclicals/documents/hf_jp-ii_enc_25031995_evangelium-vitae.html.

24  International Theological Commission, "Communion and Stewardship," 25, accessed January 11, 2017, http://www.vatican.va/roman_curia/congregations/cfaith/cti_documents/rc_con_cfaith_doc_20040723_communion-stewardship_en.html.

25  Aquinas, *Summa theologiae*, I-II 113.9.

The concept of dignity assumed the central place in Christian ethics in
the 20th century. The centrality of dignity coincided, naturally, with the
refinement of its definition. For instance, in *Gaudium et Spes* dignity was
often mentioned, but never clearly defined. However, the theological
community, including John Paul II, the U.S. Catholic bishops, and
Benedict XVI have given specificity to this core concept. According to John
Paul II, human dignity meant that each person possessed inestimable value
and incomparable worth.[26] His moral positions on the rights of workers,
sexual ethics, the use of in vitro fertilization, etc...all derive their inspiration
from the value of each human person.[27] The U.S. Catholic bishops defined
dignity as the "transcendent worth" of each person.[28] Like John Paul, the
bishops maintain that personal worth cannot be measured. Along the
same lines, Benedict argued that "man has unassailable value without
distinction. At every state man is in the image of God."[29] This is the case
because "God sees divine image in each being; embryo, disabled, etc...."[30]
Benedict further refined his definition by calling the world to recognize the
transcendent value of each person.[31] Pope Francis, citing John Paul II, wrote,
"To believe in a Father who loves all men and women with an infinite love
means realizing that 'he thereby confers upon them an infinite dignity.'"[32]
It is this notion of the value of the person that is present in *The Ethical
and Religious Directives for Catholic Health Care Services* (hereafter ERDs).
The *ERDs* guide the moral practices of each Catholic health facility in the
United States and are regularly revised by the United States Conference
of Catholic Bishops. The most recent edition of the *ERDs* underscores the

---

26  John Paul II, *Evangelium Vitae*, 2 and 96.

27  Charles Curran, *The Moral Theology of John Paul II* (Washington D.C.: Georgetown University
    Press, 2005): 94.

28  United States Conference of Catholic Bishops, "Economic Justice for All," 28, accessed
    January 11, 2017, http://www.usccb.org/upload/economic_justice_for_all.pdf.

29  Benedict XVI, *Dignitas Personae*, 7, accessed January 11, 2017, http://www.vatican.va/
    roman_curia/congregations/cfaith/documents/rc_con_cfaith_doc_20081208_dignitas-
    personae_en.html.

30  Benedict XVI, 16.

31  Benedict XVI, "Address to the United Nations, 2008," accessed January 11, 2017, http://
    w2.vatican.va/content/benedict-xvi/en/speeches/2008/april/documents/hf_ben-xvi_
    spe_20080418_un-visit.html.

32  Francis, *Evangelii Gaudium*, 178, accessed January 11, 2017, https://w2.vatican.va/content/
    francesco/en/apost_exhortations/documents/papa-francesco_esortazione-ap_20131124_
    evangelii-gaudium.html.

fact that every person, regardless of health status, is a "unique person of incomparable worth."[33]

At a number of points in recent history the church has recognized human dignity as the grounding principle of Catholic ethics.[34] While discussing ethical business practices Pope Benedict wrote, "On this subject the Church's social doctrine can make a specific contribution, since it is based on man's creation 'in the image of God' (Gen 1:27), a datum which gives rise to the inviolable dignity of the human person and the transcendent value of natural moral norms."[35] The church's key contribution to business ethics, or any ethics for that matter, is its notion of personhood and personal dignity. Theologians Todd Salzman and Michael Lawler have acknowledged the importance of dignity in ethics, as they assert that dignity is "widely recognized as the central moral principle in Christian ethics."[36]

## III. PERSONHOOD, LOVE AND CATHOLIC HEALTH CARE ETHICS

At this point, one might say: So what? So what if the Roman Catholic approach to personhood differs from the colloquial view? What difference does it make? Isn't this just an academic disagreement? In this section I will show just how consequential this disagreement is. As I suggested in the introduction, these are not "ivory tower" questions. The answer to the question affects decisions about who lives and who dies, who is allowed to live, or is allowed to be killed, and who receives medical care and treatment, and who is denied care and treatment.

---

33  The United States Conference of Catholic Bishops, *The Ethical and Religious Directives for Catholic Health Care Services*, #3, accessed January 11, 2017, http://www.usccb.org/issues-and-action/human-life-and-dignity/health-care/upload/Ethical-Religious-Directives-Catholic-Health-Care-Services-fifth-edition-2009.pdf.

34  See, for instance, St. John XXIII, *Mater et magister*, 220, accessed January 11, 2017, http://w2.vatican.va/content/john-xxiii/en/encyclicals/documents/hf_j-xxiii_enc_15051961_mater.html.

35  Benedict XVI, *Caritas in Veritate*, 45.

36  Todd Salzman and Michael Lawler, "Method and Catholic Theological Ethics in the Twenty-First Century," *Theological Studies* 74 (2013): 911.

The official Catholic position on every issue in medical ethics reflects both an understanding of personhood as well as what is called the primacy of charity. I have already explained what personhood is, but what is the primacy of charity? First, charity is the virtue, or good character trait, by which a person loves both God and neighbor. This "double love" is the heart of Catholic ethics. Catholic ethics is not an ethics of sin avoidance or rule-following, it is an ethics of love. What is love? It is, in the words of Pope Benedict XVI, "to desire that person's good and to take effective steps to secure it."[37] Christian love is not merely emotional, but engages the whole person and is always realized in actions. Further, the theological tradition has consistently maintained that love of God and love of neighbor are inseparable.

But why has the Catholic tradition insisted upon the inseparability of the love of God and neighbor? Why must a Christian love her neighbor if she is to love God? Again, we find help in Aquinas. His treatment of charity contains the Christian tradition's clearest explanation of the connection of the two loves. In his masterwork, the *Summa Theologiae*, Aquinas explained the interconnection of the love of God and neighbor through an analogy to human friendship.

> Friendship extends to a person in two ways: first in respect of himself, and in this way friendship never extends but to one's friends: secondly, it extends to someone in respect of another, as, when a man has friendship for a certain person, for his sake he loves all belonging to him, be they children, servants, or connected with him in any way. Indeed so much do we love our friends, that for their sake we love all who belong to them, even if they hurt or hate us; so that, in this way, the friendship of charity extends even to our enemies, whom we love out of charity in relation to God, to Whom the friendship of charity is chiefly directed.[38]

---

37  Benedict XVI, *Caritas in Veritate*, 7.
38  Aquinas, *Summa Theologiae*, II-II, 23.1 ad 2.

For example, if my friend Kate has a friend, Brendan, I should relate to Brendan in relation to Kate. Because Kate loves Brendan, I, too, should love Brendan. Aquinas takes for granted that one should love the friends of one's friend. Common experience corroborates this. For someone to love me, they must also love my sons and my wife. If they harm or hate my family, the relationship with that friend will be damaged. Similarly, Christians are called to relate to the world in relation to how their friend, God, relates to the world. Earlier I emphasized the fact that God sees God's image in all persons, has gifted them with transcendent value, and loves all persons. Because God loves all persons, regardless of intellectual status or moral character, those who love God should also love all persons.

Returning to Aquinas' analogy, we find that while we may love all of our family members equally, there are some that we might love preferentially. For instance, we often first love the weak and vulnerable in our family. We care first for the children, elderly, the disabled of our families, and then serve the adult, able-bodied members. The God revealed by Jesus Christ acts similarly. God is partial; He is a God who opts for the poor, the weak and the vulnerable of the human family. The Christians who follow this God should exercise a preferential love for the beloved of God. Christians should first serve the children, the poor, the sick, the disabled and the elderly. In sum, God's priorities should drive the moral priorities of those who worship God.

## *The Implications of the Catholic and Colloquial Approaches to Personhood*

While the Catholic accounts of personhood and charity influence the concrete moral norms that affect the care of all patients, socially and physically vulnerable persons receive special attention in Directive 3 of the *ERDs*.

> Catholic health care should distinguish itself by service to and advocacy for those people whose social condition puts them at the margins of our society and makes them particularly vulnerable to discrimination: the poor, the uninsured and the underinsured; children and the unborn; single parents; the elderly; those with incurable diseases and chemical

> dependencies; racial minorities; immigrant and refugees…person(s) with mental or physical disabilities….[39]

Here the bishops call Catholic health care institutions to serve those with social and physical conditions that put them at risk for not "counting" as persons. Because the unborn, the young and old, the drug addicted, the undocumented, the disabled, the dying and the poor often lack autonomy and suffer from low quality of life, their value is regularly unrecognized in society. The colloquial view implies that these human beings are either non-persons (in the case of the fetus) or lesser persons than the strong and intellectually able (in the case of the disabled and permanently unconscious). As a result, they are often deprioritized for care and are considered suitable candidates for medically-assisted killing. Abortion, infanticide, physician-assisted suicide and euthanasia are moral options within the colloquial view of the person because their "limited" value can be compared against other important values. Recall Mary Anne Warren's argument for abortion. Because the fetus is not a person, it does not have the value of a person or the right to life. The mother, in the exercise of her right to freely choose the course of her life, can terminate the pregnancy. Here, personal freedom can outweigh the value of another person.

The Catholic approach rejects any attempt to compare the value of a person against other relative values such as freedom or wealth. The unborn, the weak, the poor, the disabled, and the suffering are the transcendently valued beloved of God. The God revealed by Jesus is a God who stands on their side. But, as previously noted, these are the very people who are at risk for being ignored as persons. In addition, there is, according to Pope Francis, a globalized "indifference to suffering."[40] Today people are cultivated to attend to their own vision of the pleasurable life and, therefore, typically make little space for the suffering of others.

---

39  United States Conference of Catholic Bishops, *The Ethical and Religious Directives for Catholic Health Care Services*, Directive, 3.

40  Francis, *Misericordiae Vultus*, 15, accessed January 11, 2017, https://w2.vatican.va/content/francesco/en/bulls/documents/papa-francesco_bolla_20150411_misericordiae-vultus.html.

In the face of this indifference Catholic health care should prioritize the well-being of the socially and physically vulnerable. Mercy, not indifference or annihilation, is the Christian response to those who suffer with social stigma and physical pain. Mercy is one of the principal ways in which Christian love is enacted. Mercy is love's response to those in pain. It is the virtue by which a person suffers with the suffering and attempts to "dispel the misery of the other."[41] The goal of Francis' Jubilee Year of Mercy in 2016 was to move Catholics toward those persons who are weak, forgotten, and who suffer. Francis is no masochist, however. Suffering is an evil, but it is real. The only situation worse than suffering is suffering alone.

Instead of indifference, the merciful never allow the suffering to suffer alone. They practice the works of mercy, such as feeding the hungry, clothing the naked, and caring for the sick. They are not indifferent to the unwed pregnant teenager, or to the couple whose fetal child has spina bifida.

The loving and merciful response to these women and men is to show them that "you are not alone." Implicit within this offer of loving care is the recognition that their fetuses are images of God, no matter their social or physical condition, and should be treated as transcendently valuable persons.

The loving and merciful response to the terminally ill patient is to offer him an authentic "death with dignity." Human dignity is not concerned with the control of one's bodily functions or intellectual capacity, it is about the value of a person. In this account, a dignified death is one in which the person's immeasurable value is recognized and in which others share in his burdens.

The loving and merciful response to the poor is to invite them into Catholic health facilities and to provide them care based on need, not wealth.[42] The need-based distribution of care is unique because it says and shows to the poor and the world that the poor are as deserving of medical treatment and care as the rich, because they are as valuable as the rich. They are full persons.

---

41  *Summa Theologiae*, I 21.3.
42  *The Ethical and Religious Directives*, 1.

Showing love and mercy to the suffering does not, however, require Catholic health care to provide all life-sustaining treatments at all times. The Catholic tradition is not "vitalist." Vitalism is a commitment to prolong life in every single instance because life is the greatest good. As I've argued, love of God and neighbor is the greatest good for the human person, not life.

In practice, this means that according to official church teaching, it is morally permissible to remove ventilators, assisted nutrition and hydration, dialysis, chemotherapy, and any other medical treatment when the burden to the patient and the community outweighs the benefit to the patient.[43] In short, allowing oneself or another to die of natural causes is not morally equivalent to either killing someone or helping him end his life.

## CONCLUSION

The Catholic approach to personhood provides deep insights into these issues. It is a much richer approach than a "no" to certain procedures. For instance, the church's "no" to direct abortion is the product of a great "yes" to personal dignity and universal love. Admittedly, it is a more difficult way of relating to the vulnerable and suffering than being indifferent to them, or worse, killing them. The Catholic approach to personhood and love asks us to suffer, too; to bear the burdens of the mother and child, the disabled, the dying, the poor.

Ours is an age in which the colloquial, "performance-based" notion of personhood is increasingly powerful and in which there is widespread indifference to suffering. In such a time, the annihilation of suffering emerges as an attractive solution. For those abandoned by family and society, abortion seems to be the solution to unwanted pregnancy. For those who equate dignity with control of one's faculties, physician-assisted suicide seems to be the solution to terminal illness. It is in this context that one of the central tasks of Catholic health care must be to witness to the value of all persons. This is the prophetic mission of Catholic health care. This mission is realized when Catholics say and show to the suffering: "You are a person, you are valuable, you are loved, and you are not alone."

---

43  *The Ethical and Religious Directives*, #57.

## DISCUSSION QUESTIONS

**1.** What are the essential aspects of the Catholic approach to personhood?

**2.** Imagine you are engaged in conversation with a person whose colloquial notion of personhood led them to moral positions that violated the dignity of persons regarding either physician-assisted suicide or the care of poor and homeless patients. How might you help them understand how the Catholic position on personhood drives the church's perspectives on how to care for the dying and the poor?

**3.** How might a Catholic health care facility and the employees of the facility communicate with and demonstrate to the suffering that they are a person, they are valuable, they are loved, and they are not alone? Is there a way to institutionalize this, or is it a matter of individual employees taking the initiative to practice mercy?

CHAPTER SUMMARY

This chapter introduces readers to the theological conversation
about God and suffering as that conversation has developed
through the centuries and continues in contemporary thought.
It discusses the ways in which those engaged in Catholic health
care confront the reality of suffering every day and describes
various dimensions of human suffering. The author takes note
of the "implicit theologies" of suffering that are present in the
minds of most believers. Then he explores key perspectives on
suffering in the Hebrew and Christian Scriptures and among
some contemporary thinkers. The author also draws on the
distinct ways in which the four evangelists relate the death of
Jesus and connects this with the "varieties of faith" that are
reflective of the Christian experience.

## 2.2 GOD'S PRESENCE IN OUR SUFFERING

———

Fr. Robin Ryan, CP, Ph.D.
*Associate Professor of Systematic Theology*
*Catholic Theological Union*

E VEN IF THEY HAVE NEVER TAKEN A SINGLE COURSE in theology, people who work in Catholic health care are familiar with the experience of suffering and, to a certain degree, with "theologies" of suffering. Every day they encounter human suffering in its many guises: the person injured in an automobile accident arriving by ambulance at the door of the emergency room; the woman whose breast biopsy reveals cancer; the stroke patient trying so hard to articulate his words; the nursing home resident with memory loss sitting alone and staring off into space; the homeless person in need of medical care but having no health insurance; the woman who has been battered by her husband or boyfriend; the family struggling to make end-of-life decisions about a loved one; the nurse or doctor grieving the loss of a patient. These experiences leave a mark on the soul, and they raise difficult questions about life's meaning and purpose. For people of faith, they evoke urgent questions about God and God's relation to those who are suffering.

Two questions that people have posed to me are deeply ingrained in my memory. Some years ago, after giving a talk on the topic of prayer in times of suffering, a woman told me about her husband's amazing escape from injury after a horrific automobile accident. The state trooper who arrived at the scene called it a "miracle." As people of faith, they expressed their sincere gratitude to God for her husband's survival. A few months later, however, the teenage daughter of close friends of theirs was killed in an automobile crash. In their attempts to comfort their friends, they did not know what to say. So she asked, "In this situation, how should we be speaking about God?" The second question was asked by my sister, after my oldest brother was diagnosed with glioblastoma. Feeling that it was useless to pray for healing given the diagnosis of this virulent form of brain cancer, she suggested that perhaps we should simply pray for acceptance of the outcome. She asked, "How should we be praying?"

Two compelling questions, asked with urgency: How should we be talking *about* God when our friends have just lost their daughter in an automobile accident? How should we be talking *to* God when our brother is suffering from brain cancer? While these particular situations may be distinctive, the questions are not; such questions are asked, explicitly or in the silent recesses of the heart, by countless people of faith who are experiencing suffering. We find these questions at health care facilities of all kinds, even though they often lie beneath the surface of ordinary conversation and interaction.

## IMPLICIT THEOLOGIES

Most people of faith have an implicit theology of suffering within them, though these are often unexpressed. The sources of this theology derive from a variety of influences: a person's earliest education in the faith; favorite scenes, stories or verses from the Bible; statements about suffering that one has read or heard in church or elsewhere. A number of theological assumptions and convictions are evident in familiar maxims that are sometimes articulated in situations of suffering: "I cannot explain why this is happening, but I am sure that God knows what he is doing;" "Remember, God has a plan for us;" "There's a reason for everything;" "God never gives us a bigger cross than we can bear;" "Our faith is tested and purified in the crucible of suffering;" "Suffering is just part of life;" "God is there with you in your suffering — God is suffering, too."

I mention these frequently heard "proverbs" not to endorse any of them but simply to emphasize the fact that most people of faith have some implicit theology of God and suffering. People typically make such statements as ways of expressing compassion for others and in the attempt to find meaning in perplexing situations. Sometimes it is easier to fit an experience of suffering into a structure of meaning that involves a questionable image of God than it is simply to stand before the mystery. The challenge for believers is to explore the content of their implicit theologies and to allow these ways of thinking about God to enter into conversation with the tradition, as the tradition is expressed in the Bible, the teachings of the church, and the writings of spiritual masters and theologians. In the course of that sustained dialogue our personal theologies become illumined, enriched and refined.

## EVIL AND SUFFERING

The Judeo-Christian tradition has consistently affirmed the intrinsic goodness of creation. It has reiterated this conviction against various forms of *dualism* that have arisen through the centuries. Dualistic strains of thought typically posit two absolute metaphysical principles — one that is the ultimate source of goodness/light and the other that is the origin of evil/darkness. These metaphysical principles are viewed as hostile to one another. Dualistic thinking usually envisions the world we know as the result of a fall or flaw in some heavenly realm that existed before creation. The material world is a kind of prison from which one needs to escape. Christian thinkers have responded to such scenarios by insisting that the world is the good gift of a good God, even if it has been wounded by sin. And in Christ, the Word of God truly became flesh (Jn 1:14), inextricably connected with creation and all that is "earthy." Thus the material world is the place where God's saving purposes are being accomplished. For Christians, salvation entails the salvation *of* the world, not salvation *from* the world. Human history and all of creation are the objects of God's saving work in Jesus Christ.

From this perspective, suffering has been viewed as the result of evil, which is usually divided theologically into two distinct categories: moral evil and physical (natural) evil. Moral evil is the wrongdoing committed by human beings; it is people inflicting suffering on other people and, in so doing, upon themselves. Theologians, past and present, have argued that the origin of moral evil is not to be traced to God in any sense. Having gifted human beings with freedom, God permits such evil but does not directly cause it. As mentioned above, those who work in Catholic health care encounter the suffering that results from moral evil in many forms, including the effects of violent crime, domestic abuse, the neglect of children and the elderly and the marginalization of the poor. While Christian theology traces the source of moral evil to those who commit it, the complexity entailed in social conditioning and psychological motivation can lend an air of mystery to it. It is difficult to ascertain what could have been going through the minds of the perpetrators of the Nazi war crimes, the 1994 Rwandan genocide, or the wanton gang violence that afflicts scores of people in our cities.

Much of the suffering that health care professionals encounter originates from what theologians have traditionally labeled as "physical" or "natural" evil: physical illness and disease; the debility and decline that accompany the aging process; the deleterious effects of genetic abnormalities; mental illness resulting from chemical imbalance; injuries due to natural disasters; etc. In recent years, the findings of evolutionary science have compelled theologians to address physical/natural evil more directly. They have probed more deeply into the costs entailed in evolution. These costs include pain (in sentient creatures), physical decline, death, and the extinction of entire species. Saint Paul marvels at the "groaning" of all creation, which is in "labor pains" awaiting its redemption (Rom 8:18-25). Theologian Elizabeth Johnson observes: "How stunning to think that massive death is intrinsic to the process of evolution."[1] In dialogue with evolutionary science, many contemporary theologians acknowledge that such loss and death have been necessary for the cosmos to attain the level of development and the intensification of beauty that is found in it. Here theologians often assert that in creating an evolving world, God limited God's Self in order to allow creation to be and to develop. Just as God respects the free will of human beings in history, so God also respects the free processes involved in the emergence of the universe, allowing creation to be and to develop through

---

1    Elizabeth Johnson, *Ask the Beasts: Darwin and the God of Love* (London: Bloomsbury, 2014): 184.

the subtle interplay of natural law, chance and time. Johnson suggests
that the affliction that we experience in the natural world arises "from below"
rather than "by direct divine will."[2] Christian theologians also connect the
"agony" of creation to the death of Jesus. In the cross of Jesus we can perceive
God's solidarity with and compassion for every creature that suffers. This is
a cutting edge area for theology today, one that has caused theologians to
re-think their understanding of God's relation to creation. Denis Edwards,
a theologian who dialogues with scientists, cautions that "in any authentically
*theological* approach to natural evil, we must stand with the Book of Job
(chapters 38 – 42) before the mystery of God and God's creation, and
acknowledge that there is a great deal that we do not know."[3]

## DIMENSIONS OF SUFFERING

Human suffering has many distinct faces. Rather than attempt to construct
a precise definition of suffering that would encompass its multiple
manifestations, it seems more helpful to reflect upon dimensions of
suffering. Canadian theologian Phil Zylla enumerates four dimensions of
human suffering: physical pain, psychological anguish, social degradation
and spiritual despondency.[4] Health care professionals are very familiar with
the suffering that comes from *physical pain*. Chronic pain can be utterly
debilitating for body and spirit. Advances in the field of palliative care
are positive developments that have led to the alleviation of the physical
discomfort experienced by the sick and dying and have given consolation
to their loved ones. *Psychological anguish* is an aspect of suffering that can
be more intense than physical pain. As Zylla points out, at the root of the
psychological dimension of suffering is fear: fear of the unknown, of pain,
of a difficult future, of death. Such anguish also can be caused by the deep
wound inflicted by the loss of a loved one. There is also a *social* dimension
to suffering. Sometimes the physically or mentally ill, and persons with
disabilities, are ignored, avoided or even abandoned. The long-term
care resident who seldom receives a visitor suffers alienation from the

---

2    Johnson, 191.
3    Denis Edwards, *The God of Evolution: A Trinitarian Theology* (Mahwah, NJ: Paulist Press, 1999):
     36 (emphasis author's).
4    Zylla, *The Roots of Sorrow: A Pastoral Theology of Suffering* (Waco, TX: Baylor University Press,
     2012): 58 – 69.

community. The mentally ill homeless person who wanders the streets may suffer intense isolation. To suffer *spiritual despondency* is "to experience the eclipse of hope itself, which leads us to experience a growing distance from God."[5] A person may well feel that God has abandoned her or him, echoing the prayer of the suffering Christ found in the Gospel of Mark: "My God, my God, why have you forsaken me?" (Mk 15:34). This sense of desolation can lead to a crisis of faith and of personal meaning in one's life.

It is impossible to "measure" the suffering of another, or even one's own suffering, for that matter. But attention to these dimensions of suffering can provide insights about the intensity of suffering that is experienced, and it can inform protocols of health care. The more dimensions of suffering that a person experiences, the greater the intensity of that suffering. One may experience serious physical discomfort but have faithful personal support, a deep faith and a strong will to live. On the other hand, an elderly person who feels very alone in life may have a less serious physical illness or condition but may be suffering intensely. For Catholic health care to respond effectively to those it serves, it must attend to all of the dimensions of human suffering.

## BIBLICAL PERSPECTIVES ON SUFFERING

Sometimes people ask, "What does the Bible say about God and human suffering?" Actually, the Bible says a lot of different things about God and suffering. There is no single, uniform message about suffering in the Judeo-Christian Scriptures, and this pluralism can be confusing. There are a number of different interpretations of the experience of suffering in the Hebrew Scriptures and the New Testament. Daniel Harrington and other biblical scholars elucidate these distinct biblical themes for us.[6]

---

5   Zylla, 63.

6   Daniel Harrington, *Why Do We Suffer? A Scriptural Approach to the Human Condition* (Franklin, WI: Sheed & Ward, 2000). See also Daniel Simundson, *Faith Under Fire: Biblical Interpretations of Suffering* (Minneapolis: Augsburg Publishing, 1980). I also discuss these biblical perspectives on suffering in Ryan, *God and the Mystery of Human Suffering: A Theological Conversation Across the Ages* (New York: Paulist Press, 2011): 19 – 81.

## THE OLD TESTAMENT

One theme found throughout the Hebrew Scriptures is the *theory of retribution*. Righteous people are rewarded with blessing, while those who do evil are cursed with misfortune. Since belief in life after death developed gradually and appears in only a few passages in the Old Testament, the effects of reward and punishment are usually viewed as limited to earthly existence. This view is found in the Book of Deuteronomy and in the theological history of Israel composed by the Deuteronomistic authors, found in the books of Joshua through Second Kings. Looking back on the history of their own people, these authors interpret Israel's national fortunes to be a direct result of their fidelity or infidelity to their covenant with God. This interpretation had its roots in the preaching of Israel's great prophets, who warned the people about impending disaster because of pervasive idolatry and injustice. The theology of retribution is also found in some of the Wisdom literature, e.g., the Book of Proverbs. There is a corporate and cross-generational dimension to this theory of retribution. The sins of one person affect the entire community, and the sins of ancestors can cause trouble for their descendants (see Ex 34:6-7). This theory of retribution attests to a limited insight: there is a grain of truth to the adage that a person reaps what he or she sows. And in our own day and time, the history of racism and the ecological crisis show that the conduct of one generation does affect later generations. Nevertheless, the people of Israel came to recognize that this explanation was much too simple to account for every experience of suffering. If one reverses the formula that sin leads to suffering and assumes that the presence of suffering must be an indication of some wrongdoing, then the harmful effects of this perspective become manifest. Pastoral ministers witness the harm that can be done when a sick person is convinced that his or her illness is a form of punishment for past wrongdoings.

A second prominent theme in the Hebrew Bible is the *cry of lament*. The theory of retribution evinces reflection on the experience of suffering from a distance in time. When biblical peoples were more immediate to the experience of suffering, they cried out to God. Of all the psalms within the Bible, laments comprise the greatest number. The Hebrew Scriptures bear direct and compelling testimony to the crying out of the sufferer. They show that the Hebrew ideal was not that of suffering alone or in silence. Lament psalms are usually emphatic in their confession of trust that God will listen to the petitioner and respond with aid. Walter Brueggemann observes, "The world of lament speech thus is based on the premise that the speech of Israel draws God into the trouble. God will act and life will be restored."[7] At the same time, biblical laments are striking for their realistic descriptions of the experience of suffering and for the boldness with which people of faith express their sentiments to God. Laments offer eloquent testimony to the fact that for the Hebrew people the God of the covenant was so real, so close at hand and directly involved in their lives, that they knew they could, and even should, cry out to God. And that was precisely the way in which God remained real for them, even amidst experiences of suffering that defied explanation. This tradition of lament has direct relevance for the emotional and spiritual care of the sick and dying.

The Book of Job represents a third Old Testament perspective on suffering. It is another compelling expression of the place of lament in the tradition of ancient Israel, and it poses the most direct challenge to the doctrine of retribution. The author of the Book of Job, thought by scholars to have been written after the Babylonian exile (6th century BCE), adapted an ancient folktale about a legendary wise person who was tested, found to be faithful, and subsequently rewarded for faithfulness. The author reshaped this story by inserting a series of dialogues between Job and his "friends" and concluded the book with two lengthy speeches by God. In so doing the biblical author refashioned the original story according to his own purposes and aims.

In this classic story, the life of Job — the paradigmatic righteous person — is turned upside down by a series of catastrophes that result in unspeakable personal suffering. In their lengthy, repetitive monologues, Job's friends articulate the theology of retribution, and they become increasingly impatient with Job's refusal to acquiesce to that traditional teaching. They are convinced that Job's misfortunes must be the consequence of some sin. Job, however, perseveres in professing his innocence despite the traditional

---

7    Walter Brueggemann, *Israel's Praise: Doxology Against Idolatry and Ideology* (Philadelphia: Fortress, 1988): 143.

doctrine. He is convinced that the order of divine justice has been disrupted, and he wants to present his legal case before the divine tribunal. When God finally speaks "out of the storm" (Jb 38:1), Job is reduced to reverent silence, and he eventually "repents" in dust and ashes (Jb 42:6). God never accuses Job of any sin; rather God acts as a wisdom teacher, directing Job's attention to the marvels of nature and suggesting that despite the reality of innocent suffering chaos does not reign in the universe.[8] Nowhere in these speeches does God directly answer the questions that Job has posed throughout the story.

Interpretations of the Book of Job vary widely and never seem to capture the entirety of the message. Nevertheless, several key ideas emerge with relative clarity. First, the story demonstrates that the doctrine of retribution is inadequate to the experience of suffering. There is such a thing as innocent suffering. Second, the book is a further biblical witness to the importance of lament in the tradition of ancient Israel. Job's bold crying out to God is an expression of his faith in the God of the covenant. Finally, the experience of God's presence in the midst of suffering is transformative for Job. While he receives no explanation for his predicament, he is assured of God's presence and care for him and for all creatures. Job, the suffering one, is granted an experience of communion with God.

Elie Wiesel, the prominent Holocaust survivor and Nobel Peace Prize laureate who died in 2016, commented eloquently on the relevance of the Book of Job for modern people, especially for Jews.[9] Wiesel noted that during the days after World War II, Job could be seen on every road of Europe. He observed that in the Jewish tradition people continue to turn to Job's words when they are grappling with suffering: "In times of stress it is to his words that we turn to express our anger, revolt or resignation. He belongs to our most intimate landscape, the most vulnerable part of our past."[10] Wiesel expressed his admiration for Job's courage in arguing his case before God, and he registered his protest at Job's repentance: "Much

---

8  See Dianne Bergant, *Job, Ecclesiastes*, Old Testament Message Series, vol. 82 (Wilmington, DE: Glazier, 1982): 213.

9  See Elie Wiesel, "Job: Our Contemporary," in *Messengers of God: Biblical Portraits and Legends*, trans. Marion Wiesel (New York: Summit Books, 1976): 211 – 35.

10  Wiesel, 211.

as I admired Job's passionate rebellion, I am deeply troubled by his hasty abdication."[11] Relating the biblical tradition of lament to his own prayer as a Holocaust survivor, Wiesel commented, "What I try to do is speak to God. Even when I speak against God, I speak to God. And even if I am angry with God, I try to show God my anger. But even that is a profession, not a denial of God."[12]

Fourth, the theme of *sacrifice* is also part of Hebrew reflection on the experience of suffering. Drawing a connection between suffering and sacrifice represented an attempt to find positive meaning in suffering, suggesting that some good can be accomplished through the experience of suffering. Sacrifice was an integral element of the covenant tradition of Israel, with various meanings assigned to it. It was not viewed as a human means for appeasing an angry God. Rather, sacrifices in Israel were ways of bridging the gap between God and humanity, allowing human beings to enter the presence of God. Sacrifices entailed "a gradual movement toward and through sacred space and an approach to God."[13]

The most influential interpretation of the suffering of Israel in sacrificial terms is found in Second Isaiah (chapters 40 – 55 of the Book of Isaiah). As the Babylonian exile was coming to an end, an anonymous author spoke a word of profound hope to the exiles. In four poems, we meet the figure of the "servant," whose experience is depicted as emblematic of Israel (Is 42:1-9; 49:1-6; 50:4-11; 52:13-53:12). The fourth servant poem manifests the clearest interpretation of the servant's suffering in terms of sacrifice: "Surely he has borne our infirmities and carried our diseases; yet we accounted him stricken, struck down by God and afflicted. But he was wounded for our transgressions, crushed for our iniquities . . ." (Is 53:5-6; a passage read in the Catholic liturgy for Good Friday). The servant, who is without any exalted status, performs a singular service on behalf of the people and is granted a "portion among the great" (Is 53:12). The identity

---

11   Wiesel, 233.

12   Wiesel in Ekkehard Schuster and Reinhold Boschert-Kimmig, *Hope Against Hope: Johann Baptist Metz and Elie Wiesel Speak Out on the Holocaust*, trans. J. Matthew Ashley (New York: Paulist Press, 1999): 91.

13   Christian Eberhart, *The Sacrifice of Jesus: Understanding Atonement Biblically* (Minneapolis: Fortress Press, 2011): 71.

of this servant has long been a matter of debate among biblical scholars, with interpretations that pose both collective and individual possibilities. Whatever the precise identity, it is clear that the servant's suffering is viewed as having positive significance for the entire nation. This servant poem influenced the early Christian community in its interpretation of the meaning and effects of the death of Jesus (e.g., see Acts 8:26-40). The sacrificial interpretation of suffering is deeply embedded in the Christian imagination. It is an interpretation that has been critiqued by many modern theologians, especially for its misuse in ways that served to keep oppressed people from rightfully asserting themselves. Still, it remains part of our biblical and theological tradition as a perspective that accentuates the opportunity for good that is present in suffering.

The fifth Old Testament perspective on suffering is found in *apocalyptic* literature. This biblical perspective is found in parts of certain prophetic books (e.g., Zechariah) and in the Book of Daniel. It is certainly reflected in the Book of Revelation in the New Testament as well. Apocalyptic writings are difficult to interpret because they narrate revelations from heavenly beings communicated in code language that is replete with sometimes bizarre symbolism. Fundamentally, however, apocalyptic literature embodies a message of hope offered to people who are suffering in oppressive situations. Apocalyptic authors attempt to keep hope alive for the oppressed by announcing a climactic intervention by God that will put an end to suffering and vindicate the righteous. They exhort believers to trust in God and to await God's decisive, saving action on their behalf. The Book of Daniel, the clearest example of apocalyptic writing in the Old Testament, reflects the situation of the people of Israel under the oppressive rule of Antiochus IV Epiphanes (175 – 164 BCE). By narrating a story set four centuries earlier during the Babylonian exile, the author presents a compelling message to the suffering people of his own day: God is sovereign over human history; the power of evildoers is only temporary; believers must trust in God and remain faithful in the present. In a certain way, the apocalyptic perspective embraces the doctrine of retribution, though retribution is delayed to a future time, an end-time of definitive divine action when God's kingdom will come. Apocalyptic literature does not offer a clear explanation as to why the sovereign God allows the forces of evil to wreak havoc in the world. It does offer a path through suffering by counseling steadfast trust in the fidelity and justice of God. Sometimes it suggests that the faith of believers is purified and strengthened by their endurance in the face of oppression.

A sixth Old Testament theme related to the experience of suffering is the *pathos of God*. For the Hebrew people God was transcendent, absolutely holy; but God was also near, present to and with God's people. God's transcendence was actualized in God's nearness to God's people. Thus in some way God even participated in the misery of humanity. As one Old Testament scholar puts it, "His [God's] pain for the world is never the wailing sympathy of an uninvolved onlooker, but the genuine pain of one who is directly affected, the suffering of a comrade, who takes upon himself a part of the burden."[14] Even when God is viewed as sending the people into exile, God goes into exile with them — God accompanies them. Speaking as the voice of God, the prophet Jeremiah says, "Is Ephraim not my favored son, the child in whom I delight? Often as I threaten him, I still remember him with favor; my heart stirs for him, I must show him mercy, says the LORD" (Jer 31:20). Terence Fretheim categorizes Old Testament passages about divine suffering according to a threefold schema: God suffers *because* of the people's rejection; God empathizes *with* the people who are suffering; and God suffers *for* the people — God bears their burdens.[15] The suffering of God is articulated in the context of the foundational reality of covenant: God becomes bound to the people of Israel and so is personally affected by their response. This biblical portrait of divine compassion is very important for a Christian approach to persons who are sick, disabled or dying.

## THE NEW TESTAMENT

The earliest disciples of Jesus, as well as the authors of the writings that became the books of the New Testament, assumed the various perspectives on suffering that we have explored. Their Scriptures were the Hebrew Scriptures. They were convinced that the God who had been revealed in Jesus was the same God who had entered into a covenant relationship

---

14   E.Gerstenberger in E. Gerstenberger and W. Schrage, *Suffering*, trans. John E. Steely, (Nashville: Abingdon Press, 1980): 99.

15   Terence Fretheim, *The Suffering of God* (Philadelphia: Fortress Press, 1984): 108.

with the people of Israel. At the same time, they were also convinced
that something entirely new had taken place in Jesus' ministry, death and
resurrection. His ministry and destiny, even his very person, had shone new
light on the character of God and God's relationship to the human family.
This disclosure illumined the way in which Christians thought about the
presence of God in the midst of suffering and death.

Contemporary theologians stress that if we want to explore the meaning of
God's revelation in Jesus we must pay close attention to his public ministry.
We should not focus solely on his death and resurrection, isolating these
climactic events from all that preceded them. If we ignore the ministry
of Jesus, we may well end up with a distorted notion of God. When we
do reflect on his public ministry we discover that its major focus was his
proclamation of the reign (kingdom) of God. The Gospel of Mark presents
Jesus' initial proclamation this way: "This is the time of fulfillment. The
kingdom of God is at hand. Repent, and believe in the gospel" (Mk 1:15).
The symbol of the reign of God was rooted in the longing of Israel for the
God of the covenant to come in power and establish God's rule. It referred
to the dynamic state of affairs in which the love of God would become
the governing force in people's lives and throughout creation. In Jesus'
proclamation, there is an inherent tension between the future and the
present dimensions of God's reign. On the one hand, his preaching alludes
to "God's future display of power over all creation and the acknowledgment
of it by all created things."[16] At the same time, Jesus makes the reign of God
present through his words, his deeds and his very person. Jesus' healings,
exorcisms and table fellowship are integral dimensions of his proclamations
of God's reign. The Gospel accounts of Jesus' ministry show that when
God's reign became present in and through him, *people found life.* Jesus
acted against all the forces that drained life out of people. And his life-
giving presence affected the whole person, body and spirit. As one scholar
puts it, "Jesus himself was less engaged in interpreting suffering than he was
in actively working to overcome it."[17]

---

16   Harrington, *Why Do We Suffer?*, 90.
17   W. Schrage, in Gerstenberger and Schrage, *Suffering*, 139.

The experience of the death and resurrection of Jesus focused early Christian reflection on the mystery of suffering. It is important to recognize the scandal that Jesus' death was for many people. It was death by crucifixion, the most horrific form of execution in the Roman Empire, reserved for enemies of the state and rebellious slaves and designed to be a deterrent to anyone who might think of opposing the empire. To proclaim that someone who had died in this cruel and cursed manner was Savior and Lord sounded like utter foolishness to many people, as Paul acknowledges in his First Letter to the Corinthians (1 Cor 1:18-25). Yet, in light of the experience of the risen Christ, this was exactly what the first Christians confessed. They soon attributed salvific meaning to his death. This is evident in the early creedal formula quoted by Paul in 1 Cor 15:3-8, which includes the affirmation that "Christ died for our sins in accordance with the scriptures." Reflecting from the vantage point of the resurrection, believers soon proclaimed the death of Jesus not simply as a tragic injustice but as in some mysterious way intrinsic to God's saving activity on behalf of the human family. The Easter experience led disciples to envision the death of Jesus not just as a brutal, unjust state execution, but as an act of loving service by Jesus that culminated a life of loving service. And this experience taught them that God can be found in the suffering person, even in one undergoing a shameful death by crucifixion.[18] Easter also disclosed to them that God's signature activity is to bring life out of death. The crucified and risen Jesus became for Christians the love of God made flesh.

New Testament writers sought to inculcate in believers an attitude of identification with the crucified and risen Jesus. When they searched for the presence of God in suffering, they turned their gaze to the destiny of Jesus. This was particularly true in regard to suffering that was endured because of fidelity to Christ and his Gospel. When Paul speaks of his sufferings as an apostle, he expresses his conviction that his personal trials have been an opportunity for a closer union with Christ and a source of benefit for the church (see, for example, 2 Cor 11:16-12:10). In a lyrical passage, Paul describes the life of faith in terms of identification with the crucified Jesus: "I have been crucified with Christ; yet I live, no longer I, but Christ lives in

---

18  See Gerald O'Collins, *Christology: A Biblical, Historical and Systematic Study of Jesus*, 2nd ed. (Oxford: Oxford University Press, 2009): 107.

me; insofar as I now live in the flesh, I live by faith in the Son of God who has loved me and given himself up for me" (Gal 2:19-20). The First Letter of Peter, written to Christians who were enduring opposition for their faith, lifts up Christ as the exemplar of faith in the midst of adversity (2:21-25), and it articulates a spirituality of Christian witness. Believers can find reason for joy because through suffering their faith is purified and they are given an opportunity to bear witness to their belief in Christ.

## THEOLOGICAL REFLECTION

### *Divine Compassion*

In their grappling with the mystery of suffering, contemporary theologians emphasize that the God of the Bible is the God of compassion. This is the God revealed to Moses in the burning bush as saying, "I have witnessed the affliction of my people in Egypt and have heard their cry of complaint against their slave drivers, so I know well what they are suffering" (Ex 3:7). This is also the God of Jesus Christ, whom Paul names "the Father of compassion and God of all encouragement, who encourages us in our every affliction, so that we may be able to encourage those who are in any affliction with the encouragement with which we ourselves are encouraged by God" (2 Cor 1:3-4). When Mark narrates the story of Jesus' cleansing of the leper, he describes Jesus as "moved with pity" at the sight of this outcast person who begs for his help. The Greek term employed by the evangelist (*splanchnistheis*), suggests a deep, visceral reaction on the part of Jesus. Throughout his public ministry, Jesus discloses the God who is moved with compassion for all those who are suffering.

Through the centuries, the Christian theological tradition has struggled to interpret the meaning of divine compassion. Classical thinkers like Augustine of Hippo and Thomas Aquinas have argued that the transcendent perfection of God entails God's immutability (unchangeableness) and, consequently, God's impassibility (immunity from suffering). Thus, for Aquinas God is compassionate insofar as God acts to dispel the misery of beloved creatures, but not in the sense that God "suffers with" creatures who suffer. At the same time, the Christian tradition has never been content

with a God whose transcendent perfection would preclude closeness
to the pain and tragedy that pervade human history. It has appealed to
belief in the incarnation, affirming that in the passion of Jesus the Son of
God truly suffered, though in his human nature not his divine nature. A
number of modern theologians have challenged the classical principles
of divine immutability and impassibility, arguing that the ability to freely
enter into the suffering of another represents a perfection, not a limitation
or deficiency. The German theologian Jürgen Moltmann famously
asserted, "Were God incapable of suffering in any respect, and therefore
in an absolute sense, then he would also be incapable of love."[19] Elizabeth
Johnson contends that, from a feminist perspective, "the idea that God
might permit great suffering while at the same time remaining unaffected
by the distress of beloved creatures is not seriously imaginable."[20]

Whether one ascribes to divine impassibility or conceives of a God whose
being is impinged upon by our sufferings, the Christian tradition presents
God as intimately close to every suffering person. Through the incarnation
God has in a certain way united God's Self with every human being and
thus with all people who suffer. A pastoral minister can confidently assure
a person who is suffering that God knows her or his experience from the
inside. In his encyclical *Spe Salvi*, Pope Benedict XVI affirmed that God
"desired to suffer for us and with us." The pope quotes an expression of the
12th-century theologian Bernard of Clairvaux: "God cannot suffer, but he
can *suffer with*." Referring to the incarnation and passion of Jesus, Benedict
says that God "became man [sic] in order to *suffer with* man in an utterly
real way" (n. 39).

This belief in divine compassion challenges Christian believers to exercise
genuine compassion toward all of those who suffer. Phil Zylla suggests that,
because suffering is unattractive and threatening to us, our natural response
to it is one of indifference.[21] We must make a concerted effort to overcome
this indifference in order to move into the suffering of others with active

19   Jürgen Moltmann, *The Crucified God: The Cross of Christ as the Foundation and Criticism of
       Christian Theology*, trans. R.A. Wilson and John Bowden (New York: Harper & Row 1974): 230.
20   Elizabeth Johnson, *She Who Is: The Mystery of God in Feminist Theological Discourse*
       (New York: Crossroad, 1992): 253.
21   Zylla, *The Roots of Sorrow*, 93.

help. Through the grace of the Holy Spirit, we are empowered to align our character with God's own character by becoming men and women of genuine compassion for others.

## *Varieties of Faith*

The Judeo-Christian tradition demonstrates that faith is "a many-splendored thing." Through the centuries, faith in the God of Abraham and Sarah and of Jesus has encompassed a rich variety of expressions, from the arguing of Job to the loud lamentations of the psalmists and the protest of Elie Wiesel laboring under the haunting shadow of Auschwitz. This same faith also has been manifested in the lives of many ordinary believers who have exhibited profound trust in God even in moments of great personal suffering.

It is instructive to consider the distinct ways in which the four Gospels portray the final moments of the dying Jesus. While retaining their distinctive nuances in their narratives of the passion,[22] both Mark and Matthew depict Jesus as uttering the opening line of Psalm 22: "My God, my God, why have you forsaken me?" (Mk 15:34; Mt 27:46). Jesus cries out in agony as he experiences the fierce assault of death. Luke portrays Jesus as praying the words of Psalm 31: "Father into your hands I commend my spirit" (Lk 23:46; Ps 31:5). There is a sense of serenity here as Jesus entrusts his life into the hands of his Abba-God. In the Gospel of John, the crucifixion is the hour of glory, and Jesus' final words are, "It is finished" (Jn 19:30). Jesus has accomplished his mission. This variety found in the passion narratives is pastorally and spiritually important for us because people die differently; even people of strong faith die differently. Some struggle to the very end against the assault of death and experience the depths of darkness, as did the Jesus of Mark and Matthew. Others move

---

22  Donald Senior points out the subtle changes that Matthew makes to Mark's terminology in depicting the death of Jesus. The Gospel of Matthew reads: "But Jesus cried out again in a loud voice, and gave up his spirit" (27:50). Matthew's use of the Greek term "to cry out" implies that "at the very moment of his death Jesus once more prays the words of Psalm 22." And the Greek word he employs to describe Jesus' death as "giving up his spirit" (distinct from Mark's "expires") suggests that Jesus "prays in lament but also entrusts his very being to God his Father and the author and source of all life." Matthew's version highlights the obedience and trust of Jesus and is less stark than that of Mark. See Senior, *Why the Cross?* (Nashville: Abingdon Press, 2014): 48.

into an acceptance of death and manifest a deep sense of peace, like the
Jesus of Luke's passion narrative. Still others are convinced that they have
accomplished the mission given to them by God and envision their death as
a homecoming to God, like the Jesus of John's Gospel. The diversity among
these Gospel portraits suggests that each manner of dying can be a *dying
with Christ*. Each way can be an expression of faith, a grasping onto the
hand of God. For the Christian tradition, there is more than one way that
people of faith may respond to the experience of suffering.

## Responding to Challenging Questions

The questions posed to me by my sister and by the woman who attended
the talk on prayer pertained to how Christian believers should talk *to* God
and *about* God when confronted with the intractable mystery of suffering.
Should we pray for healing for our brother diagnosed with glioblastoma, or
simply ask for the ability to accept the outcome? After much thought, my
answer was that we should pray for healing. That is the only human thing
to do — to pray for healing when one's brother is sick. A truly human
prayer is a genuinely Christian prayer.[23] And we could be confident that our
prayer would be answered. It might not be answered in a cure (as it was not
in Tom's case), but it could well lead to spiritual healing and peace for our
brother as well as consolation and strength for our family. The God revealed
in Jesus' response to the leper is the God of compassion and healing.

The question posed by the woman whose husband had narrowly escaped
serious injury and whose friends had lost their teenage daughter defied
any rational explanation. Hesitating and stammering, I said that she and
her husband found themselves immersed in the realm of mystery in their
dilemma and that there were no satisfying theological explanations to be
given. I suggested that the invitation for Christians is to continue to believe
that God was present in each of those situations, faithfully at work from
within to bring life out of death. Though my response may have sounded
hollow to the woman who posed the question, it was the only way I knew
to answer. Nevertheless, the belief that God is always present and at work
to bring life out of death — even in the most rationally incomprehensible

---

23   See Karl Rahner, *On Prayer* (Collegeville, MN: Liturgical Press, 1993): 65 – 80.

situation — lies at the heart of the Christian faith. It is grounded in Christian faith in the saving life, death and resurrection of Jesus. This conviction is reflected in the famous words of Paul (often read at funerals) in his Letter to the Romans. After speaking about the groaning of creation, Paul shares his own bedrock conviction: "For I am convinced that neither death, nor life, nor angels, nor principalities, nor present things, nor future things, nor powers, nor height, nor depth, nor any other creature, will be able to separate us from the love of God in Christ Jesus our Lord" (Rom 8: 38-39). Paul does not provide a solution to the mystery of suffering, but he does profess his profound hope in a God who is faithful, the God who brought life out of death for Jesus. This bringing life out of death is God's signature activity. Christians cling to the hope that this is what God is always doing on behalf of God's beloved daughters and sons. It is this hope that undergirds and empowers the compassionate care that Catholics are called to offer to persons who are sick, disabled or dying.

## DISCUSSION QUESTIONS

1. Are there "favorite sayings" that you employ when faced with situations of suffering? What do those "sayings" imply about suffering? What do they imply about God?

2. Have you experienced times of crying out in lament to God? What was that experience like?

3. What have I learned about God and suffering from the people I have served?

========= CHAPTER SUMMARY =========

Health care touches the psychological, spiritual and religious
aspects of a human being. Moreover, health care organizations
sponsored by Christian churches are ministries to those who
believe in life after death. From the seventeenth to the early
twentieth century, theology has criticized approaches to death
and life after death and has sought to express them in light
of the New Testament and of the human person. This essay
presents ideas from recent Christian theologies about dying
and life beyond death. These insights offer new approaches to
traditional religious ideas about life after death, judgment and
purgative maturing, heaven and punishment.

## 2.3 CATHOLIC HEALTH CARE'S MINISTRY TO THE FUTURE

Fr. Thomas F. O'Meara, OP, Ph.D.
*Emeritus Professor, Department of Theology*
*University of Notre Dame*

HEALTH CARE IN ITS MANY INSTITUTIONS AND personnel touches the psychological, spiritual and religious aspects of a human being. Moreover, in health care centers sponsored by Christian churches, there are specific ministers to ecclesial grace through words and sacraments, and an atmosphere of faith and hope strives in various ways to make Gospel ideas and values explicit. Doing this in the concrete world of health care is a challenge. However, as many persons believe in life after death, Christian ministry may also be of service not only to life in the here and now but also to what faith imagines, believes and hopes about the future.

Since the 1970s, the Catholic Church in the United States has seen a remarkable expansion, a true explosion of ministry. From a former era of religious women operating health care centers and a solitary priest serving as a part-time chaplain, thousands of baptized lay persons have entered into formal ministries in the diocese and parish, including many into the world of health care. Edward Hahnenberg writes: "Today there are more than 38,000 professionally prepared lay ministers employed in the U.S. — more than the number of diocesan priests. And their numbers continue to grow. These lay leaders have come to be called *lay ecclesial ministers*.

They are a standard feature of contemporary church life, and a welcome source of ministerial vitality. They represent, however, only a tiny fraction of the tens of thousands of lay women and men who serve in unpaid occasional, but no less important ministries."[1]

The recent expansion of ministry leads to additional ministries and to their ecclesial context. Ministry to health care institutions may come from a community of Catholics not from a particular parish or cluster of parishes. The ministry of Catholic health care institutions is not parish-based; rather, it is often sponsored by new canonical structures that transcend a particular diocese, but that are overseen by the bishop and diocese. Theology is the thinking side of ministry. Health care sponsors, administrators and ministers need theology to unfold faith and create strong bonds between the church and specific health care ministries. Theological approaches inform ministry to the sick. Theology critiques old approaches to death and life after death and expresses a deeper understanding of the New Testament and of the human person. Both look towards what the future might be.

## ESCHATOLOGY, A THEOLOGY OF THE FUTURE

Infirm men and women are concerned about their health now and in the future, immediately and in the long term. The practice of medicine works tirelessly for the health of those seeking to live. Many patients, however, do not continue to live; they pass into and through death. Health care takes place amid discussions and decisions about life and death, amid conversations between the dying and those around them in the present. Ministries to the sick and dying — medical and religious, liturgical and psychological — are involved with the future and with life beyond death.

---

1 Hahnenberg, *Theology for Ministry* (Collegeville, MN: Liturgical Press, 2014), 113. "We can honestly say that we have been living through one of the most significant periods of ministerial transformation in the history of the church" (113). Charles Bouchard writes of "the complexity of the term itself and the enormous ecclesial change it signifies" ('Health Care as 'Ministry': Common Usage, Confused Theology," *Health Progress* 89 [2008]: 26 – 30; see O'Meara, "Ministry to Presence: The Hospital and the Spirit," *Hospital Progress* 55 [1974]: 62 – 65).

The following pages present some ideas from recent Christian theologies
about dying and life beyond death. These insights are few and brief,
although they can be challenging and inspirational. Traditionally, Christian
theology about the future has been named *eschatology*: the Greek-derived
term means reflection on future, ultimate realities. Eschatology, the theology
of the future, has in recent years gone beyond traditional understandings
of judgment, purgatory and heaven to develop new consoling possibilities.[2]
There is no lack of studies from recent years offering insights into death
and judgment, purification and eternal life, the uncertain life in hell and
the social life of those living beyond death in eternal life. Fr. Edward
Schillebeeckx, OP, observed that we should see a theology of the future, first,
as the expression of our belief that history is in God's hands. That history of
the world will reach a special fulfillment through Jesus Christ who embodies
the life and teaching of the future.[3] The mystery of death
and the Christian teaching about life after death throw light on aspects
of health care. What are some of the new insights stimulated by Christian
faith and eschatology?

A summary of those insights would include a resistance to the idea that
all temporality ends with death and a belief in new modes of duration
extending beyond death. There is the illuminating idea that at death a
person proceeds at once to the afterlife. There are also views that what
follows death is not bodily punishment but self-illumination and maturity.
Eternal happiness would draw new realities and relationships from the

---

2    For overviews on recent eschatology see Peter Phan, "Roman Catholic Theology," Jerry Walls,
     ed., *The Oxford Handbook of Eschatology* (Oxford: Oxford University Press, 2008): 215 – 32;
     *Living into Death. Dying into Life. A Christian Theology of Death and Life Eternal* (Hobe Sound,
     FL: Lectio, 2014); Monika Hellwig, *What Are They Saying about Death and Christian Hope?*
     (New York: Paulist Press, 1978) 59 – 60. After the 1960s there are modern eschatological
     theologies by Karl Rahner, Zachary Hayes, Joseph Ratzinger, Joseph Bracken, Gisbert
     Greshake, John Shields and Peter Phan. Recently with their own lists of sources are studies
     by Thomas P. Rausch, *Eschatology, Liturgy, and Christology. Toward Recovering an Eschatological
     Imagination* (Collegeville, MN.: Liturgical Press, 2012); Dermot Lane, *Keeping Hope Alive.
     Stirrings in Christian Theology* (New York: Paulist Press, 1996); Brian Robinette, *Grammars
     of Resurrection. A Christian Theology of Presence and Absence* (New York: Crossroad, 2009);
     Harold Coward, ed., *Life after Death in World Religions* (Maryknoll, NY: Orbis, 1997); William
     La Due, *The Trinity Guide to Eschatology* (New York: Continuum, 2004).
3    Schillebeeckx, "The Interpretation of Eschatology," *The Problem of Eschatology, Concilium* 41
     (New York: Paulist Press, 1969), 54. There are different eschatologies at work in health care
     ministry just as there are different views of Jesus, of liturgy, and of the revelation of God.

billions of people who have lived and from distant peoples as eternal life opens out into the cosmos with civilizations' many cultures and liturgies. Finally, the opposite to all eschatological life, hell, may not be eternal punishment but brings a total annihilation of the person's existence.

These ideas are both critiques of previous thinking and richer approaches to life after death. In all of this is the assertion of faith that God sustains each life through a divine love that has various plans. Let us look at a few of these theologies.

### DEATH

Why do people die? More and more, medical research succeeds in exploring death's physical causes, while psychology seeks to help those who feel its nearness. The biological nature of death limits all living things, including human beings. Living cells are preprogrammed by their genetic code to stop the dividing processes after a certain number of divisions have occurred — and so to die. Empirically, death comes from the winding down of a biological life, from infections and decline.

There is an awareness today that death comes from human beings and their world and not directly from God. When human beings cause others' violent deaths, God witnesses and permits the act of human freedom that chooses to acquire a weapon and shoot someone, but God does not cause or endorse that action. Deaths from animals, reptiles, and parasites are directly occasioned by an imprudent entry into their areas. Death also can be caused by an individual's biological activities such as addiction, or a serious lack of care for one's health.

Death is usually a complex event, both an external decline and an interior condition. Death is more than something that occurs abruptly through organic failure or a traffic accident. God does not cause an illness; rather, God created a universe in which some organisms injure others as both seek their own lives and goals. Sickness does not exist to punish a person or to test faith and courage. Viruses, bacteria, parasites and cancers do not exist for destructive purposes but to further their own specific ecosystems as active beings in the universe with their own nature and function. They may come into conflict with human organs and vital processes. When their effect is injurious to people, they are not in themselves evil but are pursuing their own natures. If there is an unfortunate intersection of creatures, it is not due to a direct, divine instrument inserting misery into a person's life.

Modern psychologies and philosophies ponder how a human being is active and not purely passive in dying. Fr. Karl Rahner, SJ, wrote: "Death is the event in which the very person becomes a definitive self. It is certainly and eminently a topic for theology. Death is an occurrence which concerns a person as whole, as a unity of nature and person, that is, a being who, on the one hand, even prior to personal free decisions is constituted in existence in a certain way…, and, on the other hand, disposes of herself freely, so that he is finally what he freely wills to consider himself to be."[4] The longing of human nature and the affirmations of religious belief both assert possible life beyond death. Christian faith holds that a deeper plan for intelligent creatures includes a richer, future life. Health care at the end of life is a privileged place, for there we brush closely to our ultimate destiny. The present and the future find in the world of health care a place for thinking about non-clinical aspects of medicine. We now turn to some insights about these realms.

## LIFE BEYOND DEATH: A JOURNEY

Faith affirms that there is life beyond death. Religions have fashioned rituals mourning the death of family members, soldiers, or children. Monuments, anniversaries, poems and songs proclaim life after death. Few societies or religions embrace an empty fatalism asserting that there is no future life. Many people believe there is life after death.[5] Human beings in every age have wondered about whether there is "more." Christians believe that

---

4   Rahner, "Death," *Encyclopedia of Theology: The Concise* Sacramentum Mundi (New York: Seabury Press, 1975), 329. Peter Phan has written magisterially on Rahner and eschatology: Phan, *Living into Death. Dying into Life. A Christian Theology of Death and Life Eternal* (Hobe Sound, FL: Lectio, 2014); *Eternity in Time. A Study of Karl Rahner's Eschatology* (Cranberry, NJ: Associated University Presses, 1988), 203; *Responses to 101 Questions on Death and Eternal Life* (New York: Paulist Press, 1997).

5   A 2015 poll by Pew Research revealed that 72% of Americans believe in heaven and 59% in hell. http://www.pewresearch.org/fact-tank/2015/11/10/most-americans-believe-in-heaven-and-hell/

human history has been graced by a special sharing of God's eternal life. Jesus calls this life — deeper, kinder, in the future — the "reign of God." The goal of his preaching was to announce a "more abundant life." So life on Earth has been and is a history of salvation. God seeks us out and offers us special ways of living. Christian theologians through the centuries have taught that life, death and everlasting life comprise a journey with stages. Ministry works not only to sustain courage in the seriously ill but to prepare people for death, to prepare them for what may be inevitable but in the belief that it is a passage rather than a conclusion. Contemporary theologies of death as liberation and self-determination bring a new direction.

Life after death is no longer pictured as a castle of frightening, unpleasant chambers or one of timeless, pleasant entertainments for the soul. Nor is God waiting for us in a courtroom on the other side of the great barrier. Beyond Earth, there is a rich future flowing from God's depths.

Does life after death imply some kind of time? Time can be perceived as not a failure disappearing into death but a momentum towards a future where there are new kinds of time other than time on Earth. Thinking about the future involves imagining different "times," further realms of life for myself and others. Perhaps the future will not remove all duration, since duration is an aspect of human existence. New ways of existence bring a transfiguration of time through a communication and communion with God. Scientific hypotheses about parallel times and multiverses suggest that unglimpsed forms of temporality lie ahead. Fr. Bernard Sesboüé, SJ, writes: "Divine eternity is so much eternity that it is capable of assuming the reality of time into itself, transcending, while respecting, it at one and the same time. In freely creating the world and, with it, time, God has already put himself in a relationship with time which he embraces as a unity."[6] Time ends not in absence but in a new vitalizing presence of God.

Death is a stage on a journey. As dying does not lead a person to an afterlife of prisons or resorts, it yields at once to a future life, perhaps

---

6    Sesboüé, *The Resurrection and the Life* (Collegeville, MN: Liturgical Press, 1996), 71; see G. Lafont, *A Theological Journey: Christian Faith and Human Salvation* (Collegeville, MN: Liturgical Press, 2007): 81.

several future forms of life. While Catholic traditions placed stages on the journey between dying and entering eternal life (judgment, transformation, purification and education), some believers have thought that the dead move quickly to final moments of the journey. In the Roman catacombs, near the resting places of their loved ones, believers inscribed in Greek or Latin their belief that the dead persons were right after death "in peace." For them, judgment and heaven came immediately, while delays and purifications were unknown.

Recent theologians warn against paying too much attention to an "interim state,"[7] a time of waiting marked by negative delays and frightening punishments and an incomplete existence of a soul separated from the body living a ghostly life. Believers unfortunately pictured heaven as a place for souls and not the full human person; there the soul moves from floor to floor as in a clinic or a courthouse.[8] Life, however, is always a personal journey. God has created existence on Earth so that it leads into new ways of space and time, individuality and relationship.

## JUDGMENT

Is there an evaluation of each person's life? St. Thomas Aquinas gave an interesting reason for why there should be a serious evaluation of each person's life. He did not refer to crimes with punishments nor did he connect judgment with past evil or present pain. Moving in a different direction, he argued that as the universe nourishes being and life by giving each reality its proper place, so each human being needs to find his or her own identity, his or her "place," which would fashion existence now and in the future. "The judgment of each person individually by his works belongs

---

7   *The Baker Evangelical Dictionary of the Bible* says: Christians hold that there will be decisive events in the future: the resurrection of all, the return of the Risen Christ, and a new age. Many people physically die before those events. The state of being between an individuals' death and eschatological events is often called an "intermediate state" and could include a moment of judgment or a process of purgation.

8   Karl Rahner writes: "The genesis of the idea of an intermediate state in the Middle Ages was a stage in the history of theology, but no more than that. It is the attempt to reconcile the collective and the individual view of eschatological fulfillment." ("The Intermediate State," *Theological Investigations* 17 (New York: Crossroad, 1981), 118; see Peter Phan, "The Intermediate State," *Eternity in Time* 117 – 32 and Peter Müller-Goldkuhle, "Post-Biblical Developments in Eschatological Thought," *The Problem of Eschatology, Concilium* 41, 24 – 41.

to the governing of the universe."[9] Judgment is a further work of the God who created beings out of love. This is a "last" judgment not because it comes at the end of a particular life but because it sums up a life. It is not final because it distributes penalties but because it looks at the total orientation of a life so that the human being can emerge into the light of fuller reality. German theologians Alois Kothgasser and Clemens Sedmak wrote: "Love your own story and history. It is the way in which God has involved himself with you."[10]

Discernment about an individual life — who is the judge? Who will judge me? What are the standards by which I will be judged? Is the judge prone to understanding — or to contempt? Is the legal code of that court obedience to the rules or to the dogmas of a particular religion? Peoples' attitudes towards a judge are marked by their experiences of human judges who sometimes are legalistic and mean-spirited. There is a further source of anxiety: the possibility of unknown rules. The standard by which one is judged might be partly unknown. And that judge may be slow to be merciful.

Who judges me? Angels or saints? Our ancestors or intelligent creatures from other planets? Jesus alludes to people as judges in the future — the Apostles and their followers will sit on 12 thrones in judgment.[11] Interestingly, for Aquinas, human judges will be people who have led a simple life, despising the avarice and power that causes so much suffering on Earth.[12]

Only one Gospel text describes a solemn and formal judgment by God or Jesus of men and women (Mt 25: 31-39). At the end of time, we are taken to a court with a theatrical setting. The judgment's standard is surprising. The Redeemer of the human race, the man Jesus, is central; the measure of a person's good and evil is not according to rules obeyed or scorned

---

9    Aquinas, *Summa Theologiae, Supplementum*, q. 88, a. 1, c.

10   Alois Kothgasser and Clemens Sedmak, *Geben und Vergeben. Von der Kunst neu zu beginnen* (Innsbruck: Topos, 2014): 126.

11   Matthew 19:28 – 29.

12   Aquinas, *Summa Theologiae, Supplementum* q. 89, a. 2. For Aquinas purgatory exists not mainly as a time of growth but as a time of punishment for offenses against God. The one punished indirectly accepts the punishment because it leads to something good (*Summa Theologiae, Supplement* qq. 1 & 4).

but respect for and assistance to human and social life. The standard that separates the good from the evil is a person's treatment of other human beings, particularly marginal and needy people:

> All the nations will be gathered before him, and he will separate people one from another as a shepherd separates the sheep from the goats, and he will put the sheep at his right hand and the goats at the left. Then the king will say to those at his right hand, "Come, you that are blessed by my Father, inherit the kingdom prepared for you from the foundation of the world; for I was hungry and you gave me food, I was thirsty and you gave me something to drink, I was a stranger and you welcomed me, I was naked and you gave me clothing, I was sick and you took care of me, I was in prison and you visited me.[13]

The standard is not whether one knows celestial doctrines or fears hellish punishments but life itself, meeting other people in a humane way.

## MATURING AND PURIFICATION

When someone is dying, she is leaving not only a weakened body but the depth and breadth of a terrestrial life. There might be fears repressed or exaggerated disappointment, unjustified anger at self or misdirected anger towards God, anger at family or the rejection of a religious organization that does not represent well God's mercy. Not just Roman Catholics but other religious groups, past and present, have thought that there might be an intermediate period between death and new life. "Purgatory" became a commonly used word in religion and even in secular contexts. Purgatory is not prominent in the Bible, but it has been prominent in popular Catholic piety of recent centuries.[14] The purgatory of hell-like suffering joined to precise calculations for times of confinement, however, is not church dogma but the product of popular myths. That place was not so much a purification as a punishment for penalties due. The dramatic agenda of punishments after death is not grounded in the image of God given by Jesus.

---

13   Matthew 25: 31 – 39.

14   See Zachary Hayes, "The Purgatorial View," in *Four Views on Hell*, ed. William Crockett (Grand Rapids: Zondervan, 1996): 100f.

Christians of the first centuries believed that death led at once to participation in the resurrection into a new life. After some centuries, however, the deaths of so many baptized whose lives had not been virtuous raised the issue of a temporary state, a period of purification, maturity or punishment. Clement of Alexandria in the early third century spoke of a fire of purification accompanying a course of education. (A few centuries later, symbolic "fire" became real fire.) Jacques Le Goff, the scholar of medieval history, writes: "When, between the second and fourth centuries, Christianity set itself to thinking about the situation in which souls find themselves between the death of the individual and the Last Judgment, and when in the fourth century, the greatest Fathers of the church conceived of the idea that certain sinners might be saved — most probably by being subjected to a trial of some sort — a new belief was born, a belief that gradually matured until in the twelfth century it became the belief in Purgatory."[15] In the Christian West, purgatory was viewed as a mediating time of isolation and punishment. At the end of the Middle Ages, an emphasis on ongoing purification led to the church exerting its authority in providing information and control over the time a person would spend in purgatory; this in turn led to the avarice and commercialism of partial and plenary indulgences. A purgatorial realm, well organized and manipulated, was a catalyst for the Protestant Reformation. The Council of Trent said only that there is a "*purgatorium*" (a place or a process or an assistance) to help those who have died so that they might be drawn towards heaven, and these processes are helped by the prayers of people on earth.[16] The Catholic Church teaches only that "purgatory exists, and the souls detained there

---

15   Jacques Le Goff, *The Birth of* Purgatory (Chicago: University of Chicago Press, 1981), 3; on the emergence of purgatory in the third century and the modifications of the following centuries see Joseph Ratzinger, *Eschatology, Death and Eternal Life* (Washington, D. C.: The Catholic University of America Press, 1988), 218 – 32; and Isabel Moreira, *Heaven's Purge. Purgatory in Late Antiquity* (Oxford: University Press, 2010), 206ff.

16   The Council of Trent in Denziger, *Enchiridion Symbolorum, Definitionum et Declarationum de rebus fidei et morum* #1580. The bishops deliberating at Trent urged pastors to teach against superstitious practices and beliefs claiming to give details about people in purgatory. The term *limbo* was introduced by Saint Albert the Great in the thirteenth century to designate a state of deprivation of blissful union with God which was not a state of punishment or torment. This idea accommodated the unresolved question about good people before the time of Christ and of children dying unbaptized. At the same time, the overwhelming weight of tradition asserts the universal salvific will of God as the context within which all such questions must be asked.

are helped by the prayers of the faithful."[17] The mechanics of indulgences, however, with their artificial temporality of "quarantines" and "years" has no claim to accuracy. Faith and liturgy can at no time give precise information about people's journeys — God's kindness assists all in this life and in the next, although how and to what extent remains unknown. Aquinas' words about praying for the dead retain uncertainty and vagueness. "Through the way of prayer there can be a change in the activity of attaining the goal while they are on their journey…. Prayer might diminish the penalty or have some similar effect."[18] Like everything in the realm of the kingdom of God, the important agent is God, and brief human actions do not control God. Lighting a candle serves as a symbol of faith in the love and activity of Jesus touching one of his brothers and sisters, not a subtraction of time to be served.

Purification is a valuable time of learning and growth after death. As persons encounter the absolute eschatological reality, God, they are taught and changed as love guides the person immature in faith and selfish in behavior to care for others. Rahner observed: "Purgatory would mean that the person, even after surrendering its bodily structure and through that surrender, experiences in its freely posited self-determination more clearly and acutely its own harmony or disharmony with the objective right order of the world."[19] If a process of purgation holds some pain, it is because an individual had formed his or her personality in ways hostile to true fulfillment, and so a purification of disharmony through love could be in a positive way painful. After looking at the writings of theologians from recent years, Harvey Egan concludes: "Abandoning a legalist view of purgatory as a place of torture located between heaven and earth in favor of understanding purgatory as an encounter with Jesus Christ, or God, or the Holy Spirit, and with the mystical body and the cosmos that purifies and transforms the multidimensional social person that we are has many advantages.....It comprehends the 'cleansing fires' as the 'dark, loving

---

17  Denziger, *Enchiridion Symbolorum…* # 998, 983 "The decisive documents do not impose any obligation as regards fire, a place of purification, the duration, or the kind and intrinsic nature of the punishment" (Elmar Klinger, "Purgatory," *Encyclopedia of Theology. The Concise Sacramentum Mundi* 1320).
18  Aquinas, *Summa Theologiae, Supplement*, q. 71, a. 1, c.
19  Rahner, "Death," 331.

spiritual fire' of the Holy Spirit, Christ, the communion of saints and also of creation itself. It shifts the theological discourse away from extrinsic, legalistic and mythological terminology to intrinsic, personalistic and more pastorally useful categories."[20] Still, how God's love works in the dead — its intensity and its duration — remains unknown. Thomas Rausch sums up:

> The idea of some kind of purification before we enter into the presence of God in his majesty makes sense....How and when this happens remains a mystery. Does it happen after death or perhaps in the process of dying — a time often filled with memories, remorse, and hope — or perhaps even during this life. What seems to make most sense today is the idea that purgatory happens in that personal encounter with God that takes place at death.[21]

A mysterious future from a loving divine presence has been revealed: the dying person waits for the arrival of a parent and friend.

## RESURRECTION

Jesus risen from the dead announces in the days after Easter that his life is beyond death and will last. He does not return permanently to our world limited by matter and death but goes into a new world of life, community and exploration. Jesus is not a ghost: he talks with people, he eats — he even cooks. He moves and meets human beings in the locations and times he chooses. The Gospels tell us that the Risen Jesus is a human being but different in terms of space, time and matter. The forecast, beginning and model of the resurrection of billions of human beings on Earth is the resurrection of Jesus of Nazareth. He is the source and channel of divine power reaching into the graves of all. Fr. Dermot Lane sums up:

---

20  Harvey Egan, "In Purgatory We Shall All Be Mystics," *Theological Studies* 73 (2012): 888.

21  Rausch, *Eschatology, Liturgy and Christology* 113. "If, then, we can hardly deny an interval in a person's destiny between death and the corporeal fulfillment of this person as a whole, then neither can anything decisive be said against the notion of a personal maturation in this interval....The question is not yet settled with regard to the sense in which and the degree to which temporal categories can still be applied here." Rahner, *Foundations of Christian Faith* (New York: Seabury Press, 1978): 442.

We can say what the eschatological reality of Jesus is not. It is not a physical resuscitation or a return to historical existence; it is not simply something that happened to the disciples but rather something that occurred objectively to Jesus and therefore had a transforming effect on the disciples; it is not simply a response to or an interpretation of the life of Jesus but a new reality subsequent to the death of Jesus affecting the disciples. That reality is new but not purely spiritual; being risen embraces the whole person of Jesus as transformed. The resurrection of Jesus is God's eschatological action on the life and death of Jesus within history.[22]

Jesus' resurrection is a statement and a forecast of the resurrection of all men and women. Rausch concludes:

The eschatological role of Jesus cannot be taken from him. For Jesus is not just a man in whom the Spirit of God dwells; he is more than a model or exemplar, teaching God's special love for the poor. Jesus is God's Word become flesh, God with us, who lives in the divine presence and too is already bringing the *eschaton*.[23]

All people are predestined to heaven. Good and evil, love and sin, are not partners in a dialectic. There are not two parallel highways, one leading to heaven and one leading to hell; eschatology does not lead to doors marked "Heaven" and "Hell." There is one path: God has created all intelligent creatures on Earth to share in kinds of life given by divine creative love, and faith asserts that a deeper life, coming from God's plan and love, will confront and conquer death. Heaven is not a geographical paradise but a state of human existence following a transformation.

Today some theologians conceive of resurrection occurring in an instant, right after death or not long after death. Rahner reflects:

---

22  Lane, *Keeping Hope Alive. Stirrings in Christian Theology* (Eugene, OR: Wipf & Stock, 2005), 106.

23  *Rausch, Eschatology, Liturgy and Christology* 160; see Michael Skelley, *The Liturgy of the World: Karl Rahner's Theology of Worship* (Collegeville, MN: Liturgical Press, 1991).

It is not an issue of faith whether what we call the resurrection of the body in the narrower sense takes place at the end of collective history or is thought of as a moment occurring simultaneously [with death] in the one process by which a person achieves his or her definite orientation at the time of his or her own death.[24]

Process and person are the subjects of human future, not soul and waiting.

Although the seriously sick person seems to be more and more alone as she dies, Christian faith calls attention to all those, seen and unseen, who are around the person on a passage through dying. The cosmos and its risen individuals will reflect each other. To die is to move on to a realm unknown, a transfigured cosmos. Jesus' resurrection transforms space, time and matter, and thereby lays the foundation for wider relationships in the universe. Life on Earth exists in a universe of stars and planets, and the future of the totality of creation is one of God's plans. Christian faith and hope look to when the "human race as well as the entire world will be fully re-established in Christ."[25] Rahner concludes that the glorified body of each person in the wider dynamic of resurrection becomes "a full expression of the enduring relation of the glorified person to the cosmos as a whole."[26] God will make galaxies and their intelligent civilizations new. A widespread and lasting transformation of man and his world no longer comes from creation's evolution but reveals a creative power of God. Grace after death personalizes people so that they are eminently social, and so their relationships would extend out into the wider realms of the universe empowered by the resurrection. God is the source and destiny of further forms of the universe, and their reality remains mysterious and varied. In the eschaton there is a rich process of vitalization for intellectual beings and for the cosmos around them.

---

24  Rahner, "Easter and Hope," *The Great Church Year* (New York: Crossroad, 1993): 185.

25  Vatican II, *Constitution on the Church*, chapter 7, # 48.

26  Rahner, *On the Theology of Death* (New York: Herder and Herder, 1961): 26.

## HELL

Descriptions and images of hell aim at making sin unattractive. Unfortunately, as centuries passed, their goal shifted to making believers miserable. Joseph Ratzinger wrote:

> Theology cannot be primarily devoted to an objectivating speculation on the other world. It must apply itself above all to bring out the real relevance of the affirmation of a hell for human existence. It is not the task of theology to go into details about supposed facts of the next life, such as the number of the damned and the severity of their pains and so on.[27]

Popular views that it is easy to slip into hell or that some are predestined to hell regardless of their lives are shallow and false. A hell easy to fall into is repugnant to the divine Wisdom and Love who have created beings for their own lives and happy destinies.

Religions depict hell as a prison with a fiery backdrop in which devils and evil people move sadly, but such pictures of the tortured are not based in revelation.[28] Those images of hell are the product of human religions drawing on popular legends. Hans Küng concludes:

> Hell is not to be understood mythologically as a place in the upper or underworld but theologically as an exclusion from the companionship of the living God, described in a variety of images but nevertheless unimaginable, as the absolutely final possibility of distance from God....The New Testament statements about hell are not meant to supply information about a hereafter to satisfy curiosity and fantasy.[29]

---

27  Ratzinger, "Hölle. Kirch. Lehramt," *Lexikon für Theologie und Kirche* V (Freiburg: Herder, 1960): 448.
28  A survey of hell's depictions in art is found in Alice K. Turner, *The History of Hell* (New York: Harcourt Brace & Company, 1993).
29  Hans Küng, *Eternal Life* (Garden City, NY: Doubleday, 1984): 141f.

God is not concerned with punishing his creatures. The evil, selfish person does not move on to a future resort for criminals or to a noisy theatrical club for the corrupt. What we call "hell" is emptiness. Satan's inferno is not an ugly slum, the counterpart to the kingdom of God and heaven. Reality, love and mercy are the healthy milieu of human life on earth and a deeper life given in the future through God's presence, while hell is the opposite of life. And so, it is no life at all — not even a miserable life.

Is hell eternal? An everlasting time that has no conclusion? Can a human say "No" so forcefully and repeatedly that it becomes the constant, unchanging force in an eternal existence? Why should any punishment last "forever"? A true God never frustrates creation and never punishes directly. What purpose does it serve to punish an intelligent creature eternally? If all meaning and hope are gone in hell, existence has no reason to continue. Fr. John R. Sachs, SJ, writes against an eternal hell:

> Sin is a horrible reality and God does not 'raise it up' and 'save' it for eternity. And it makes little sense to imagine God as simply abandoning the sinner to his or her 'No' just as it makes no sense to imagine that 'the saved' are merely confirmed in the state of their imperfect 'Yes' to God.[30]

Whatever life those fixed in evil have after death is not life at all but is the continuance of dying.

> Perhaps one should be content to speak of the indefinite (and so, non-definite!) persistence or endurance of a free 'no' to God but not of its finality or eternity. As long as human freedom tries to refuse God, it fails to reach the finality for which it is created, for this finality comes not from human freedom in itself, but from and in God. Until human freedom has chosen God, it has not found its way to finality, and therefore cannot be said to be in a definitive, absolutely irrevocable stance against God. Perhaps it can be said that it is yet bound in the realm and process of death.[31]

---

30  Sachs, "Current Eschatology: Universal Salvation and the Problem of Hell," *Theological Studies* 52 (1991): 252.

31  Sachs, 252.

The human being thoroughly opposed to love has chosen what in the eschaton a kind of non-existence is, in fact, a kind of non-existence. Its entry is annihilation. This word centers on the Latin "*nihil,*" nothing. Annihilation is not pain or a punishment. It is the termination of a life that has been directed by the person towards what opposes life and so ends up as nowhere and nothing.

## MINISTERING INTO THE FUTURE

To the extent that health care places life over death and to the extent that faith presumes life after death, they face the future in its various forms. While faith and psychology, in fact, do not hold much information about the future, still they are subtly penetrated by the human hope that terminal illness is not the absolute end. The preceding pages have not pursued precise questions and controversies about eschatology, for instance, about near-death experiences or ecclesiastical indulgences. Religious mathematics about a purgatory and childish pictures of hell dissolve when faith sees death as continuing the journey of life. Far from offering picturesque details about a next life, Christian theology is quite limited. Reflections on what the past and present tell us about the future are sparse. Ministry to the dying person, in sacrament and word, soon ends in silence.

For Catholic Christianity words can only go so far and then grace must come into creation and humanity and become sacrament. The liturgy and the sacramental are eschatological. From its first decades, the Christian community gave the ill a consecrated oil: that anointing signified and imparted a strengthening of body and soul. This was for a journey through illness. Further, when approaching death the believer receives the Eucharistic bread, and that long ago was named "*viaticum.*" That is the Latin word for food destined for a journey.[32] Today the church is rediscovering the forward direction of all the sacraments and liturgical texts.

---

32  See James Schellman's article on Viaticum, pp. 187 – 193.

The past of religion and faith's existence today are always being drawn into the future.[33] In ministering to people on Earth, those in the varied realm of health care serve the lives of their patients and their future.

## DISCUSSION QUESTIONS

**1.** What are some ways in which time is present and influential in dying?

**2.** What are some ideas on "purgatory" that go beyond punishment?

**3.** What creates and leads to what is called "hell"?

---

33  See Catherine Vincie, "Lay Ecclesial Ministry and Ritual," Zeni Fox, ed., *Lay Ecclesial Ministry. Pathways toward the Future* (New York: Rowman & Littlefield, 2010): 85 – 100; Antonio Spadaro, Cybertheology. *Thinking Christianity in the Era of the Internet* (New York: Fordham University Press, 2014).

# III

# SACRAMENTS AND LITURGY IN HEALTH CARE

CHAPTER SUMMARY

This chapter offers one view on how participation in liturgy,
in Christian ritual practice, has the power to transform us.
It suggests that like an encounter with a "text," the world
of liturgy interacts with our world. We are invited to
take a risk of faith and let the world of the liturgy become
our world. By integrating the liturgical experience of Scripture,
prayer, ritual offering, eating and drinking, etc., we are
transformed by the Gospel values embedded in the liturgy.
Of course, God transforms us toward the truth and the good,
but does so through very human means — bodily/soulful
participation in the liturgy.

# 3.1 THE TRANSFORMATIVE POWER OF LITURGY IN CATHOLIC HEALTH CARE
## Reprinted from *Health Progress*
## July–August 2009

---

Sr. Catherine Vincie, RSHM, Ph.D.
*Adjunct Professor*
*Aquinas Institute of Theology*

T O BE HUMAN IS TO EXPERIENCE CHANGE. WE ARE creatures who grow and mature at every level of our person-hood: body, mind and spirit. Although physical change, whether it be growth or decline, has a certain inevitability about it, other dimensions of the human experience are more open ended. Even if the outer landscape of our lives stays somewhat the same over a lifetime (and this is surely not the norm), our inner landscape experiences significant growth and change as we relate to others and to the world. Truly, any life experience has the potential to bring about human transformation as new insights and knowledge alter our way of seeing the world and ourselves and, ultimately, our way of being in the world.

We might even say that the human person has an inherent drive toward change and growth. When are all our questions about the world fully answered? When can we say we have enough insight into the workings of nature, of individuals or of society? Just as our minds constantly crave new knowledge, we have within us, according to the Christian understanding of personhood, a drive toward the infinite (which we call God). Christians understand the human person to be a transcendent being. At our best, we are always seeking and yearning for the "more" that life can give us: more insight, more truth, more love, a greater experience of the real. When we achieve this "more," we are transformed. Our hearts can grow bigger, our desire for the good increases, our spirits soar, and our behaviors change as we integrate new experiences and understandings.

Yet we know from past experience that such experiences leave us only temporarily satisfied. In our infinite quest for the divine in this life and the next, we find ourselves once again longing for more as the effects of our new insights and experiences diminish.

Further, our curiosity is not quenched merely in knowing that we can change. We want to know how it happens. What facilitates transformation for the good? What can we participate in, what can we immerse ourselves in that will stretch our minds and spirits and change our behavior accordingly?

In particular, we might ask what religion in general and Christianity in particular bring to our quest for transformation. What spiritual disciplines have the potential to transform us? Perhaps the most obvious of these is the practice of corporate prayer, or liturgy.

## LITURGY AS ENCOUNTER WITH RISK

Christianity in all its varieties shares a common tradition of gathering on Sundays for corporate prayer, praise and petition for the world and for each individual. Although the structure of the worship assembly may differ from denomination to denomination, nearly all share common elements. These include readings from the Scriptures and responses of praise, professions of belief and requests for forgiveness and blessing, as well as ritual acts of offering and sharing of a ritual meal. Whatever the particular complexions of the religious services, we can call them "liturgical services" or "liturgies" for our purposes here. (While Roman Catholics tend to call the celebration of the Eucharist or Mass "liturgy," there are many more kinds of Catholic services, all of which go by the general term liturgy; for example, Liturgy of the Hours, Communion services, celebrations of other sacraments).

Having clarified our terms, we can turn to exploring what it is that makes liturgical services transformative for us.

The question can be answered from two perspectives: the phenomenological — that is, how do liturgical events affect those who participate in them, and the theological — how do Christian communities understand God's action in the liturgy?

The second perspective is the more profound because Christianity posits that the spirit of God, who is our source and our end, drives all transformation for good. The "more" we can grow toward and into divinity, the more we can thus become the singular person God created us to be. And because that growth is God's ultimate desire for us, God actively relates to us in varied circumstances to facilitate this growth and change.

As for the phenomenological dimension, the field of hermeneutics, or interpretation theory, has much to teach us, and it has been richly employed in the field of liturgical theology in recent years. From both a linguistic and a philosophical perspective, hermeneutics explores the interaction between a person and a "text," whether the text consists of words on a page or a work of art, music or dance, or a liturgical celebration. Hermeneutics asks: How does the text, which stands on its own, come to be understood by a thinking, feeling person? How, in an encounter with a text, is a person changed?

Philosopher Paul Ricoeur, in his writings on hermeneutics, speaks of the encounter between a human subject and a text (let's call it *Hamlet*) as an event of interpretation. In this event, the text with its horizon or meaning comes into contact with a human subject, or person, with her or his own horizon of meaning and experience.[1] In a true encounter, a person does not simply impose a meaning on *Hamlet* from the outside, or from her or his own limited perspective alone. Rather, the encounter consists of a dynamic interchange between the text, which has something to offer, and the individual, who likewise has something to give. Ricoeur suggests that every text projects a world in which to live. The interpreter, then, is invited to take a risk and enter the world that is presented. It is in this leap of faith

---

1   Paul Ricoeur, *Interpretation Theory: Discourse and the Surplus of Meaning* (Fort Worth, Texas: Texas Christian University Press, 1976), passim, and "The Hermeneutics of Symbol I and II" in *The Conflict of Interpretations* (Evanston, Ill.: Northwestern University Press, 1974): 287 – 334.

and openness that we and our worlds can change. We open ourselves to the possibility of the new that the text offers us and, in doing so, risk that we will never be the same again. Whether the change will be for good or ill depends upon which worlds we allow to enter our horizon. It matters with *what* we interact, and it matters *how* we integrate it.

In exploring how we can be transformed by liturgy, we need to think of it as our text. It projects a world and invites each one of us to take it on as her or his own. The Scriptures, for instance, propose a world of hope in the face of death and gloom; they offer a word of reconciliation for the sinner and healing for those ill; they offer love and redemption for the Earth and its people, especially those most despised by our societies.

Beyond the Word, the liturgy invites us to participate in ritual acts, and these, too, project a possible world. For example, the most revered Christian action is to remember in ritual form the great things our God has done, especially in Christ Jesus, "who on the night before he died took bread, said the blessing and gave it to his disciples …." As Catholics understand this ritual, we take bread and wine, fruit of the earth and work of human hands. We offer this bread and wine back to the God who has first offered it to us, who then blesses and transforms them into the Body and Blood of Christ and returns them to us as gifts so that we may become one with Him and with each other.

In other words, at the end of this dialogue of offer and counter offer, we ritually take into our own bodies the body of the Lord presented to us in sacramental form. We take the risk of allowing His body to become ours.

As with the interpretation of *Hamlet*, where we let the world that Shakespeare imagined shape our own, in the liturgy we allow the world of God shown forth in Christ Jesus in Word and sacrament to become our world. In offering ourselves for the sake of another, even to the point of death, we live out in ritual the way of life that we call Christian. And our participation in that ritual, from a strictly phenomenological perspective, comes with strings. To place oneself in dialogue with the world projected by the Christian liturgy (be that Eucharist, reconciliation, marriage) is to risk allowing that world to become ours. The very process of interpretation engages us in a dialogue that begs for our vulnerability to the new, and thus to transformation.

Because liturgical participation is holistic, meaning that it engages our whole person, it has great potential to change us. We take in that world not just with our minds, but also with our senses. The sounds, the smells, the sights of the liturgy have profound effects upon our inner emotional, psychic and spiritual life. We don't just give voice to our belief that the cross of Christ is a sign of salvation; we sign ourselves repeatedly with our hands, with oil or with ashes. We sing the meaning of Christmas and Easter with hymnody that sounds through our body in ways that speaking alone cannot do. We walk in procession with the bodies of our beloved dead, blessing them with the holy water of baptism.

The liturgy presents Christians not only with God's Word, but also with God's offer of divine relationship. To that offer we are asked to make a response. We can accept that offer and move deeper into the transformation that is at the heart of our lives. Or we can reject the offer and stay the same, or worse, retreat from the "more" we are called to be.

## GOD MEETS US WHERE WE ARE

But what, exactly, is the theology of this transformation? What is the Christian, and more specifically, the Catholic view?

We already adverted to some issues when we spoke about the Eucharist and its ability to transform those who participate in the ritual enactment. By freely entering into the ritual event, we "buy into" its meaning, appropriate it, and are transformed. Further, we noted earlier that God is both our source and our end, and intends to incorporate us into God's own life. The church has consistently taught that God achieves this by taking the human experience deeply into account. God respects what God has made.

As early as the second century, Christian theologians, in continuity with the Hebrew tradition, have insisted on the role of the body, and the material world, in salvation. The Christian writer Tertullian, for example, claimed "the body is the hinge of salvation." By this he meant that, because we are embodied creatures, God works with us according to the capacities of our bodies. Thus Tertullian writes that we wash the body so that the soul may be cleansed; we anoint the body so that the spirit may be sanctified. There is no other way for God to relate to us but through the very constitution of our person — through body, soul and spirit and, by extension, through the materiality of the world.

Against those who would argue that creation is evil, as various groups have done over time, early Christian practice affirmed the goodness of the material world. In our ritual remembrance of Christ Jesus, we use very material gifts of bread and wine. In fact, an "offertory procession" with these gifts was inserted into the Eucharistic celebration by the end of the 2nd century to stress that God works with us through physical realities.

What we find in Tertullian is the beginning of what we call a sacramental theology. In other words, God, who desires union with us now and in the life to come, uses our ritual celebrations to achieve the kind of transformation God desires for us and that we long for. The Christian community began with the faith statement, made manifest in Jesus, that God desires our transformation into the divine, and then, gradually, developed a theology of how this is accomplished. The community came to understand and teach that through ritual participation, through liturgy, we participate in the reality signified, which is always God's desire for our salvation. Through ritual washing, for instance, we image in ourselves Jesus' experience of being called God's beloved. As Paul described it in a metaphor, we die with Christ in baptism and are raised with him. In Eucharistic sharing, we come to share in the very divinity of Christ and so come into union with him and with his whole mystical body, the Christian community. Through the laying on of hands and anointing, we are given the Spirit.

## PARTICIPATION COMES WITH STRINGS

The church, as agent of Christ on Earth, continually celebrates through ritual words and actions the mighty works of God for our salvation. In doing so it provides the means through which Christians can participate in that reality. God's grace operates through human means. As stated previously, through appropriation of divine realities, we are invited to integrate them with our whole person and modify accordingly our behavior in the world.

From a theological perspective, then, we can say the liturgical participation comes with strings. Ethical behavior flows from ritual transformation. By acting in the world as God would have us act, we have the potential for transforming not only ourselves, but also all our relationships and the world we share. That too we accomplish with God's grace. Not only does God work transformation in us through liturgical participation, God works *through* us for the transformation of the world.

### DISCUSSION QUESTIONS

1. Consider how one liturgical experience has touched you and possibly transformed you.

2. Why do you think we can go to liturgy and remain unmoved?

3. What do we have to contribute to the possibility of liturgy transforming us?

CHAPTER SUMMARY

This chapter examines the history of Catholic health care in
the United States through the story of one congregation,
the Sisters of Charity of the Incarnate Word of Houston, Texas.
It outlines what the author believes to be the essential
elements of Catholic health care and why that ministry has
historically made such a distinctive contribution to the church
and society alike. Finally, the chapter asks whether it is
possible, under dramatically new conditions, for Catholic health
care to continue to make a distinctive contribution and
what steps would be necessary to assure the future of a
truly Catholic health ministry.

## 3.2 LESSONS FROM HISTORY
## ON INSTITUTIONAL SACRAMENTALITY

—————

Fr. David Gentry-Akin, S.T.D.
*Professor, Theology and Religious Studies*
*St. Mary's College of California*

### A FOUNDING STORY

"O UR LORD JESUS CHRIST, SUFFERING IN A
*multitude of persons of sick and infirm of every kind, seeks
relief at your hands.*" With these words, Bishop Claude
Marie Dubuis, the second missionary bishop of Texas,
made an appeal to Mother Angelique Hiver, superior of the monastery
of the Incarnate Word in Lyons, France, for sisters willing to come to
the Gulf Coast of Texas to care for the sick, the poor and orphans. While
the Monastery of the Incarnate Word was a cloistered convent, Mother
Angelique told Bishop Dubuis that if he could find some young women
who felt a call to journey to Texas and undertake this missionary apostolate,
she would train them at her monastery and give them the spirituality of
the Incarnate Word nuns, founded by Jeanne Chezard de Matel in 1633.
Three courageous women who were willing to embark on this adventure
responded to Bishop Dubuis' appeal. They first went to the Monastery
of the Incarnate Word for a three-day novitiate, and then sailed for Texas,
landing in Galveston on October 25, 1866.

This is a brief sketch of the literally hundreds of incredible stories about courageous and visionary missionary endeavors on the part of women religious throughout the history of the Catholic Church in the United States.[1] They came in response to every human need — from education to health care, to care for the poor, for immigrants, and for other disenfranchised persons and communities. There is abundant evidence of these stories.[2] This article focuses on one of the stories and the implications it represents for Catholic health care.

## ESSENTIAL ELEMENTS OF INSTITUTIONALIZED CATHOLIC MINISTRY

If we analyze Bishop Dubuis' words, we find a number of theological assertions about the nature of Catholic health care:

**1. It is an ecclesial enterprise in which the bishops of the church have historically been involved.** Studies of the early church often note that Jesus started a movement that initially appeared to be one for reform and renewal within his Jewish faith. It gradually became a new religious movement, building on ancient Judaism but also incorporating new elements introduced by Jesus and his followers. After the death of Jesus, this charismatic movement grew to incorporate people from diverse cultures, languages and religious backgrounds. As first-hand witnesses of Jesus' ministry died out, the church evolved from a charismatic, and often rather chaotic, movement into an organized institutional reality. As any good sociologist will tell us, this phenomenon is common in social groups: the charismatic leader dies and his followers are left trying to figure out what to do next. Christians believe, however, that the particular social and historical movement which was to become the church was unique in one essential respect: this movement is the work of God, guided by God's Holy Spirit.

---

1    It should be noted that impressive contributions have been made by religious orders of men as well. While most of these have been in the area of education and care for the poor, congregations such as the Alexian Brothers, the Camillians, and the Hospitaller Brothers of Saint John of God deserve special mention.

2    One of the most impressive of recent offerings is the 56-minute documentary DVD *Women and Spirit: Catholic Sisters in America*, narrated by NPR's Cokie Roberts and produced by the Leadership Conference of Women Religious (LCWR). See www.womenandspirit.org.

Already in the time of St. Paul, we see a structure of ministry led by bishops who are assisted by deacons and presbyters. We see this more hierarchical pattern of organization being accompanied by the less structured and often somewhat more chaotic phenomenon of charisms, or gifts, for ministry: prophecy, teaching, miracle working, healing, speaking in tongues, interpreting tongues, etc.[3] These two phenomena — the hierarchical and the charismatic — coexist throughout history, often with tension. The former favors "order" for the good of the whole, while the latter favors the disruptive inbreaking of God's Spirit, which often interrupts patterns of order so as to make room for the emergence of something new. The impulse in Roman Catholicism — one that has been named as the "analogical" impulse or the "both/and" impulse — is one that seeks to affirm both of these phenomena: the need for order, and the necessity of not being so strictly ordered that the maintenance of the structures becomes more important than fostering the movement of the Spirit that the structures are designed to protect and facilitate.

Following the example of the apostle Paul in his own missionary journeys, Bishop Dubuis became a missionary in the foreign land of Texas in the New World. His life was marked by his evangelical poverty and humility and his witness to vast human suffering: *"Our Lord Jesus Christ, suffering in a multitude of persons, seeks relief at your hands."* On one of his journeys home to raise funds and recruit ministers for mission territory, Bishop Dubuis did what many others had done before him: he approached the superior of a convent of nuns who were well known to him, a convent founded under the particular charisms of Jeanne Chezard de Matel, and asked for their help in his new missionary diocese. Their response — unlike the one he hoped for of sending their own cloistered sisters — was to offer to share their charism with a group of women who felt called to this new missionary adventure. And thus, a new religious family was born, gifted with the spirituality of an older family in the church, and equipped for the missionary challenge of bringing health care, education and other social and spiritual relief to the people of Texas. It was a partnership that wedded hierarchy with charism, "order" with the gifts of a particular group of women who felt a call to embrace the reality of vast "disorder" in the chaotic environment of 19th-century Texas.

---

3   Cf. for example, Romans 12:6 – 8 and I Corinthians 12:27 – 31.

Such a pattern of hierarchical and charismatic cooperation has marked the life of the Catholic Church for 2,000 years. Like any other human activity, the church's life and endeavors are marked by human sin and imperfection. Even as we believe that the Catholic Church is the work of God and the memory and guarantor of the life and ministry of his son Jesus, we have to acknowledge that the church is nevertheless made up of sinful men and women who do not always get it right. But, as the adage goes, we cannot allow "the perfect to be the enemy of the good": we have to seek to do the good we can, knowing that we will not always get it right, and that sometimes our own sinfulness, blindness and weakness may cause us to get it very wrong. According to Paul's theology, the church is truly, and not just figuratively or symbolically, the "body of Christ" in the world today. A holy body because it is Christ's, but a body not without the wounds of sin, because it is made up of men and women who are sometimes sinful and shortsighted. As albeit imperfect human beings, our bodies and the institutions they create are essential if the ministry of Jesus is to be enfleshed, incarnated among real men and women, and not merely an esoteric, disembodied and ultimately escapist spiritual ideal.

**2. Catholic health care is explicitly Christological.** As Conor Kelly notes in his contribution to this volume, this Christological focus is at the heart of all true Christian ministry. It is, quite simply, Jesus Christ that we recognize, and seek to love and serve in the persons who come to us for care:

> "For I was hungry and you gave me food, I was thirsty and you gave me drink, a stranger and you welcomed me, naked and you clothed me, ill and you cared for me, in prison and you visited me.' Then the righteous will answer him and say, 'Lord, when did we see you hungry and feed you, or thirsty and give you drink? When did we see you a stranger and welcome you, or naked and clothe you? When did we see you ill or in prison, and visit you?' And the king will say to them in reply, 'Amen, I say to you, whatever you did for one of these least brothers [and sisters] of mine, you did for me'." [4]

---

4    See Matthew 25:35 – 40.

We seek to recognize, love and serve Christ in all persons because doing so is integral to *being* Christian. The Catholic spiritual impulse is to scan the horizon looking for signs of Christ's presence, and, when he presents himself "in his most distressing disguise," to seek to minister to his suffering in the flesh of contemporary men and women.[5] We do this not because we have a morbid obsession with suffering, but because we hope that suffering can be relieved, that death is not the end, and that our efforts contribute to the realization of God's reign among us. As Pope Benedict XVI wrote:

> Only when the future is certain as a positive reality does it become possible to live the present as well. So now we can say: Christianity was not only "good news" — the communication of a hitherto unknown content. In our language we would say: the Christian message was not only "informative" but "performative." That means: the Gospel is not merely a communication of things that can be known — it is one that makes things happen and is life-changing. The dark door of time, of the future, has been thrown open. The one who has hope lives differently; the one who hopes has been granted the gift of a new life.[6]

**3. Catholic health care is profoundly incarnational.** As Christians, our focus is Christological. As Catholic Christians, we place a special emphasis on the idea that Christ is not merely identified with the historical Jesus who lived as a Palestinian Jew in the first century CE. Rather, Christ's presence permeates all of created reality, so that God, through Christ, is immanent to created reality, is to be experienced *in* and *through* created reality, rather than by seeking to escape or transcend it.[7] This point bears repeating: the Catholic spiritual impulse is one that seeks God *in* and *through* the reality of God's creation, rather than in some disembodied attempt to *escape* or *transcend* creation. Embodied, material, earthly reality is the mode of God's presence to us. As Ignatius of Loyola and so many other wisdom teachers of the tradition tell us, our task is "to find God in all things." This means that joy and suffering are both to be understood and appreciated as modes of

---

5　An image used frequently in the writings and talks of St. Mother Teresa of Calcutta.

6　Benedict, XVI, *Spe Salvi*, §2.

7　See Thomas P. Rausch, SJ, *Being Catholic in a Culture of Choice* (Collegeville, MN: Liturgical Press, 2006): 34.

God's presence among us. This results in our taking the human needs of real persons with the utmost seriousness. We have a profound conviction that it is Christ himself to whom we minister when we reach out to those who are suffering, that the suffering of Christ continues in the suffering of men and women today. Christ, St. Paul tells us, emptied himself of Godlikeness in order to share our human condition. God's love is so strong that it impels God to abandon his own prerogatives as God in order to share fully in what it means to be human. His body is broken and his blood poured out for us. In a desire to re-enact his sacrifice, holy women and men throughout the ages have put themselves at his service, to be broken and poured out for others as he was. This impulse might best be named as one of "identification" or of profound "solidarity." Our care and concern for others is so all-encompassing that we seek to be one with them in their suffering. We come to see Christ, and ourselves, in the person who is hurting. Of course, we never do this perfectly. In our spiritual life, it is often two steps forward and one step back. The spiritual life is all about continuing on that quest in spite of our failures and disappointments, to cling stubbornly and tenaciously to the idea that Christ is here, even in those moments when my own human blindness and sinfulness do not allow me to perceive him easily.

**4. As Catholic Christians, we seek to see Christ in all persons without distinction, whether those persons see Christ in themselves or not.**
Catholic health care has never been restricted to Catholics or other Christians. The Sisters of Charity of the Incarnate Word of Galveston, Texas, ministered to everyone who came to them without distinction. Their vows of chastity, poverty and obedience, their prayer life, and religious habits made it clear to all that they were clearly and unambiguously Catholic. This lack of ambiguity about their identity enabled the sisters to remain rooted in their theological and spiritual motivation for ministry even while serving everyone who came to them. The sisters' days were marked, not only by the work of caring for the sick and poor, but by significant spiritual practices: morning and evening prayer, meditation, the sacrifice of the Mass, the recitation of the rosary, retreats and hours of adoration before the Blessed Sacrament. All of this was designed to support the sisters in their own spiritual growth, so that their increasing self-knowledge and spiritual maturity would be accompanied by an equally powerful ability to recognize Christ in the world around them, particularly among persons

who were suffering. If the work of alleviating suffering was to be effective both spiritually and existentially, it was essential that the sisters nurture within themselves the aptitude for "dreaming dreams and seeing visions."[8] This aptitude is essentially a mystical one, the ability to go beyond the surface into the depth of things. It is an aptitude that can only be cultivated through deep prayer and contemplation. It is not a shallow undertaking.

**5. Most initiatives in Catholic health care have been lay driven.**
Catholic religious women often have been erroneously identified more with the clergy than with the laity. In fact, while these women voluntarily became members of specific religious movements with a particular spirituality and a particular ministerial focus, they were *lay* women taking the Gospel imperative with the utmost seriousness and responding to it wholeheartedly, with all that they had and were. While such focused commitment is found among lay persons who are not members of religious orders, it is less common and often does not take the form of institutional ministries.

## WHAT MAKES AN INSTITUTION CATHOLIC?

What makes a Catholic hospital, clinic, elementary school or college a "Catholic" institution? Is it enough that it be named for a saint? Is it enough that it have a chapel? That patient rooms be adorned with a crucifix? That Mass and the sacraments be periodically available? That the hospital dedicate a certain percentage of its revenue to the care of the poor? That the hospital not perform certain procedures that are considered violations of Catholic medical ethics? Or, is something else required that we have not fully recognized and are not fully accounting for? This is an important conversation in Catholic health care that requires our ongoing attention and investment.

These elements, while often taken as the overt markers of Catholic identity, are necessary but far from sufficient. What made Catholic institutions unique in the past was the presence of the religious virtuosos who inhabited them, who guided and governed them, and who gave to them a particular religious quality. The concept of the religious virtuoso was first proposed by the sociologist Max Weber. According to Weber, all religions contain a

---

8   Cf. Joel, 2:28.

majority of "average" adherents, together with a minority of virtuosi who make the pursuit, realization and embodiment of the ideals of the religion their primary life focus.[9] These virtuosi model for others what the fullest possible attainment of the religious ideal might look like in a given tradition. While they are always in the vast minority relative to the total number of followers of any given tradition, they exert enormous imaginative influence on the tradition. Many of them become cultural icons, whose lifestyles bear witness to the degrees of holiness that the practice of a given tradition might effect in the life of an individual believer.

Many people of an older generation can describe how much comfort it brought to them, when they were in a Catholic hospital suffering from an illness, recovering from surgery or accompanying a seriously ill child, to have a sister come by and visit with them. While priests generally had more theological education and were the ones entrusted with access to the sacraments, the sisters brought a ministry of accompaniment, of presence, of empathy, of spiritual identification with the suffering of the patient that often was more important, existentially, to the suffering person than the ministrations of a priest. The sisters were present in greater numbers and more ubiquitous, so people felt surrounded by the sacred by virtue of their presence and the conscious intentionality with which they went about their ministry. The sisters rarely resorted to verbal proclamations of their faith. They did not need to. Their very lives and witness were a living homily that preached volumes.

The quality of the sisters' witness — lived daily through prayer and charity for those in need — was, more than anything else, what made their hospitals "Catholic". These women were the "living witnesses" to the deeper reality that Christians believe is present in the daily round of life, with its births and its deaths, its joys and its sorrows.[10] Their lives of *prayer, witness,* and *accompaniment* gave the Catholic enterprise its uniquely Catholic and spiritual character. As Blessed Pope Paul VI once wrote:

---

9    See Max Weber, *The Sociology of Religion*, (Boston: Beacon Press): 1993.

10   Mother Jeanne Chezard de Matel, foundress of the Order of the Incarnate Word and Blessed Sacrament, used the term "gospels of love" to describe what she hoped each of her Sisters would become. See *Life of the Reverend Mother Jeanne Chezard de Matel* by Mother Saint Pierre of Jesus, trans. Henry Churchill Semple, SJ (San Antonio, Texas: Convent of the Incarnate Word, 1922).

Above all the Gospel must be proclaimed by witness. Take a Christian or a handful of Christians who, in the midst of their own community, show their capacity for understanding and acceptance, their sharing of life and destiny with other people, their solidarity with the efforts of all for whatever is noble and good. Let us suppose that, in addition, they radiate in an altogether simple and unaffected way their faith in values that go beyond current values, and their hope in something that is not seen and that one would not dare to imagine. Through this wordless witness these Christians stir up irresistible questions in the hearts of those who see how they live: Why are they like this? Why do they live in this way? What or who is it that inspires them? Why are they in our midst? Such a witness is already a silent proclamation of the Good News and a very powerful and effective one. Here we have an initial act of evangelization.[11]

*Lumen Gentium*, the Dogmatic Constitution on the Church decreed by the Second Vatican Council, makes clear the call to holiness is a universal call, extending to all of the members of the Body of Christ.[12] *Apostolicam Actuositatem*, the Apostolate of the Laity also decreed by the Second Vatican Council, makes it clear that all baptized persons are called to participate in the apostolic activity of the church. With these two documents, the Council clearly opted for an ecclesial model whereby all are called to holiness according to their way of life, including the option for the particular forms of consecrated life that cultivate holiness in unique and particular ways. In cultivating a particular Gospel charism in an institutional ministry such as a school, college, hospital, clinic, or other social service institution, the issue is whether a sufficient number of people have embraced that charism radically enough that it is actually operative in that institution, or whether it is merely the echo of a spirit that was present in the past but which no longer really animates the institution in any profound way. As Sr. Patricia Wittberg, SC, points out in her important work on religious virtuosity, our institutions have gone from being places in which the religious virtuosos did most of the ministry, to being places in which they were accompanied by significant numbers of laity who were more or less committed to the

---

11   Paul VI. *Evangelii Nuntiandi*, §21.
12   See *Lumen Gentium*, Chapter 5, "The Universal Call to Holiness in the Church".

religious vision of the ministry, to places which were merely administered by the religious virtuosos, and now, to organizations that are often merely sponsored by the religious virtuosos where few if any may actually be present in the day-to-day life of the institution.[13] The question is whether this kind of sponsorship is sufficient, or whether we need a much more robust model whereby associates are called upon to embrace the charism with the utmost seriousness and to seek to live it out with the same zeal as the religious virtuosos once did.

## THE UNIQUENESS OF CATHOLIC INSTITUTIONAL MINISTRIES

Whether serving human needs through health, education or social services, the uniqueness of Catholic ministry is found in the *conscious intention* that accompanies the doing and the *depth of spiritual vision* that underlies the doing.

In every Catholic ministry, there must always be a consciousness that something much deeper is going on. The formation and prayer life of the sisters conditioned them always to be on the lookout for the depth dimension, the sacred dimension, the God dimension, of human experience and to seek ways of witnessing to that dimension. This was the fundamental perspective that gave Catholic institutions their reason for being and that set them apart. These ministries took on a kind of sacramental character: consecrated by the prayer and work of the religious virtuosos, they gave a constant witness to the sacramental nature of all of reality. Prayer, work, rest, joy and sorrow, human efforts to relieve suffering and promote healing, and even scientific advances in treatment, were all seen as a means of witnessing to and ministering to the presence of Christ in the human person.

As sacramental people, Catholics stress the value of the deeper spiritual dimension of reality that animates and permeates the material world. This reality cannot be discerned in its essence, but only in its effects. The institutions Catholics founded such as schools, orphanages, hospitals and

---

13    Sr. Patricia Wittberg, SC, *From Piety to Professionalism and Back: Transformations of Organized Religious Virtuosity* (New York: Lexington Books, 2006): 11.

health clinics, became visible, palpable signs of God's kingdom and God's commonwealth among us even now. As Darren Henson notes elsewhere in this volume, Catholics believe that our celebration of the Eucharist is not only a remembrance of past events, but a sacramental action in which we bring those events into the present. We believe the Eucharistic celebration is a foretaste of the Kingdom of God in which we become so identified with God that we ourselves are "deified". Our institutions are certainly bound by the human limitations of time and space, but they are meant to be signs of God's grace at work among us, to point us toward the reality of God's reign in our world and to remind us of our responsibility for cooperating with God in making that reality ever more present.

## THE CRISIS CREATED BY THE DECLINE IN THE NUMBERS OF APOSTOLIC WOMEN RELIGIOUS

### *A Turning Point: Where Do We Go from Here?*

With the decline of the religious virtuosos of the past — the sisters, brothers, and priests who once served these institutions in large numbers — we are faced with the issue of how to fill the important role that they once filled. Some believe we can address this problem by cultivating traditional vocations to priesthood and religious life; others feel we must identify and prepare lay candidates. Whatever approach we take, the underlying need is an urgent one to protect against the risk of becoming purely secular organizations and to preserve our identity as the healing ministry of the Catholic Church. It is not enough to think that everyone who comes to be employed by a Catholic institution will somehow catch the spirit that formerly inspired the religious virtuosi. We must be intentional in identifying and forming this new generation.

The market poses major challenges as well. While some Catholic hospitals continue to be located in the inner cities and minister to the poor in those cities, many others have abandoned the inner city and moved to the suburbs, almost completely replicating their private and for-profit counterparts. Others have been sold to investor-owned systems. Sometimes they retain the Catholic name and are under contract to remain in compliance with the *Ethical and Religious Directives for Catholic Health Care Services*. These moves alone are not enough to preserve Catholic identity.

Our hospitals have always employed a diverse staff. There was never a requirement that every nurse, physician, therapist or technician be Catholic. Some physicians actually chose to work at Catholic hospitals because they intuited a special quality in the ethos of the place. We value this diversity, but we must take care to nourish and sustain a strong sense of mission and Catholic identity.

## A PRESCRIPTION FOR THE HEALTH OF CATHOLIC HEALTH MINISTRIES

With all this in mind, what steps are necessary to strengthen the Catholic identity and culture of our ministries?

**1.** We need to put much greater attention and energy into the identification and formation of a new generation of Catholic religious virtuosos for leadership of our ministries. These persons should be formed in the Catholic faith and values and be able to demonstrate a commitment to fostering those values in the day-to-day management of Catholic institutions. We need people who witness to the values of Catholic health care at every level of the organization including governance, executive leadership, medical staffs and support staff as well. We will continue to value diversity among our staff and need to acknowledge that we cannot sustain a vital ministry of the church without a significant number of committed Catholics who understand their faith and see their work as part of their vocation.

**2.** We must also do a much better job of educating people about careers in Catholic health care and ways to contribute to the ministry. Many young people are seeking a path in life that provides a meaningful way to make a difference. At my own institution, I work with many young people who are discerning their vocations. Some are drawn to religious life and priesthood, and others are drawn to other forms of ministry and participation in the life of the church. Many are drawn to the study of theology, but few are aware of the possibilities for a life of ministry. Even fewer would even know about a career in mission leadership, health care ethics or chaplaincy. Catholic colleges and universities must take an active role in identifying candidates for these ministries.

**3.** Our Catholic educational institutions must develop new professional programs such as the mission leadership programs offered by Aquinas Institute in St. Louis and Loyola University in Chicago. They should also explore ways to provide a Catholic dimension to programs in health administration, nursing and pre-medicine to help students consider vocational possibilities within these careers.

**4.** We also need to continue to develop substantive formation programs that involve theology and spiritual formation. These programs can be developed by an individual system or through a collaboration of systems with assistance from a university or school of theology. The Catholic Health Association has developed an extensive variety of programs for ongoing formation of sponsors, executives, mission leaders and others throughout Catholic health care.

**5.** Liturgical life is the lifeblood of Catholicism. In addition to various "Catholic markers" such as chapels, crucifixes, religious statues, and religious art, Catholic institutions should be places where the liturgical life of the church is lived, where the sacraments are celebrated and made available and where important feast days are celebrated.

Daily Mass should be celebrated whenever possible. Communion and Anointing of the Sick should be available for the patients and visitors who seek these sacraments. There should be chaplains who can pray with people and offer spiritual comfort and emotional support. Prayer should start every staff meeting throughout the organization. The inspiration and guidance of the Holy Spirit should be invoked every time administrators reflect on the ministry and engage in discernment around important decisions about the future of the ministry. We should be conscious at all times that Catholic health care is a ministry first and a business second. It is a ministry not just to healing the body, but to the whole person, body, mind and spirit.

## CONCLUSION

Recently I was visiting with Alice, whose 50-year-old son Michael, had been taken to the hospital with chest pains and subsequently died. As I visited with the family a few days after this tragedy, they told me of the cold and impersonal way they had been treated in the hospital. Michael had been taken to the emergency room and they were waiting alone in a small room for what seemed to them like a very long time. Finally, a physician came into the room and told them bluntly, "We were not able to save him." This information was given without any context for what had caused Michael to be brought to the hospital in the first place. A few minutes later, the chaplain dutifully appeared to drop off a box of tissues. The chaplain seemed hurried and uncomfortable and did not stay with them to help them process any of what had transpired so suddenly. They were left alone in their shock and grief for a time, and then a clerk appeared to have them sign papers about the disposition of Michael's body.

The encounter they described was functional, cold and impersonal. It lacked a personal or pastoral dimension. If we lose sight of our ministerial identity, we risk losing our focus on witnessing to Christ in caring for the suffering of others. Do we risk marginalizing our own core traditions to remake our institutions in the image of our secular counterparts? Do we capitulate to prevailing secularism in our society to broaden our reach? We must preserve the great spiritual heritage we have received so that we do not leave each person alone in her or his effort to try to make meaning from the suffering and tragedy that are an inevitable part of the human condition.

We owe it to the sisters who preceded us, the "memory, the heart and the guarantors" of our Catholic identity and mission, as well as to the spiritual tradition we have inherited.[14] As the Hebrew prophet Habakkuk reminds us:

> I will stand at my guardpost, and station myself upon the rampart, and keep watch to see what God will say to me, and what answer God will give to my complaint. Then Adonai answered me and said: Write down the vision clearly upon the tablets so that one can read it readily. For the

---

14   The late Br. John Johnston, FSC, former superior general of the Brothers of the Christian Schools, chose these words to describe the role that he felt the Christian Brothers were called to play in their institutions, where they are largely engaged in collaboration with lay women and men who greatly outnumber them.

vision still has its time, presses on to fulfillment, and will not disappoint. If it delays, wait for it, it will surely come, it will not be late.[15]

Pope Francis reminds us that, while Christian faith is certainly made up of dogmas, codes of behavior and ritual practices, our faith is not in a system of belief but in the person of Jesus Christ. Believing that God became human, that God became one of us in the person of Jesus, is the faith conviction that leads us to assert that God lives in each one of us, in every person. Therefore every person is an utterly unique and unrepeatable *imago dei* (image of God) who is to be respected and reverenced for who she or he is: *Each of us is the result of a thought of God. Each of us is willed. Each of us is loved. Each of us is necessary.*[16] To embody this conviction in real and practical ways is the reason Catholic institutions exist and why they are still desperately needed in our broken and troubled world. They were founded not merely as delivery systems for education, health care, or social work, but as institutions that — while providing these goods and providing them well — would accompany the provision of these goods with an even greater gift: an evangelical witness to the fact that "the Word became Flesh and dwelt among us" and that that Word continues to be enfleshed among us still.[17]

## DISCUSSION QUESTIONS

1. What do you find most inspiring about the founding story related in the article? Perhaps you know other founding stories. Why do they continue to capture our imagination and to inspire us?

2. What do you think about what the author outlines as essential elements in Catholic health care? Do you agree that these elements are essential? Are there elements you find missing from his list?

3. What is the greatest challenge facing the future of a health care ministry that is distinctively Catholic? What are some concrete steps that could be taken to begin to address those challenges boldly and decisively? Do you see those steps being taken in the ministry in which you are involved?

---

15   Habakkuk 2:1 – 3.
16   Benedict XVI, Homily at Mass of his papal inauguration, April 24, 2005.
17   Cf. John 1:14.

CHAPTER SUMMARY

Eucharist is considered by the church to be the "source and
summit" of the church's life, but we have tended to see it more
as a service we offer to staff and families in our health care
facilities rather than as a point of theological reflection. We view
it as devotional, but not always an opportunity for catechesis.

This chapter examines various parts of the Eucharistic liturgy —
e.g., the liturgy of the Word, the offering, the communion
rite — to see how they can expand our understanding of the
ministry of health care. It concludes with three examples
of eucharistic celebrations in health care settings to show
how these celebrations strengthen the ministry and reflect
its ultimate meaning back to us.

# 3.3 EUCHARIST AS THE HEART
# OF THE MINISTRY

---

Darren M. Henson, Ph.D.

*System Vice President, Mission and Discernment*

*Presence Health*

I N ITS INAUGURAL DOCUMENT, SACROSANCTUM CONCILIUM, the Constitution on the Sacred Liturgy, the Second Vatican Council declared the liturgy, particularly the Sunday celebration of the Eucharist, as the font and summit of all activity and ministry of the Church.[1] It also described every liturgical action as "a sacred action surpassing all others; no other action of the Church can equal its efficacy."[2]

This chapter explores the relationship between the Eucharistic liturgy and Catholic health ministries. It expresses the necessity of an encounter with the living and real presence of Christ in word and sacrament for the healing ministries of Catholic health systems today.

## LITURGY — SOURCE AND SUMMIT

The grounding of the church's entire ministry in the Eucharistic celebration as its source and summit by the Second Vatican Council reflected theological movements that were taking place prior to the council.

---

1   *Sacrosanctum Concilium*, (Constitution on the Sacred Liturgy, 1963) §10.
2   *Sacrosanctum Concilium*, §7.

In the U.S., Benedictine scholar Fr. Virgil Michel wrote and lectured widely on the connection between the liturgy and social justice and other areas of contemporary life.[3] Similarly, women and men of the religious congregations that founded Catholic health care in the U.S. also connected liturgical practices in their ministry to the sick and dying. For the vowed religious involved in health care, prayer provided the foundation for their life and ministry. The American Catholic historian Christopher Kauffman observed how the Eucharistic liturgy influenced the work of the nuns in hospital wards.[4] Having encountered Christ in the proclaimed Word and having partaken of his body and blood in the Eucharist, the nuns were sent forth from Mass to tend to the body of Christ in ailing patients.

Religious often felt torn between prayer in the chapel and time on patient wards,[5] especially as health care became more complex and technologically sophisticated. The rhythms of daily prayer steeped the women and men religious in the life, death and resurrection of Jesus, giving them hope that the current suffering of patients would not be the last word and that God's saving grace and the fruit of the resurrection would come. The Eucharist sustained the sacredness of caring for the sick; in 1963, *Sacrosanctum Concilium* ratified the connection.

The centrality of the Eucharist for the church's activity and its healing ministry flows from our belief that the sacraments are encounters with the living presence of God. Belgian theologian Edward Schillebeeckx shaped this understanding of sacraments by expanding the medieval notion of sacrament as a sign of grace to an encounter with God. Jesus is

3   Virgil George Michel, *The Social Question: Essays on Capitalism and Christianity*, Ed. Robert L. Spaeth (Collegeville, MN: St. John's University, 1987). See also, Robert Tuzik, *Reynold Hillenbrand: The Reform of the Catholic Liturgy and the Call to Social Action* (Chicago: Hillenbrand Books, 2010).

4   Christopher J. Kauffman, *Ministry and Meaning: A Religious History of Catholic Health Care in the United States* (New York: Crossroad, 1995): 57, 88, 152 – 53.

5   Fr. Edward Stokes, SJ, referred to the tension women religious administrators were experiencing between their vocations and their duties when he asked: "Should the [sister] administrator think of the work in the hospital apostolate as first a series of spiritual exercises, and after that work on the floor, in the office, going about to various medical meetings and so back to prayer?" ("Integration of Religious Life and Hospital Administration," *Hospital Progress* [June 1963] 91, 96 at 95). For a fuller picture of this shift, see C. Bouchard, "Did Anyone Realize What Was Ahead? Catholic Health Care After Vatican II" (*Health Progress* November – December 2015.).

the primordial sacrament or "the personal visible realization of the divine grace of redemption."[6] When Jesus rose from the dead and ascended into heaven, he entrusted his disciples with the Holy Spirit to be a community perpetuating his ministry to heal the sick (Mt 10:8; Lk. 9:2), to preach and teach the Good News (Mk 16:15) and to baptize all nations (Mt 28:19). As a community of believers, the church became the presence and "the visible realization of [Christ's] saving reality in history. The Church is a visible communion of grace."[7] Schillebeeckx's sacramental theology provided context for the council's vision that all ministries flow from the Eucharistic banquet.

Not only the council's first document, but also its final document, *Lumen Gentium*, highlight a renewed sacramental and ecclesial theology. *Lumen Gentium* identified the entirety of the People of God as an image of the church.[8] It also named the church as sacrament par excellence as the visible and living realization of God's saving activity and love — and affirmed the role of the lay faithful as integral to the flourishing of the church's ministry. *Lumen Gentium* anchored the laity's participation in ecclesial ministry in the sacraments, "especially holy Eucharist... Now the laity are called in a special way to make the Church present and operative in those places and circumstances where only through them can it become the salt of the earth."[9]

During the more than 50 years since Vatican II, Catholic health care has emerged as a place where many laypersons have answered the call to serve. Growing complexities in American health care prompted religious congregations to seek out qualified laypersons whose expertise and commitment could help advance the mission of Catholic health care.

Today, lay professionals in corporate positions with multiple demands on their time find it difficult to routinely foster a life influenced by the liturgical-sacramental life of the church. Liturgist Rita Ferrone admits

---

6   Schillebeeckx, *Christ the Sacrament of the Encounter with God*, trans. Paul Barrett (Franklin, WI: Sheed & Ward, 1963), 15. Emphasis original in the author's text.

7   Schillebeeckx, 47.

8   *Lumen Gentium*, (The Dogmatic Constitution on the Church, 1964). Chapter II, §§9 – 17. See also Chapter IV, §§30 – 38.

9   *Lumen Gentium*, §33.

that even though the council envisions the liturgy as the center of Christian life, it competes with many other things in people's lives and with other church activities.

Two misperceptions stand in the way of experiencing the fruitfulness of a sacramental-liturgical life — doing and getting. First, skeptics and churchgoers bemoan that they do not "do" anything at Mass. Far too many presume that absent a specialized role, Mass is somehow less. The importance of the assembly of people gathered together for Mass has not been convincingly articulated widely or boldly enough.

Second, most Catholics equate going to Mass with getting Communion. Pastoral ministers muse that Ash Wednesday and Palm Sunday are popular because everyone gets something tangible and immediate — ashes and palms. One of the difficulties of fostering a habit of liturgical participation is that the effects of sacramental-liturgical practices emerge over time. Our consumer-oriented and technologically driven society leads people to expect a tangible result that comes immediately.[10] What we need is a greater focus on liturgical formation and recognition of the deep encounter with God's richness, beauty and life-giving grace in the Eucharist.

## THE NATURE OF LITURGY

Theologian Aidan Kavanagh taught that something far more profound occurs in worship than just knocking at God's door. Worship is not merely a unidirectional ritual in which the faithful offer praise, thanksgiving and prayers to God. Rather, and more importantly, the living God is present and offers divine mercy, love and grace to the gathered faithful. Kavanagh writes, this "is not a theological theory; it is a real presence which is there to affect, grace and change the world. It is an active real presence of God accomplishing his purpose as he will by the gift of himself in his

---

10  Vincent J. Miller, *Consuming Religion: Christian Faith and Practice in a Consumer Culture*, (New York: Bloomsbury Academic, 2005). Relatedly, see how market forces distort authentic spiritual practices and commodifies works of mercy in Michael L. Budde and Robert W. Brimlow, *Christianity Incorporated: How Big Business is Buying the Church* (Grand Rapids, MI: Brazos, Press, 2002).

Son through the Holy Spirit."[11] Liturgy is not something separate from the church, nor just one ecclesiastical action, but the church being itself. Kavanagh describes, "It is simply the church living its 'bread and butter' life of faith under grace, a life in which God in Christ is encountered regularly and dependably as in no other way for the life of the world."[12]

What one "gets" from the liturgy is a healing of our understanding about God and a healing of distorted visions of the world and of ourselves. By situating the faithful in the very midst of the paschal mystery — the life, death, resurrection and ascension, and outpouring of the Holy Spirit upon God's people and all of creation, the liturgy heals. Women and men religious possessed a unique capacity to abide with the suffering, often without cures, largely because the rhythms of their daily prayer steeped them in the life, death and resurrection of Jesus.

Bruce Morrill insists that today, "the specific content of this paschal mystery needs to be repeatedly expounded through word and sacrament lest we lose sight of what God we are worshipping."[13] The liturgy reminds us of a merciful, loving God in a way that is alive and real amid the messiness and blessedness of our lives. It makes present to us God's saving acts and places before the living God our needs, prayers, petitions, praise and thanksgiving.

Liturgy celebrates God's saving love. The word 'salvation' shares an etymological root with the word 'health.' Both relate to the Latin word *salus*, as in a salve, a healing ointment or a soothing of wounds.[14] Thus, liturgy has a healing role, albeit different from medicine alone. At the beginning of the liturgy, the priest often references "these saving mysteries" which he and the assembly are about to encounter. One might hear instead "these healing mysteries." Morrill suggests that the liturgy prompts a renegotiated

---

11  Kavanagh, *On Liturgical Theology* (Collegeville, MN: Liturgical Press, 1992): 8.

12  Kavanagh, 8; See also 74 – 76. For an illuminating text on the liturgical-sacramental practice sustaining the life of the world, see Alexander Schmemann, *For the Life of the World*, (Crestwood, NY: St. Vladimir's Seminary Press, 2000).

13  Bruce Morrill, *Divine Worship and Human Healing: Liturgical Theology at the Margins of Life and Death*, (Collegeville, MN: Liturgical Press, 2009): 10.

14  Susan K. Wood, "The Paschal Mystery: The Intersection of Ecclesiology and Sacramental Theology in the Care of the Sick," in *Recovering the Riches of Anointing: a Study of the Sacrament of the Sick*, ed. Genevieve Glen (Collegeville, MN: Liturgical Press, 2002): 5 – 7.

understanding of sickness itself. In other words, sacraments and liturgy are not primarily about getting something but rather "about being more deeply aware of oneself and others as the very site of the loving faithfulness and gracious mercy of God, in whatever condition we find ourselves."[15]

Today Catholic health care has been hiring primarily for expertise, bringing the necessary gifts and skills of lay women and men. An unintended consequence of such a pluralistic approach could be a workforce and senior leadership — including possibly members of governance and sponsorship — who have a tenuous or perhaps no connection to the sacramental-liturgical life of the church. The intimacy described by Kauffman that once linked the Eucharistic celebration to care for the sick and dying fades behind organizational pressures to demonstrate excellence in patient satisfaction, technological advancement, clinical prowess and financial stability. Nevertheless, post Vatican II theology affirms the inherent dignity of women and men to grow in holiness, with the Eucharistic liturgy as the primary conduit.

## THE EUCHARISTIC LITURGY AND CATHOLIC HEALTH CARE'S HEALING MINISTRY

The liturgy is the privileged place where worshippers give thanks and praise to God and enter into God's vision for a healed world. It is the source and summit because it directs and nourishes the lives of the worshippers in an encounter with the living God in two ways, through the Liturgy of the Word and the Liturgy of the Eucharist.

## LITURGY OF THE WORD

In the first part of Mass, the Liturgy of the Word orients worshippers to the Bible. There we see God's faithful and abiding presence from the first moments of creation. Cardinal Walter Kasper notes that the Hebrew Scriptures tell of a merciful God who sees the people's misery, hears their cries and responds with mercy.[16] The biblical word does not relate

---

15  Morrill, 17. Emphasis original to the author's text.
16  Walter Kasper, *Mercy: The Essence of the Gospel and the Key to Christian Life*, trans. William Madges, (New York: Paulist Press, 2014): 41 – 46.

historically accurate or precise events. After all, scripture scholars agree that the Bible is not merely a book, but rather a library of different books and genres. The point of bringing alive the biblical text is to tell the story of salvation — how God's merciful and loving care heals the world from the tragedies of sickness, violence, sin and death.[17]

Each Eucharistic liturgy has an initial reading taken from either Hebrew Scripture or the New Testament followed by a psalm that echoes a key theme from the scripture just proclaimed. Psalms express the richness of nearly every human emotion ranging from lament, grief, and despair to praise, elation, heartfelt gratitude, serenity, and more. The psalms offer some point of meaningful connection for people, whether they are a health care professional or a patient.

The Gospel reading and the homily stand as a high point in the Liturgy of the Word. Many church-goers will associate a particular Sunday Mass with the story recounted in the Gospel. Kasper describes how Jesus embodies God's mercy. God's reign comes through many kinds of healing such as exorcising evil spirits or dominating powers that harm human life. In the Synoptic Gospels, for example, mercy is encountered in Christ's healing and helping acts, particularly in his loving response time and again to those who cry out "Have mercy on us" (Mt 9:27; Mk 10:47; Lk 23:34-43).[18]

If we believe that the Gospel stories tell of Jesus' saving activity in the world, then they must tell us something about healing. It is not necessary for the story to recount a cure or a rising from the dead to have significance for those in health care. It may more broadly illuminate how as hearers of the Word we might renegotiate our own understanding of life, of God or of our own small role in advancing healing, love and mercy in the world around us. Such is the point of the homily. It ought to explain some aspect of the readings and nurture the Christian life and hope in life to come.

During the Nicene Creed, people stand to profess their faith. The creed arose from the early church's deep reflection on the biblical form of life.

---

17  *Dei Verbum, The Dogmatic Constitution on Divine Revelation*, 1965.
18  Kasper, 61 – 72.

It provides a pattern for one's own life, and concludes with a profound statement of belief in God's fidelity and ultimate triumph over death — "life of the world to come." The Liturgy of the Word draws to a close with the prayers of the faithful for the church, the salvation or healing of the world, those who are burdened and the local community. Almost always the petitions include remembrance of those who have died.[19] Here again, the liturgy expresses a healing dimension and expands the vision of healing beyond that of physical cures.

The Liturgy of the Word prepares worshippers to recognize and celebrate the living presence of Christ in their midst in the very presence of the Eucharist. It transports our associates from the flurry of spreadsheets, emails, data, productivity reports and quality charts of their daily work to a vastly different, transcendent aspect of life.

## LITURGY OF THE EUCHARIST

Like the Liturgy of the Word, the Liturgy of the Eucharist consists of multiple components. These include the preparation of gifts or the offering, the epiclesis, and the rite of communion.

## OFFERING

The Liturgy of the Eucharist begins with the preparation of the gifts brought forth to the altar and offered to the priest in thanksgiving to God. As a kid I saw this as an exciting procession of the bread and wine from the back of the church to the priest at the altar. When our family brought the gifts to the altar, I carried the vessel with nervous wonder. The offering also provides the opportunity to collect monetary gifts for the parish and other church ministries.

---

19  *General Instruction of the Roman Missal*, United States Conference of Catholic Bishops (Washington, D.C., 2002) §70. In one preeminent resource with sample prayers the final petition is always for those who have died, see Jay Cormier, *Hear Our Prayer: Prayer of the Faithful for Sundays, Holy Days, and Ritual Masses* (Collegeville, MN: Liturgical Press, 1995).

The priest describes the simple gifts of bread and wine as "fruit of the earth and work of human hands." To early Christian communities, however, these gifts reflect the very lifeblood of the gathered assembly. God's bountiful creation provided the fruit and grain, and the people freely offer them in sacrifice and thanksgiving back to God. This reflects a true sense of gift.[20] The gifts of bread and wine came not from the assembly's surplus, but from their very substance.

In contemporary celebrations of Mass, we can see beyond the mere utilitarian function of bringing the bread, wine and collection to the priest to the story of our lives placed at the altar of God in thanksgiving for all that has been given to us. As the gifts make their way from among the gathered faithful we can see our own hopes and dreams, sufferings and disappointments, joys and excitement, all presented to God.

## THE EPICLESIS

Once the gifts come to the altar, the priest leads a series of prayers that include the epiclesis, which is a calling down of the Holy Spirit upon the gifts of bread and wine, as well as all those in the gathered assembly.[21] This is a powerful image, especially for people in health care. A bedrock of clinical care is listening to the pattern of a patient's heart. The Spirit animates life, and, at the same time, it blows where it wills (Jn 3:8), serving as an instrument of change. The epiclesis implies that this sacramental celebration, in part, is offered to change us into the image of Christ whose body and blood we take into ours.

The Holy Spirit also offers gifts of wisdom and understanding, right judgment and courage, knowledge and reverence, wonder and awe.[22] All these gifts are precious to clinicians and health care leaders. Another image

---

20  Louis-Marie Chauvet, *The Sacraments: The Word of God at the Mercy of the Body,* trans. by Madeleine Beaumont, (Collegeville, MN: Liturgical Press, 2001): 99 – 109; 266 – 316.
21  Chauvet, *The Sacraments: The Word of God at the Mercy of the Body,* trans by Madeleine Beaumont, (Collegeville, MN: Liturgical Press): 2001, 129 – 43; 155 – 70.
22  See the ritual for celebrating the sacrament of Confirmation which calls upon the Holy Spirit as a helper and guide with these particular gifts. *The Rite of Christian Initiation of Adults,* (New York Catholic Book Publishing Co, 1988): §493.

of the Holy Spirit is that of consoler. Nurses, therapists and other care professionals might envision this divine consoler coming upon to them during the epiclesis. The Spirit consoles and gifts them with compassion and empathy for those whose burdens they help to bear. This pneumatological dimension of the Eucharistic celebration offers fertile ground for meditation and reflection.[23]

## THE COMMUNION RITE

The reception of Communion is the consummation of the Mass. The faithful bring the totality of their lives, to receive this "bread come down from heaven." The altar, like the cross, is a place of sacrifice. But it is simultaneously the Passover meal, where we remember Jesus' passing from death into the new life of the Resurrection. Every time we approach the altar, we confront the cross of human mortality but with the fullness of Christian hope and the faith that Christ has transformed death by his grace and resurrection.

The reality of human dying understood within the context of the Eucharist and the Resurrection that motivates the mission of Catholic health care in its care for the elderly, the terminally ill and the dying has long been a hallmark of Catholic health care ministry. The Eucharist presents a larger horizon of hope than simply medical treatments — a hope that stretches toward eternity and draws worshippers into the reality of God's reign. There, sin, sickness and death no longer cause suffering or disarray because the fullness of life and flourishing abound. This gives hope to those confronting imminent death and to those caring for them.

Eucharistic imagery is rich with healing motifs. I will mention two in particular. First, prior to receiving the bread and wine — themselves images of the broken body and outpoured blood of Christ — the assembly prays for healing in the words of the Roman centurion, who had begged Jesus to heal his suffering servant, "Lord I am not worthy that you should enter under my roof, but only say the word and my soul shall be healed" (Mt 8:5-13). Worshippers also ask to be healed in the belief that

---

23   Chauvet, 509 – 30.

the Eucharist brings about hope and healing. The second example is the prayer after Communion, which often contains healing images and prayers for a seamlessness between heaven and earth or body and soul. In one example the priest prays, "May this heavenly mystery, O Lord, restore us in mind and body…"[24] Another petitions, "Grant…that we may be refreshed and nourished by the Sacrament which we have received, so as to be transformed into what we consume."[25] As a foretaste of the heavenly banquet, these prayers reflect the Eucharist that nourishes, restores and heals our lives by its power to transcend the earthly for the heavenly.

The Eucharist is a powerful symbol of unity for Catholic health care. It reflects the unity among those who carry out the healing ministry as members of interdisciplinary teams connected by a shared mission. Eucharist strengthens one's vocation and expertise to benefit others and the common good.

The Eucharistic communion binds us to the mystical body of Christ throughout the world, thereby binding us to all who suffer and all who rejoice. Fr. Bernard Häring noted that when receiving the Eucharist we are confronted with the question of "whether we want to be and act as mutually responsible members of the Body of Christ. A truly Eucharistic, grateful memory will help us to say our responsible 'Amen' when the need of others appeals to our active love."[26] A Eucharistic spirituality fosters a sense of communion with patients and enables caregivers to cultivate empathy and Christian love.

In addition, the Eucharist reflects a communion with the whole church and all who partake of the Eucharist throughout the world. For members of the Catholic health ministry, the Liturgy of the Word and the Liturgy of the Eucharist reveal God's mercy that heals and brings bodies from all creation into an integrated wholeness.

---

24  Prayer After Communion, 26th Sunday in Ordinary Time, in *The Roman Missal,* Third Typical Edition.

25  Prayer After Communion, 27th Sunday in Ordinary Time.

26  Bernard Häring, *In Pursuit of Wholeness: Healing in Today's Church,* (Ligouri, MO: Ligouri Publications, 1985): 82.

## THREE VIGNETTES

Three examples of how the liturgy impacts the deep personal experience
of health care professionals will help to illustrate how the liturgy
intersects with the church's healing ministry. The first describes a Mass of
thanksgiving with leaders from a health system. The second reflects on the
liturgical experience at the annual Catholic Health Association's Catholic
Health Assembly. The final example considers the experience of the daily
Eucharistic celebration of those in an acute care hospital.

## MASS OF THANKSGIVING

When a formation cohort of leaders from Presence Health in Chicago
concluded their 18-month journey, we ritualized this culmination with a
Eucharistic liturgy. For some in the cohort this was a new experience. The
setting was intimate yet magnificent. The health care leaders gathered in
St. James Chapel, once a part of Quigley High School Seminary and now
the heart of the chancery offices for the Archdiocese of Chicago. Presence
Health's system offices are located nearby in downtown Chicago.

The Liturgy of the Word for that day fortuitously pointed to profound
connections for those in health care. The first reading came from the
prophet Jeremiah (7:23-28), who spoke of a new, unbreakable and
unmerited covenant God makes with God's people. The prophet speaks
of God's unrelenting faithfulness and love, despite human infidelity and
hardness of heart. How profound that leaders of Presence Health celebrated
a Mass of thanksgiving with scriptural readings radically affirming
God's abiding presence even in the face of imperfections and injustices
experienced in life.

The Gospel passage, Luke 11:14-23, recounted Jesus healing a man once
made mute by a demon. Besides describing the healing, the passage
presented Jesus probing his listeners to consider that which stands at
the center of their lives. For the leaders who just completed a formation
program, the Gospel prompted them to consider their own commitments
to furthering the mission of the healing ministry. Reflecting on the liturgical
experience, cohort participants expressed being deeply touched. Regardless

of whether they could pinpoint theological meanings, the ritual had a significant impact on them. They recognized that they had stood on holy ground. Eucharist, which literally means to give thanks, was present to them in full measure. The celebration provided the opportunity for a thanksgiving for the formation experience, and a way for leaders to join together in thanking God for the privilege of serving this healing ministry.

Other Catholic health systems celebrate Eucharistic liturgies on similar occasions. Some have a practice of celebrating Mass when meeting with their boards of directors. Others offer a Mass at semi-annual or quarterly gatherings of senior leadership. Still others rarely or never gather at a Eucharistic celebration. Some leaders feel uncomfortable attending Catholic Mass when many members of the organization may not be Catholic, but with skilled liturgical formation, dialogue and repeated experiences, these occasions can be richly received by all.

## CATHOLIC HEALTH ASSOCIATION'S ANNUAL CATHOLIC HEALTH ASSEMBLY

When the Catholic Health Association (CHA) hosts a program, it nearly always includes a celebration of the Eucharist. During CHA's centennial anniversary celebration in June 2015, hundreds of health care leaders gathered at the Basilica of the National Shrine of the Immaculate Conception in Washington, D.C. for the opening liturgy. Cardinal Donald Wuerl, archbishop of Washington, D.C., presided. Clearly, this was a mountaintop experience. The liturgy — marked by the splendor of the national basilica, jubilant music, and a joyful congregation — not only commemorated the centennial jubilee but also magnificently displayed a rich complement of Catholic health care. The Eucharistic celebration drew together ministry leaders and CHA members along with bishops representing the ecclesial hierarchy. Just four years prior, there had been disagreement and discord over passage of the Affordable Care Act. Yet here, the liturgy reflected a healing of relationships.[27]

---

27 One of the seven commitment points in the Shared Statement of Identity for health care ministries that are members of the Catholic Health Association include acting in communion with the Church. See, https://www.chausa.org/Mission/a-shared-statement-of-identity.

A second observation regarding the Eucharist at CHA's annual Catholic Health Assembly is the spotlight it places on the liturgy's connection to social justice. Theologians have described how the liturgy reveals a pattern for living virtuously and justly.[28] CHA and its member organizations demonstrate sustained commitments to justice and social transformation, in part through their advocacy initiatives. CHA's President and Chief Executive Officer Sr. Carol Keehan, DC and the association's advocacy staff maintain offices in Washington, D.C., where they regularly meet and communicate with lawmakers and policy officials. At the assembly, CHA's advocacy experts share updates from Capitol Hill and present policy priorities. When hearing the advocacy report after a liturgical celebration, one can see how the God of justice, peace and solidarity encountered in the scriptures and the Eucharist influences the work of the ministry's advocacy.

## DAILY MASS IN ACUTE CARE SETTINGS

Many Catholic hospitals celebrate daily Eucharist in their chapels. Most celebrate Sunday Mass. In the acute care setting many of those who attend are hospital associates or family members. In chapels where nuns may have once filled the pews are now technicians in lab coats, administrators in their suits, retiree volunteers, nurses in scrubs and physicians with stethoscopes tucked into their pockets.[29] Daily Mass in the hospital chapel radiates a gravitas distinct from the daily Mass in a local parish community.

In the hospital chapel family members stand before the living God to put forth their hopes, dreams and deepest petitions for themselves and their loved ones. Their individual experience meets with the prayers of the psalms and the good news of the Gospel. Their pleadings join with the prayers of the faithful, and their burdens are laid at the altar of the Lord. Then they are fed with the gift of Christ's very life offered in the Eucharist.

---

28  See Virgil George Michel, *The Social Question: Essays on Capitalism and Christianity*, ed. Robert L. Spaeth (Collegeville, MN: St. John's University, 1987); Robert Barron, "Lex Oranidi, Lex Vivendi: The Liturgy as a Source for the Moral Life," in *Bridging the Great Divide: Musings of a Post-Liberal, Post-Conservative, Evangelical Catholic* (New York: Rowman & Littlefield Publishers, 2004): 35 – 52.

29  Karl Rahner, "The Eucharist in Our Daily Lives." *Theological Investigations*, vol. 7, trans. David Bourke, (New York: Seabury Press, 1977): 211 – 28.

These families do not pray alone. Liturgy always occurs in community. The presence of hospital associates reflects a post-conciliar church in which lay professionals, highly skilled in their own disciplines, have replaced the sisters. One sees fresh insights into the notion of a Christian vocation. Lay associates can give witness to how faith animates their lives. Staff, volunteers and other associates find sustenance in the liturgy in the way it can give meaning to the tragedy of sin and death. As Bernard Häring observed, "We shall heal what can be healed and give, or rather uncover, the meaning in what cannot be healed."[30]

The daily celebration of the Eucharist places the paschal mystery on full display in the hospital. Of course, every Eucharistic liturgy celebrates the paschal mystery. Experiencing healing in the Advent or Christmas seasons will be different than searching for meaning from one's illness in Lent or the Easter season. A full sense of Christ's life and healing actions unfolds through the liturgical year. Ritualizing this day after day in the hospital chapel communicates a fullness of God's faithful presence from life through death and to new life.

## CONCLUSION

In the bygone era of abundant vocations in religious congregations, the connections between the liturgy and care for the sick appeared with greater clarity. Today, increased visibility and focused intention are needed. Catholic health care formation programs need liturgical formation akin to that seen in parishes. There are numerous pastoral resources to help the faithful carry out the vision of the Second Vatican Council to be fully active and conscious at the liturgy so that it might more concretely serve as the source and summit of all the church's activity. Similar tools should strengthen Catholic health care's formation programs.

Catholic health care systems ought to consider more opportunities for executive leaders to experience and participate in the liturgy. System offices that are far removed from care settings and dedicated chapels do little to provide liturgical experiences. While nearly all systems have some formation

---

30  Häring, 29.

program, few, if any, have developed much in terms of a deliberate experience and reflection on the liturgy. And yet, the liturgy itself is formative.[31] Liturgy draws the faithful into the patterns and rhythms of the paschal mystery and reminds us of God's promise to heal and make all of creation whole. People need help learning how to reflect upon the liturgical experience and they need the skills to take in and interpret the unique language of the liturgy. To do this, I conclude with two suggestions.

First, formation programs can incorporate liturgical experiences at multiple times in the course of formation. They need not be Eucharistic. Exposing leaders to a Liturgy of the Word or to morning prayer, for example, can introduce prayers and patterns of the church's liturgy. This presents particular ecumenical appeal. It also gives a sense of how the readings and psalms respond differently through the liturgical seasons. These elements impact one's sense of healing and insights into the life of God. Some system offices, for example, offer a liturgical celebration throughout the weeks of Advent and Lent. Extending these into Christmas, Easter — seasons of triumph and jubilation — as well as various feasts in ordinary time would give fuller expression to the paschal mystery. Having liturgical touchpoints throughout a formation program makes the experience of a Mass of Thanksgiving or some other celebratory liturgy more significant.

Second, once a formation program concludes, its participants can continue to gather to reflect on the integration of their work in the ministry and their own practice of faith. They might focus their discussion on how their worship or a particular liturgical season feeds and nourishes their vocation and their role in the healing ministry.

This second suggestion could be one way to sustain formation within a Catholic health care ministry. Formation directors reiterate how formation never ends. Its intent is to enable the individual to always grow in a life of virtue — a process never quite complete. The liturgy seems an appropriate component for the formative process as its ongoing cycles offer the living

---

31  Philip Kenneson, "Gathering: Worship, Imagination, and Formation" in *The Blackwell Companion to Christian Ethics*, 2nd ed., edited by Stanley Hauerwas and Samuel Wells (Maiden, Mass: Blackwell Publishing, 2011): 55 – 69.

presence of Christ at different times and against different circumstances in our lives. It serves as a grounding for the unpredictable nature of life and the many changes in health care, for at the Eucharist one can count on the fidelity and mercy of God.

## DISCUSSION QUESTIONS

1. When have you experienced a Eucharistic celebration in the context of your professional work in a health ministry? Describe whether or how that Mass felt different from other Masses in which you have participated.

2. What could help you to experience healing dimensions of worship?

3. Name something in your life or ministry workplace that is in need of healing. How might the liturgy help foster a renegotiated understanding of healing, new life or human flourishing?

4. How might you approach the next Mass you attend or your own faith tradition's worship service differently with this understanding of the council's vision of the centrality of Christian worship?

CHAPTER SUMMARY

In the process of renewing its practice of the Sacrament of
Anointing of the Sick, the church needs to give more attention
to its practice of Viaticum. Viaticum as communion for the
dying, the true last rite of the church, is losing ground in
sacramental practice. This is in part a result of the interventional
technology used toward the end of life. But it also comes
from our reluctance to help the dying and their families prepare
for death in time to make use of Viaticum as a deeply
consoling sacramental means of preparation for the
passage from this life to the next.

# 3.4 SACRAMENTS FOR THE SICK AND DYING
## Reprinted from *Health Progress*
## November–December 2015

James M. Schellman, M.A.
*Vice President, Mission Integration*
*Our Lady of Lourdes Regional Medical Center*

I N "SACRAMENTAL RESOURCES UNDERUSED IN CARE," published in the January – February 2014 issue of *Health Progress*, Fr. Bruce Morrill, SJ, Ph.D., offered important insights on the church's existing ritual resources for ministry to the sick and dying and what these resources offer to these dear members of the Body of Christ and those whom they love.

Here is a brief summary of some of his central insights, in my own words:

+ The care of medical practitioners shifts in response to the condition of the patient, whether seriously, critically or terminally ill. So too should our pastoral and sacramental care of the patient respond to the distinct condition of the patient. This kind of responsiveness is presumed in the church's present ritual book, *Pastoral Care of the Sick: Rites of Anointing and Viaticum.*

+ *Pastoral Care of the Sick* offers a rich compendium of resources for accompanying the sick and their families through the whole continuum of serious, critical and terminal illness. These resources correspond to the medical realities, and they could be used more fully by our pastoral care teams in hospital and other settings. Instead, these possibilities are underused, because they often are misunderstood and ignored.

+ The reasons for this are many, not least our cultural uneasiness with and even denial of death, and our medical community's sense that death is a failure of medicine. This often leaves the terminally ill in a state of isolation. Their medical professionals begin to disengage at the point when their skills can no longer hold death at bay. Their family members are at a loss to know how to accompany them at this stage of life, a result of our culture's own denial of the reality.

+ At stake, in terms of the church's pastoral ministry to these in-need sisters and brothers and their families, is the longstanding distinction between ministry to the sick, with Anointing of the Sick as its centerpiece, and ministry to the dying, with Communion as viaticum, as the church's last rite. The distinction is still largely missing from the average Catholic's understanding and practice, and is missing as well as from the understanding and practice of many of those who serve in this ministry.

## SICKNESS, DEATH, OUR CULTURE

Medical practice in the United States excels in the development of new technologies and drug therapies that enhance the quality of life and help to extend life in ways previous generations would have considered miraculous. We are the envy of the world in our capacity to combat illness and give the seriously ill months, sometimes years of further life. But coupled with this remarkable achievement is an increasing cultural inability to face and talk about death when it is inevitable. We have lost how cultures model and pass on to succeeding generations ways to accompany those we love who are actively readying for the next life.

Our medical practice mirrors this reality. Too often physicians put off acknowledging that a patient has made the transition into active dying. This is done out of compassion for the ensuing grief of patient and family. It also is because the physician feels like a failure in being able to stave off the inevitable for at least a little longer.

# PASTORAL CARE OF THE SICK

From a faith perspective, this reluctance to give over those we love to death rests on a solid intuition. Deep in our human heart, we sense that life was not supposed to be like this, that the loss of those we love, and those who love us eventually losing us, was not the way God meant this world to be. This is an intuition arising from the whole faith story, from Genesis to Christ. God made the world a garden place of harmony and endless life. The biblical revelation is that, in the mystery of our God-given freedom, humanity chose something other than God. The result is that sin and death, alien to God's original design, entered into the story of our relationship with God, one another and the world itself. In the depths of our being, we experience a deep, heartrending brokenness, and it is this that our ministry with, in and through Christ addresses.[1]

On the basis of this deep biblical intuition, we are drawn to fight sickness with all the resources available to us: "Part of the plan laid out by God's providence is that we should fight strenuously against all sickness and carefully seek the blessings of good health, so that we may fulfill our role in human society and in the Church."[2] We each have a mission in this world from God, and as long as we can, we are to work to maintain our physical health to be of use to those who rely upon us for the work that is uniquely ours.

Along the way, there is suffering that comes to us in sickness that we can, with the help of our faith, learn to accept by understanding it in relation to Christ's own suffering for the redemptive healing of ourselves and those we love. "We should always be prepared to fill up what is lacking in Christ's sufferings for the salvation of the world as we look forward to creation's being set free in the glory of the children of God — see Colossians 1:24; Romans 8:19-20."[3] It is an astounding insight that offers the sick in their suffering a great dignity and purpose. What could possibly be lacking in Christ's suffering to achieve salvation? Apparently, only our

---

1   See "The Ministry of the Sick," by James Schellman, in *The New Dictionary of Sacramental Worship*, ed. Peter Fink (Collegeville, MN: Liturgical Press, 1990): 1165 – 67.

2   *Pastoral Care of the Sick: Rites of Anointing and Viaticum*, no. 3.

3   *Pastoral Care of the Sick*, no. 3.

willing cooperation in our own suffering as a part of Christ's. And that is difficult enough.

## THE DYING AND VIATICUM

But the real problem for us, culturally, medically and pastorally, is when the seriously sick person makes the transition to being terminally ill or actively dying. At this point, our fundamental intuition about the goodness of this life must begin to be transformed into an intuition for the life that follows this life. Too often our pastoral care of the dying is caught in the wake of our cultural reluctance to face the fact of death and the inclination of many of our medical practitioners to spare the dying and their families full knowledge of the transition to a terminal or active dying state. As a result, pastoral care frequently comes late to the process, regrettably too late to use the full resources of our faith tradition in offering a compassionate accompaniment to the dying and those who love them.

We must do better. Our people must not be deprived of the full healing ministry of Jesus Christ. For the dying, this ministry shifts its focus to a healing of mind and soul that helps ease the transition to life eternal. The centerpiece of this particular moment in our healing ministry is the celebration of Communion as viaticum with the dying person.

In its official teaching, the church has held that anointing is the sacrament for the seriously sick, some of whom may be dying, but many of whom retain the hope of being restored to a productive life in community. From this understanding, the sacrament unique to the dying is Communion as viaticum, the true last rite of the community of faith. Thus, anointing celebrated early in a serious sickness opens the door to viaticum when serious sickness becomes active dying.

Viaticum can be as full or as simple as needed for the dying person. If not held off too long, it can be done within a Mass with the family, or it can be a Communion service with a choice of various elements such as a simplified renewal of baptismal vows, sprinkling the dying person with holy water as a reminder of his or her baptism, and a special Communion text that acknowledges this particular kind of Communion: "Jesus Christ is the food for our journey; he calls us to the heavenly table."[4]

If time is short, we can do a continuous and simplified celebration of penance, anointing and viaticum. But even here, viaticum is the last act by which Christ, as the goal of the dying, becomes their own dear companion for the final journey.

## LOST SACRAMENT

Despite this official and pastoral wisdom of the church which has been in place for centuries, our actual practice has continued to treat Anointing of the Sick as the last rite. Why this is so is a larger topic than this brief article. Suffice it to say that the Second Vatican Council underlined yet again the teaching that anointing is the sacrament of the sick and viaticum the last rite of our faith community for its dying members. The council's partial success can be seen in the change over the last several decades to frequent celebrations of anointing for sick persons in parishes and homes, as well as in health care settings. It is a partial success because anointing also remains in practice in many places the last rite of the church's ministers celebrated with the dying.

To have a conversation with chaplains about why viaticum is not offered can be very instructive. On the one hand, many of our electronic medical record systems, in their "spiritual care" section, do not even include viaticum in the sacramental record. You will find, for example, Anointing of the Sick, and Communion, but not viaticum. If you ask chaplains, they often will reassure you that viaticum is being offered. But a little probing will show it is actually Communion that is being offered rather than viaticum, especially in the last days. And this frequently becomes even more difficult because of the delay in acknowledging approaching death. It can be too late to offer Communion in the unique and consoling form of viaticum.

Part of what is at stake here is the sacraments of the church being the occasion to help encourage what needs to be happening anyway. The dying

---

4    *Pastoral Care of the Sick*, no. 207.

often know that death is approaching, but they want to spare their family having to talk about it. By the same token, the family sense that death is nearing, but they wish to spare the dying person that knowledge. An opportunity can be lost to heal, reconcile, thank, celebrate — whatever is most needed and appropriate before allowing this beloved person to go forth from us. By sensitively inviting some conversation around viaticum, the chaplain can help begin a larger conversation that often is desperately needed before it is simply too late.

## ONE STORY OF VIATICUM

How can we frame the question of restoring viaticum to the dying in a way that helps us long to do better by our dying sisters and brothers and those who love them? I offer a personal story.

Some years ago, my father was several weeks in an intensive care unit after surgery and before dying. The hospital was hundreds of miles from home. I flew in on Christmas Day to surprise him and, as I thought, to try to say goodbye. Dad was on a ventilator and, though unable to speak, expressive in a way that was simply remarkable. Between facial responses and a barely legible penmanship, he was able to share more than I could have imagined. My mother was not ready to admit he was dying. Dad knew and "told" me in a conversation with Mom out of the room.

My dad had gone to daily Mass frequently. There in the hospital he had not had Communion for a couple of weeks. Knowing that the ritual book allowed for viaticum in just these circumstances, in the form of consecrated wine alone,[5] I asked one of the two priests who ministered on the unit if he would be willing to bring a little consecrated wine from Mass the next morning so that Dad could receive Communion. The priest was shocked at the request and said firmly that he could not possibly do this. I was too emotional under the circumstances of Dad's dying to try to carry the conversation further. Inexperienced in this practice as he clearly was, he may simply have been concerned about proper reverence and the possibility of spillage.

---

5   *Pastoral Care of the Sick*, no. 193.

The next day I approached the second priest, fearing similar rejection and uncertain how I should respond the second time around. When I asked him, there was a long pause and steady eye contact. He then said, "I have never done this before, but for your father, I will do it."

With some preparation of my mother, father, and a couple of siblings, we celebrated together a simple and unforgettable Communion as viaticum service. My father insisted, ventilator and all, on being in a chair next to his bed. I had never seen him so alive and ready for Communion, and he had communed many, many times in his life. Within days, he was gone to the Lord with the Lord as his Eucharistic companion for the final journey.

That dear priest did not know the ritual book of the church any better than many of us, but he knew my Dad and had learned to love him. It is that kind of love that will help us learn to do the right thing, to offer our nearly departed the full ministry of the church, which is nothing less than a Lord who so longs to accompany us to the Father that he will come to us in the humblest of ways, in a few tiny drops of wine become his very self, food for that final journey.

## DISCUSSION QUESTIONS

1. Do you have experience of the ritual of viaticum with a dying person in your life — a family member, friend or other person? Recall what it was like, who was there, and how the dying person seemed to respond to Communion in this form.

2. How frequently do you think viaticum is celebrated in your health care setting (not Communion of the Sick but the distinct form of Communion for the Dying)? Does your electronic health record allow for recording Viaticum as one of your sacramental offerings?

3. What do you believe are the obstacles to more frequent offering of viaticum to your dying patients (e.g., clinical, pastoral, practical), and how might you begin to address them?

# IV

# THE CHURCH AND HEALTH CARE

CHAPTER SUMMARY

Until recently the term "ministry" was rarely used by Catholics and,
when it was, it applied primarily to individual, internal work done by an
ordained priest or deacon to build up the internal faith life of a church
community. When laypersons began to assume some of the roles
traditionally held by priests and sisters, the generic use of ministry,
to cover both ordained and lay ministry emerged. Eventually, we extended
the use of the term beyond individual actions to corporate actions by
institutions acting in the name of the church. New public juridic persons
were formed to maintain the link with the wider church and assure
fidelity to doctrine, much as religious orders had historically done.

This new expanded notion of ministry has continued to develop.
Today it is the object of theological exploration, and it has become a
central feature of formation programs for leaders in Catholic health
care. What does it mean to be a ministry of the church? How does
this kind of corporate ministry differ from the individual ministries
most of us are familiar with? What is the role of the bishop?
How do others who may not share our faith convictions participate
or collaborate with us in this ministry?

## 4.1 THE MEANING OF MINISTRY
## IN HEALTH CARE

———————

Fr. Charles E. Bouchard, OP, S.T.D.
*Senior Director, Theology and Ethics*
*Catholic Health Association*

HE USE OF THE TERM "MINISTRY" TO DESCRIBE Catholic health care was introduced only in the 1980s but it has now become common parlance. The familiarity of this description belies the complexity of the term itself and the enormous ecclesial change it signifies. I will describe some of the questions that surround the use of this term and the challenges we face if it is to be applied in any meaningful way to Catholic health care in the future.

It would be difficult to overstate the change that has occurred in the Catholic Church with regard to the understanding of ministry since the Second Vatican Council. For at least 300 years prior to 1965, the church didn't use the word "ministry." Catholics had priests and nuns, but they didn't have ministers; in fact, "the ministry" was a Protestant term. For Catholics, the idea of ministry was intrinsically associated with ordination, especially to the priesthood. While there were "minor orders" such as acolyte, deacon, subdeacon and porter, these were largely ritual and had no real theology that involved actual Gospel service to God's people. In addition, because of the tight link between celibacy, gender and these ordained ministries, there was a tendency to confuse ministerial functions strictly with clerical modes of life.[1]

---

1   Thomas O'Meara, *Theology of Ministry*, 2nd ed. (New York: Paulist Press, 1999): 191.

The role of laypeople was viewed differently as well; the laity never thought of what they did as "ministry." They had the apostolate, which was largely their work in the world, living out their baptismal commitment as parents, teachers, workers or professionals. Sometimes they became involved in certain church groups such as the Holy Name Society, the Knights of Columbus, the St. Vincent DePaul Society or others, but these kinds of involvement and service were seen as totally distinct from sacramental ministry exercised by priests and bishops.

Fr. Thomas O'Meara, OP wrote that this relatively covert understanding of lay activity in the world is a modern development dating from after the Reformation when the church felt "that the world was hostile to it. Without direct control over society, church leaders encouraged the laity, formed by doctrine, sacraments and spiritual discipline, to transform the secular order — but slowly, implicitly and from within."[2] The development of this idea of "laity" froze all Christians who were not ordained priests into a passive state.[3]

Today the ministerial circle has widened dramatically. Coming largely from below and with little encouragement from church leaders, there has been an explosion of ministry led by the Holy Spirit. In this new wider circle, we have not only priests, deacons and bishops, but a wide variety of lay persons who exercise various ministries in the church under the auspices of a pastor or a bishop.[4] These "ecclesial" ministers are distinguished from volunteers in a number of ways: they are committed to it for a long period of time; they have sought and received education and formation; they act officially on behalf of the church and have, to varying degrees, an ecclesial status. Those who lead priestless parishes, for example, are delegated and named by the bishop and have limited canonical responsibility for the parish.

---

2   O'Meara, 189. He notes that this view is "not congenial to the Catholic mind" because it made "faith a matter of individuals and religion only for souls; second, it implied that grace was absent from the world; and third, it entrusted to the laity what was in fact an infiltration of the worlds of science and politics; finally, it divided grace from nature, handing over soul and sacrament to priests but world and history to laity."

3   O'Meara, 145, drawing on Karl Rahner.

4   An ecclesiology based on the idea of communion rather than hierarchy provides a rich conceptual framework that can accommodate both the variety of ministries and their relationship to one another.

O'Meara defines ministry as "the public activity of a baptized follower of Jesus Christ, flowing from the Spirit's charism and an individual personality on behalf of a Christian community to proclaim, serve and realize the Kingdom of God."[5] He highlights several crucial aspects of this definition.

First of all, it involves *doing something*. This distinguishes it from a religious or celibate clerical lifestyle and other modes of life, which are valuable and good in themselves but which by themselves do not constitute ministry. Second, what is done is done *for the Kingdom of God*. O'Meara points out that not every noble thing is ministry and it does not happen by accident; it must be defined specifically and narrowly and undertaken explicitly and with the intention to turn the Kingdom of God into "sacrament, word or action." Third, ministry is not private. It is always a *public action*. In the early church Jesus and the disciples proclaimed the Gospel openly and publicly. They saw the public witness of their lives as essential to the ministry of the Gospel. Fourth, ministry is from the Spirit, involves diverse gifts, and is undertaken on *behalf of Christian community*. At least in the Catholic tradition, there is no such thing as a solitary, "Lone Ranger" type of ministry. For us, all ministry is rooted in baptism and in membership in an identifiable church. This is why the issue of sponsorship is so important today — it provides the essential link between a ministry and the church from which it flows. This relationship to a wider church also enables the ministry to be a leaven, a sign and a sacrament to the world.

## CAN INSTITUTIONS MINISTER?

If this expanded idea of lay ministry by individuals is new and evolving, there is a bigger and more important question for health care, viz., in what sense can *institutions* be considered as ministries? To use O'Meara's words, can Catholic health care be a "public activity of baptized followers of Jesus

---

5    O'Meara, p. 150. Compare O'Meara's definition to a definition of the mission of the church — and therefore of the mission of health care — developed by Bishop Michael E. Putney of Townsville, Queensland, Australia, specifically for health care: "The church is a communion, but as such it is a sign and servant of what God is doing on a larger scale, reconciling the whole cosmos in Christ, the coming of the Kingdom of God. The church is always a fragile, ambiguous sign of the kingdom, but is also its servant." Michael E. Putney, "Health Care and the Church's Mission," *Health Progress*, (January – February 2004): 19.

Christ flowing from the Spirit's charism on behalf of a Christian community to proclaim, serve and realize the Kingdom of God?" Can groups or teams of the baptized function as a corporate ministry? Can these teams have an ecclesial status and a "corporate vocation" to carry out a work of the church?[6] Is this ability merely delegated or is it inherent by virtue of baptism?

It is not that this is new in practice. We have had church organizations — schools, priories, monasteries, hospitals and social service agencies — that have acted on behalf of the church for centuries. They "gave flesh" to the church's mission by preaching through works of mercy, healing and education. These organizations are recognized by canon and civil law as "moral persons" and have the same kinds of responsibilities, accountability and agency as individual persons have had.

What is new is that until recently these institutions were usually not considered "ministries" in the proper sense.[7] In addition, most of them received their mandate to act on behalf of the church not *directly*, but *indirectly* through the religious orders that sponsored them. It was these orders that were authorized by the church as moral persons; the orders then carried out their mission through the institutions they founded. It was through their sponsoring religious communities that these good works maintained their "communion" with the church. Fr. Michael Place suggested that as these apostolic works of religious communities became a more formal expression of the ministerial life of the Church, the health care ministry moved into uncharted territory.[8]

---

6  Neely McCarter, longtime president of Gordon-Conwell Seminary, wrote that "vocation doesn't only mean individual purposes; it also means mutual purposes... At the root of a creative institution is a shared sense of vocation, or if you prefer, a common calling. Both in the Jewish and Christian traditions, the presence of this calling is embraced as a gift... [which requires] a corporate sense of identity and a unifying loyalty to a set of purposes." Neely Dixon McCarter, *The President as Educator: A Study of the Seminary Presidency* (Scholars Press Studies in Theological Education: 1996): 71.

7  Indeed, the use of the word "ministry" as applied to health care only emerged recently. A quick search of past issues of *Health Progress* indicates that the term only began to be applied to health care in the mid to late 1970s, replacing the more common "apostolate." In his address as incoming board chair in 1976, Msgr. Raymond J. Pollard, referred to the healing ministry of Christ." A pastoral letter issued by the U.S. Bishops in 1981, "Health and Health Care: A Pastoral Letter of the American Bishops," as well as the use of the term "health care ministry" by John Paul II during his visit to the U.S.in 1987 brought the term into the mainstream.

8  Michael Place, "Elements of Theological Foundations of Sponsorship," *Health Progress* (November – December 2000).

The extent of the transition is apparent if we think for a moment of recent changes in the way Catholic health care is sponsored. After a several year moratorium by the Vatican, in May 2006, Bon Secours Ministries was finally approved by the Vatican as a "public juridic person" (PJP) — a church corporation analogous to a religious order but comprised of both lay and religious members. In early 2007, the Holy See's Congregation for Institutes of Consecrated Life and Societies of Apostolic Life (CICLSAL) approved St. Joseph Health Ministry as a new PJP sponsoring St. Joseph Health System of Orange.[9] Although members of the founding religious order remain members of this "person," there is no longer any religious order that sponsors the ministry and maintains its communion with the church. That relationship now exists directly between the ministry itself and the Holy See through CICLSAL. Several other PJPs have been approved since then, including Presence Health in Chicago in 2015.

These new sponsorship entities are structured in a variety of ways. Some of them consist entirely of laypersons — with no involvement of a religious order at all — or they have made provision for such exclusive lay sponsorship at some point in the future. Some PJPs are sole sponsors of a health care ministry; others are one of a number of sponsors (e.g., Catholic Health in Buffalo is sponsored jointly by Trinity Health and the Diocese of Buffalo, a traditional PJP founded long before the term came into common usage). These new organizations mark an unprecedented event in which a group of laypersons has or will eventually have exactly the same canonical responsibility for a ministry of the church that in the past was possessed only by vowed religious. There is no previous example of such a rapid transition in leadership and sponsorship of such a large ministerial endeavor of the church.

Our common use of "the ministry" in reference to Catholic health care is meant to convey that, while health care must be run in a business-like way, it is first and foremost a work of the church that is rooted in the healing mission of Jesus. Its purpose is first of all to proclaim the Gospel on behalf of the church. But practice and language have gotten ahead of

---

9    In 2016 St. Joseph Health merged with Providence Health & Services to become
     Providence St. Joseph Health.

theology. There are a number of important questions that must be answered before we can fully claim the title of "ministry" and a number of things that need careful attention to ensure that health care will remain vital long into the future.

## CHALLENGES TO THE DEVELOPMENT OF HEALTH CARE AS A MINISTRY

### *Lay ministry to corporate ministry*

I have already noted the tentative, though rapidly evolving notion of "lay ecclesial ministry." Although it is clearly here to stay, the concept is still ambiguous and ill-defined. It is bedeviled by confusion about the difference between volunteer and "career" lay ministers, the lack of accurate and consistent job titles and job descriptions, inadequate compensation, and the absence of official status. Practice varies widely from one diocese to another. Some bishops have embraced lay ecclesial ministry and recognize it by official commissioning; others have accepted it grudgingly, if at all, and see it as a temporary fix until adequate numbers of priests can be prepared.

Indeed, the Vatican itself has been ambivalent, fearing that this wider expression of "ministry" will dilute the unique identity of priesthood. A 1997 Vatican instruction described what the non-ordained do as "functions and tasks" — clearly distinct from the more sacral duties of clergy.[10] The non-ordained faithful "do not enjoy a right to such duties," the document said. Rather, they are "capable of being admitted by the sacred Pastors ... to those functions which, in accordance with the provisions of law, they can

---

10  "Interdicasterial Instruction on Certain Questions Regarding the Collaboration of the Non-Ordained Faithful in the Sacred Ministry of the Priest" (August 15, 1997): #50 – 51. The instruction invoked the distinction between "duties" of the faithful and the "office" of the ordained: "In some cases, the extension of the term 'ministry' to the *munera* belonging to the lay faithful has been permitted by the fact that the latter, to their own degree, are a participation in the one priesthood of Christ. The *officia* temporarily entrusted to them, however, are exclusively the result of a deputation by the church. Only with constant reference to the one source, the 'ministry of Christ' (...) may the term ministry be applied to a certain extent and without ambiguity to the lay faithful: that is, without it being perceived and lived as an undue aspiration to the ordained ministry or as a progressive erosion of its specific nature." This is a discouraging and fearful document that appears to be based on an assumption of scarcity, rather than fullness of grace.

discharge" or, where "[ordained] ministers are not available ... they can supply certain of their functions ... in accordance with the provisions of law."

The issue here is twofold. First, can laypeople actually function as ministers in the full sense of the word? And, if so, is their ministerial activity merely *delegated*, as the Vatican instruction suggested, or is it an expression of subsidiarity, a proper exercise of their own baptismal dignity rather than something delegated from above by those who actually possess ministerial power but occasionally allow it to be exercised by others in extraordinary circumstances?

If we are unsure about the authenticity of "ministry" exercised by individual laypersons, how can we apply the term to organizations as vast and influential as Catholic health care?

## MONEY AND MINISTRY

A second area of concern is whether the enormous scale of Catholic health care and the money required to sustain it are ultimately compatible with the idea of ministry. Some years ago, Brian Anderson argued that Catholic Charities had "lost its soul" because the huge infusions of government money required to support its activity had rendered it into an essentially government agency. This, he argued, led Catholic Charities to abandon moral responsibility and faith and to see crime as just an effect of economic and social oppression. In 2000 he wrote that Catholic Charities was more concerned with lobbying and networking for left-wing causes than in anything remotely like ministry. "Many of today's Catholic Charities agencies," he says, "pay little attention to the power of faith to transform lives."[11]

In the 1970s a group of Catholic health care leaders raised a similar concern. They said that the infusion of federal money and control that came with Medicaid and Medicare posed an insurmountable challenge to the integrity

---

11  "How Catholic Charities Lost Its Soul," *City Journal*, (New York: Manhattan Institute, Winter 2000). Although Anderson's criticism obviously is driven by a political agenda, his point is well worth considering. *City Journal* is available online (www.city-journal.org).

of our ministry. They proposed that we should get out of acute care entirely and focus on parish-based non-acute services.[12] "When the government gets in," one participant said, "the Church should get out."

More recently the advent of for-profit Catholic health care has created a new set of questions. Is it possible for a Catholic ministry to be held by an investor-owned corporation? Can this ministry of healing be structured in such a way that it also produces a financial return to disinterested investors? On one hand, there may not be much moral distinction between a health care system that generates capital through bonds and one that generates revenue by selling stock. In 2012, Ascension Health created a for-profit corporation that would raise money to rescue distressed hospitals because often these hospitals were in such bad shape that even large Catholic systems could not afford to acquire them and provide the necessary capital to improve them. This system, said the CEO at the time, would be a "mirror image" of the system's non-profit holdings, except that it would raise money differently. Unfortunately, most Catholic systems that were at risk were sold to the highest bidder — often a secular for-profit, and the Catholic corporation was eventually dissolved.[13]

On the other hand, however, is it possible for an investor-owned Catholic hospital to be fully Catholic, or will Catholic identity become just a matter of compliance to the *Ethical and Religious Directives*? Some of these Catholic, for-profit ventures seem to be working fairly well, but it remains to be seen whether they will be able to be accountable to shareholders *and* to the church.

## FORMATION FOR MINISTRY

Celeste Mueller treats the question of formation more fully elsewhere in this volume. However, a few words here, in the context of ministry, may be helpful. The formal and ecclesial way in which we have described ministry

---

12  The activities of this CHA effort, The Catholic Health Services Leadership Program, were reported in a number of articles in *Hospital Progress* in 1971. See, for example, Sr. Mary Maurita Sengelaub, RSM, "CHSLP: Expectations and Realizable Goals," *Hospital Progress* (November 1971): 58 – 62.

13  Alice Popovici, "A Catholic Foray into For-Profit Health," *National Catholic Reporter*, May 29, 2012.

always has required a relatively permanent commitment, gifts appropriate to the ministry, and theological and spiritual formation. Many health care systems realize that they must find ways to replicate the formation that was traditionally provided to priests and religious in a way that is appropriate to this new expression of lay ecclesial ministry. Some have initiated their own formation programs for senior leadership, others have established collaborations for ministry formation programs, and still others have partnered with schools of theology or universities to provide formation.

Whatever shape this formation takes, it is clear that there can be no meaningful appropriation of the term "ministry" to describe Catholic health care unless it is nourished with serious theology and spirituality at a number of levels. Senior leaders, board members and sponsors must acquire fluency in theological questions that impact health care just as they have fluency in organizational development, finance and strategic planning. They must also see that formation extends across the organization so that all leaders, employees and volunteers grasp the mission and are able to participate actively in it.

## SPONSORSHIP AND GOVERNANCE

Because Catholic health care was for most of its history sponsored by the religious institutes that founded it, the idea of sponsorship was implicit and rarely invoked as a theological or canonical reality.[14] As the numbers of religious decline and, in some cases, as the congregations come to relinquish their sponsorship role to mixed groups of lay and religious or to groups of laity, the idea of sponsorship has taken on a new and explicit dimension. The responsibilities and competencies of this new generation of sponsors will differ from those of traditional board members. While board members will continue to exercise fiduciary governance responsibility with an emphasis on the mission and assets, sponsors, on the other hand, will have specific responsibility for communion with the church. These distinct areas of responsibility will require distinct formation and commitments.

---

14  See "Canonical Dimensions of Ecclesiology: Catholic Health Care, the Bishops and Sponsors" in this volume, by Barbara Cusack, Fr. Frank Morrisey and Sr. Sharon Holland, pp. 213 – 228.

A CHA white paper on the theology of sponsorship recognized the distinctiveness of the ministry of sponsorship and linked it to important questions about ministry that we have already highlighted:

> Today we have come to recognize that the relationship we call sponsorship is itself a vital ministry in the church. Those who sponsor…act publicly on behalf of the church. They are not 'extraordinary' ministers, nor are they simply the bishop's delegates. [Their call] flows directly from the baptismal gifts of the Spirit. In their work they participate in the mediation of grace and are themselves transformed and perfected by it.[15]

The distinct nature of sponsorship may require a deeper and longer commitment than governance requires, perhaps something analogous to the members of medieval military orders that took vows and made life-long commitments as laypersons. This may sound quaint today, but it suggests how important this new form of ministry is to the vitality of Catholic health care.

## COLLABORATION AND JOINT VENTURES

When we think of ministries such as priest, deacon and directors of liturgy and pastoral care, we are thinking largely of *internal ministry*; in other words, the actions of these ministers are directed *primarily* toward members of the church community and their purpose is building up and sanctifying the people of God. In the Catholic tradition, however, there are also public ministries that extend beyond the walls of any given church community; while they also have something to do with sanctification, their *primary* purpose is realization of the Kingdom of God through work for the common good. This external, public aspect of ministry is one of the reasons Catholics got into education, health care and social service in the first place. It was a way of witnessing to the Gospel in the world and of actually cooperating with grace to help extend the reign of God beyond the church.

---

15   "Toward a Theology of Catholic Health Care Sponsorship." Available for members at CHA www.chausa.org/sponsorship. This paper opened the question of how sponsorship is a ministry, but the question needs further work, especially by ecclesiologists.

These ministries of service extended to those who were non-Catholic and non-Christian. They could not have survived without the active cooperation of other persons of good will who shared our commitment to the common good. Today, this cooperation has become more complicated as we enter into formal cooperative ventures with other faith-based and non-religious health care entities.

It is important to understand how those who are not Roman Catholic may be involved in this ministry of the church. There always have been those who see value in our ministerial work and contribute to it even though they may not have been baptized Catholic. These relationships even found their way into movies. Think for example of Horace P. Bogardus, the crusty businessman who ended up giving his new building to Fr. O'Malley and Sister Mary Benedict (Bing Crosby and Ingrid Bergman) in the 1942 film *The Bells of St. Mary's*. He did not share their faith, but he did appreciate the educational service their school provided. Or remember Sidney Poitier, who played the itinerant carpenter Homer Smith in *Lilies of the Field* (1963). Although himself Baptist, he eventually built a new chapel for a group of persistent German nuns.

Today, we have physicians, executives, board members and employees who are not Catholic, yet find meaning and vocation in their work in Catholic health care. Those who are Christian can actually *participate* in our ministry because they share with us baptism, belief in the ministerial gifts of the Holy Spirit, the healing power of Jesus, the resurrection of the dead, and the Kingdom of God whose herald Jesus is. There are real issues that divide us (interpretation of Scripture, differences in the way we understand how grace works in our lives and the origin of ministerial authority), but on a basic level, they can share in our work as *ministry* to a significant extent.[16]

There are many others involved in Catholic health care who are not Christian, but who nevertheless understand and appreciate the virtues of

---

16  The difference we have about the understanding of grace is significant in that it was the basis of the Reformation. Even today, the Catholic understanding of grace is the basis of our entire sacramental system and is at least partially responsible for our institutional commitments. We need to be careful that collaboration does not lead to the unintentional loss of this distinctive theological perspective.

mercy and compassion and who value the common good from their own
faith perspective. We have many Jewish and Muslim physicians, for example,
and I have worked with many boards that have at least one Jewish or
Muslim member.

The Jewish tradition has the notion of *tzedakah*, or a blend of justice and
charity. Jonathan Sacks, former Chief Rabbi of London, says that *tzedakah*
refers to distributive justice and is less procedural and more substantive than
legal justice. "It is difficult to translate *tzedakah* because it combines in a
single word two notions normally opposed to one another, namely charity
and justice…" Rabbi Sacks continues, "[Tzedakah] insists on the difference
between possession and ownership. Ultimately, all things are owned by God,
creator of the world. What we possess we do not own, we merely hold it in
trust for God."[17] This is almost exactly how we would describe social justice,
also biblically based and one of the animating principles of Catholic health
care. Part of our ministry is to distribute equitably the goods of health care,
which we do not own. Pope Paul VI, in his encyclical *Populorum Progressio*
(1967) made this clear when he discussed the "universal destination of
human goods."

This provides a perfect basis for involvement with us. Non-Christians
do not *participate* with us in our ministry in the same way that baptized
Christians do, but they *collaborate* with us to varying extents. I say that
they do not participate fully not only because of the difference of our faith
commitments, but also to avoid a kind of paternalism that would make
them co-workers in the Catholic faith whether they want to be or not.
It is a question of respecting others' religious beliefs but welcoming their
collaboration with us in things we all value.

Finding ways to preserve the truly ministerial and ecclesial dimension of
health care while enhancing collaboration toward the common good and
welcoming collaborators of other faiths or no faith is a challenge that
we have only begun to address. It will require far more than detailed legal
agreements, episcopal approvals and reproductive services carve-outs. It
requires formation that respects the conscience of those who work with us,

---

17   Jonathan Sacks, *The Dignity of Difference* (New York/London, Continuum 2002): 113 – 14.

while also inviting them to deepen their own spiritual awareness as
a resource for the ministry.

Sponsorship, which is described by Cusack, Morrisey and Holland in the
next chapter is a special case. Some sponsor groups include members who
are not Catholic, but because sponsors hold official canonical authority for
a ministry of the Catholic Church, I believe sponsors should be Catholic in
order to exercise this role. There are many persons who have deep faith and
are committed to our work of health care. I do not mean to suggest that
any Catholic would be a better sponsor just by virtue of being Catholic, but
I do think we need to continue to reflect on the unique role that sponsors
play and whether it is canonically or theologically appropriate to consider
persons from outside the tradition to fill these roles. It would be a loss to
the church if we opted for other-than-Catholic sponsors because of their
commitment, and missed the opportunity to prepare members of the
Catholic faithful to assume leadership of their own ministries.

## REASONS FOR HOPE

Although we face unprecedented challenges if we are to keep health care
vital as a ministry, I am by no means pessimistic. Nature and culture
(including human organizations) are perfected, not destroyed, by grace,
and grace is infinitely adaptable. This adaptability has enabled the church
to reshape itself in response to changes in culture over and over again
through the centuries. A thorough response to the issues I have identified
here — and there may be others as well — will require the serious work
of theologians, canonists and health care leaders. The challenge may be
daunting, but it is also exciting. If we can make "ministry" more than just
a descriptive term for the huge enterprise we call "Catholic Health Care,"
we will have found a profound expression of the church's sacramental life
in the world. Indeed, if Catholic health care grapples successfully with these
complex questions of ministry, it might provide a model for the church at
large to shape a new expression of ministry that includes all the baptized.

## DISCUSSION QUESTIONS

1. How has your own understanding of "ministry" changed since you became involved in Catholic health care?

2. Do you think it is possible for an institutional ministry to "evangelize," that is, to preach the Gospel? Can it do so internally — to the church itself — as well as externally to the world around it?

3. To what extent do you think Catholic health care can engage the world with specifically theological language?

Canon law is derived from and is reflective of certain theological presuppositions. Our understanding of the church (ecclesiology) creates many structures of mutual accountability that are spelled out in canon law. Two of the key relationships are those that exist between health care ministries and their sponsors (whether lay, diocesan or religious); and between the health care ministry and the bishop. The two articles that follow explain the role and responsibility of the bishop with regard to health care and the rapidly changing character of sponsorship.

They show that sponsorship itself is changing because of the development of "public juridic persons" that are filling the role formerly held by founding religious institutes. The relationship of these sponsors to the bishop is also changing because of the growing number of systems that have ministries in multiple dioceses.

## 4.2 CANONICAL DIMENSIONS OF ECCLESIOLOGY: CATHOLIC HEALTH CARE, THE BISHOP AND SPONSORS

*Editor's Note: The two articles that follow are reprinted from Health Progress.*

## 4.2.1 THE ROLE OF THE DIOCESAN BISHOP IN RELATION TO CATHOLIC HEALTH CARE[1]
### Reprinted from *Health Progress*
### July–August 2006

*By Barbara Anne Cusack, J.C.D.*

The responsibilities of the diocesan bishop are outlined in the *Ethical and Religious Directives for Catholic Health Care Services* (hereafter "ERDs") and fall into several categories: general oversight (General Introduction); pastoral appointments (Directives 21 and 22); ethical standards (Directive 37); and Catholic identity, reputation and adherence to Catholic teaching (Directives 67, 68 and 71). When one is reviewing the role of the bishop, the first question to ask in each case is "*Which* diocesan bishop has this responsibility?" It could be the bishop of the diocese in which the health care institution is located, or it could be the bishop who has jurisdiction over the hospital.

---

1    Additional material pertaining to implementation of the ERDs in specific diocesan settings was added by the author.

## GENERAL OVERSIGHT

The General Introduction to the ERDs states, "As the center of unity in
the diocese and coordinator of ministries in the local church, the diocesan
bishop fosters the mission of Catholic health care in a way that promotes
collaboration among health care leaders, providers, medical professionals,
theologians and other specialists. As pastor, the diocesan bishop is in a
unique position to encourage the faithful to greater responsibility in the
healing ministry of the church. As teacher, the diocesan bishop ensures the
moral and religious identity of the health care ministry in whatever setting
it is carried out in the diocese. As priest, the diocesan bishop oversees
the sacramental care of the sick. These responsibilities will require that
Catholic health care providers and the diocesan bishop engage in ongoing
communication on ethical and pastoral matters that require his attention."[2]

All references in the General Introduction are to the "diocesan bishop,"
and the context indicates that the diocesan bishop in question is the bishop
of the diocese in which the particular health care facility is located. He is to
"foster the mission of Catholic health care," "encourage the faithful to greater
responsibility in the healing ministry of the church," "ensure the moral and
religious identity of the health care ministry," and "oversee the sacramental
care of the sick." The encouragement is for mutual cooperation and
communication. The ERDs also cover rare situations in which reception
of sacraments by non-Catholics or administration of the sacraments by
someone other than a Catholic priest may be allowed.[3]

*Suggestions for Implementation*

> ✦ Consistent with his responsibility as diocesan bishop to "foster
> various forms of the apostolate within his diocese" and to "ensure that

---

2 United States Conference of Catholic Bishops, *Ethical and Religious Directives for Catholic
  Health Care Services*, 5th Edition (Washington, 2009), hereafter "ERDs".
3 This falls under the concept of *communicatio in sacris* (Code of Canon Law, 844, para. 4).
  "With regard to other Christians not in full communion with the Catholic Church, when the
  danger of death or other grave necessity is present, the four conditions of canon 844, §4,
  also must be present, namely, they cannot approach a minister of their own community;
  they ask for the sacraments on their own; they manifest Catholic faith in these sacraments;
  and they are properly disposed. The diocesan bishop has the responsibility to oversee this
  pastoral practice" (ERDs, Directive 20).

within the entire diocese, or in its particular districts, all works of the apostolate are coordinated under his direction" (*Code of Canon Law*, canon 394.1), the diocesan bishop welcomes communication and collaboration with Catholic health care institutions in his diocese.

+ The president of every Catholic health care institution in the diocese will send an annual report to the bishop highlighting any significant events that have occurred in the past year as well as any that are foreseen for the following one. (e.g., completion of or planning for a new wing, reorganizing structures of governance, etc.).

+ The bishop or his delegate will make a formal visit to each Catholic health care institution every three years on a rotating basis. Requests for other visits (e.g., to dedicate a new chapel or building) will continue to be scheduled as needed.

+ With regard to the reception of sacraments by baptized non-Catholics, the general sacramental guidelines of the diocese apply to Catholic health care institutions as well. Therefore, Christians not in full communion with the Catholic Church may receive the sacraments of anointing of the sick, penance and Eucharist, when the danger of death is present. The four conditions of canon 844.4, also must be present, namely, they are unable to approach a minister of their own community; they ask for the sacraments on their own; they manifest Catholic faith in these sacraments; and they are properly disposed.

## *Social Responsibility of Catholic Health Care Ministries (Part One)*

The ERDs clearly indicate that the church's social responsibility includes promotion of human dignity, the common good, responsible stewardship, respect for conscience and especially, care for the poor (Part One, Introduction). As the ERDs state, "The biblical mandate to care for the poor requires us to express this in concrete action at all levels of Catholic health care. This mandate prompts us to work to ensure that our country's health care delivery system provides adequate health care for the poor. In Catholic institutions, particular attention should be given to the health care needs of the poor, the uninsured, and the underinsured."

*Suggestions for Implementation*

+ In the annual report to the bishop, the president of the health care institution will state explicitly the manner in which this Biblical mandate of care for the poor is being fulfilled.

+ In that same report, the president will summarize local efforts and accomplishments toward achieving the goal of health care coverage for the poor.

## RESPONSIBILITY FOR PASTORAL APPOINTMENTS

While recognizing the rightful autonomy of Catholic health care administrators to determine their regular staffing needs and make decisions that address them, the bishop has special responsibility with regard to the staffing of pastoral care departments. The bishop oversees the sacramental care of the sick within the diocese. Canon 565 states, "Unless the law provides otherwise or someone legitimately has special rights, a chaplain is appointed by the local ordinary to whom it also belongs to install the one presented or to confirm the one elected."

References to "bishop" in the ERDs are to the bishop of the diocese in which the facility is located. It is not clear how these directives are intended to relate to canon 565, which deals with chaplains. Directive 21 refers to "approval or confirmation," but the canon speaks of "appointment" of chaplains (presuming this is the office being referred to here) and does not require that the diocesan bishop make the appointment; a local ordinary (i.e., a vicar general or episcopal vicar, in addition to diocesan bishop) may make such an appointment.

With regard to the director of the pastoral care staff, it is not clear who makes the appointment only that the diocesan bishop is to be "consulted" (Directive 21). Reference in Directive 22 to a "diocesan policy" implies action on the part of the diocesan bishop, since he is the only promulgator of diocesan, particular law (presuming a "policy" has the binding force of law). The "approval" by the diocesan bishop of someone other than a Catholic to be appointed as director of pastoral care refers to the bishop of the diocese where the facility is located. Again, it is not clear who actually makes the appointment. It would be important, since some of the terminology in these directives is reflective of the language surrounding ecclesiastical office, to make a determination of what is intended.

## Suggestions for Implementation

+ The administrator of any Catholic health care institution in the diocese will inform the bishop about the potential hiring of any priest or deacon to the pastoral care staff prior to offering that individual the position. The bishop reserves the right to accept or reject the proposed candidate. When presenting a priest or deacon for such a position, the administrator must supply the bishop with the cleric's full resume, a statement of suitability for ministry from his diocesan bishop or religious superior and a declaration that a criminal background check has been conducted with no concerns raised. If the individual being considered is not a U.S. citizen, documentation showing that proper Immigration and Naturalization Service regulations have been followed must also be presented (Directive 21).

+ The administrator of any Catholic health care institute in the diocese will consult with the bishop about the potential hiring of any director of the pastoral care staff prior to offering that individual the position. The bishop reserves the right to review the proposed candidate's full resume prior to granting his *nihil obstat* to the appointment by the administrator (Directive 21).

+ Directors of pastoral care in Catholic institutions must be Catholics in full communion with the church. Any exception to this policy requires explicit approval by the bishop (Directive 22).

+ Other positions within a pastoral care department of a Catholic institution may be offered to non-Catholics provided the administration has ensured that the Catholic sacramental care for Catholic patients is sufficiently provided (Directive 22).

+ Issues of concern about pastoral care in Catholic institutions, including assurance that access to the sacraments by Catholics is available, should be directed to the proper diocesan office.

## RESPONSIBILITY FOR ETHICAL STANDARDS

Even though many health care facilities and systems have their own ethicists, the final responsibility for insuring the integrity of ethical standards is the bishop's. "The relationship of the person seeking health care and the professionals providing that care is an important part of the foundation on which diagnosis and care are provided. Diagnosis and care, therefore, entail a series of decisions with ethical as well as medical dimensions. The health care professional has the knowledge and experience to pursue the goals of healing, the maintenance of health, and the compassionate care of the dying, taking into account the patient's convictions and spiritual needs, and the moral responsibilities of all concerned. . . . When the health care professional and the patient use institutional Catholic health care, they also accept its public commitment to the Church's understanding of and witness to the dignity of the human person" (ERDs, Part Three, Introduction).

The reference is clearly to the bishop of the diocese where the facility is located. It is not clear whether this bishop is to articulate these standards for consultation, or, rather, to judge whether standards established by a health care agency are sufficient.

*Suggestions for Implementation*

+ Every Catholic health care institution in the diocese is to have an ethics committee or some form of ethical consultation available (Directive 37)

+ Administrators of Catholic health care institutions in the diocese annually will forward to the bishop or his designated delegate a roster of the members of the ethics committee noting their credentials. If an ethics committee does not exist, an explanation of the system used for consultation on ethical issues is to be sent instead.

+ The bishop should be informed immediately if there is a situation at a Catholic health care institution in which there is the potential conflict with the ERDs or in which there is possible scandal to the faithful.

# RESPONSIBILITY FOR CATHOLIC IDENTITY, REPUTATION AND ADHERENCE TO CATHOLIC TEACHING

In his teaching role within the diocese, the bishop has the responsibility to ensure that entities that identify themselves as Catholic remain faithful to the teachings and morals of the church. In attempting to maintain a Catholic identity, Catholic institutions' efforts to enter into "partnerships can pose serious challenges to the viability of the identity of Catholic health care institutions and services, and their ability to implement the ERDs in a consistent way, especially when partnerships are formed with those who do not share Catholic moral principles. The risk of scandal cannot be underestimated when partnerships are not built upon common values and moral principles. Partnership opportunities for some Catholic health care providers may even threaten the continued existence of other Catholic institutions and services, particularly when partnerships are driven by financial considerations alone" (ERDs, Part Six, Introduction).

All references, the context suggests, are to the bishop of the diocese where the facility is located. The direct involvement of this diocesan bishop in the actual decision making, (e.g., his *approval* to proceed with a partnership), occurs only in cases in which the institution in question is subject to his jurisdiction. Such would be the case with a hospital owned and operated by the diocese, or a facility under the sponsorship of a religious institute of diocesan right.

In other cases, when the diocesan bishop does not have such jurisdiction, his role is more passive in that he is to indicate that he will or will not stand in the way. It is not clear who, in this latter case, actually gives the "approval" to proceed. Although Directive 71 refers to the diocesan bishop's responsibility to "assess and address" situations in which scandal has occurred or could occur, it does not explicitly state that he has the authority to issue a directive if the institution is not under his jurisdiction.

+ Administrators of Catholic institutions should inform the bishop about any pending situations that could affect the Catholic mission and identity of the institution or which could cause scandal. Decisions in these matters are to be made only after consulting with the bishop or his delegate (Directive 67).

+ "Any partnership that will affect the mission or religious and ethical identity of Catholic health care institutional services must respect church teaching and discipline. Diocesan bishops and other church authorities should be involved as such partnerships are developed, and the diocesan bishop should give the appropriate authorization before they are completed. The diocesan bishop's approval is required for partnerships sponsored by institutions subject to his governing authority; for partnerships sponsored by religious institutes of pontifical right, his *nihil obstat* should be obtained"(Directive 68).

+ "The diocesan bishop has final responsibility for assessing and addressing issues of scandal, considering not only the circumstances in his local diocese but also the regional and national implications of his decision" (Directive #71).

## ALIENATION OF PROPERTY

Alienation occurs when a "transfer of property necessarily results in the loss of Catholic identity. The work is then no longer identified as ecclesiastical, the Church has lost effective control over the undertaking, and the marketable dimensions are greatly diminished."[4] This occurs in outright sales, and sometimes in cases of formation of new canonical entities as well. In cases involving the alienation of property by public juridic persons not subject to the diocesan bishop (e.g., religious institutes of pontifical right), they are to follow their own statutes / constitutions. If it is a matter of alienation that exceeds the maximum limit, Vatican permission is required. When religious institutes of pontifical right are seeking this permission, it has been the practice of the Vatican to ask for the *votum* of the diocesan bishop of the principal seat of the institute as well as of the diocese where the property is located.

---

4    See Francis Morrisey, "Alienation and Administration: System Restructuring Often Entails Four Types of Canonical Acts," *Health Progress* (September – October, 1998): 24 – 29 for a fuller discussion of alienation.

## Suggestions for Implementation

+ Administrators in Catholic health care institutions should provide the bishop with all necessary information in a timely fashion when his *nihil obstat* is being requested for an alienation of property.

+ All reasonable care should be taken so that the successor owner of any property of a Catholic institution does not engage in activities that could give rise to scandal.

### FLUIDITY MAY BE BENEFICIAL

The practical application of the ERDs still needs time to develop. As issues arise, the ERDs' lack of specificity is sometimes evident. Given the evolving nature of health care issues and the pace of change in health care institutions, some fluidity in interpretation may be beneficial.

## 4.2.2 MINISTERIAL JURIDIC PERSONS AND THEIR COMMUNION WITH DIOCESAN BISHOPS
**Reprinted from *Health Progress***
**November–December 2016**

*By Fr. Francis G. Morrisey, OMI, Ph.D., J.C.D., and Sr. Sharon Holland, IHM, J.C.D.*

One of the basic principles underlying the application of the *Code of Canon Law* is that the apostolic activity of the faithful is to be carried out in communion with the bishop of the place where the ministry is being exercised (canon 209). This principle finds numerous applications in the church's legislation, depending on the activity and the persons involved.

Indeed, for an apostolic work to be recognized as "Catholic," it must be in communion with the church and its leadership.

While some of our apostolic works flow directly from the bishop's initiative, such as the establishment of parishes and their various activities, others are conducted by persons who offer their services to the faith community, especially through works of education, health care and social services.

## RELIGIOUS INSTITUTES MINISTERING IN A DIOCESE

For centuries, religious institutes have been sponsoring these services and helped in numerous ways to build up the faith community. Either invited into a diocese at the bishop's request, or accepted by him, they have carried out their mission in accordance with their specific charism and purpose. Sound relationships between the diocesan bishop and the religious institutes present in his diocese usually were the result of mutual consultation (canon 678.3), leading to a strong spirit of communion. Both the bishop and the superiors had their respective responsibilities. Good working relations between them fostered cooperation that led to the strengthening of the church (canon 680).

Although traditionally the religious institutes were particularly responsible for the operations of the activity, as well as for its financing and staffing, three areas in particular were entrusted to the special responsibility of the bishop: (1) the care of souls; (2) the public exercise of divine worship; and (3) other works of the apostolate (canon 678.1). This corresponds with canon 394's recognition of the bishop's responsibility to foster and coordinate works of the apostolate in the diocese.

More recently, however, the activities of religious institutes have been seriously limited because of a shortage of personnel. Institutes have had to withdraw from ministries that they had exercised oftentimes for well over a century. Providentially, however, the religious were preparing the way for being replaced by other entities involving lay people in the formal sponsorship and governance of the works. This change necessarily brought with it growing pains, and both bishops and the laity, together with religious, are seeking to find ways to continue the various apostolic activities in full communion with the church.

## THE CALL TO THE LAITY TO EXERCISE THEIR BAPTISMAL COMMITMENT

We recall that Vatican II clearly stated that the call to mission in the church arises initially not from ordination or religious profession, but rather from baptism and confirmation (canon 225). The baptized now are being called upon to live their baptismal commitment in ways that beforehand were relatively rare. The response to this call has been far beyond original expectations, so much so that in many dioceses, committed lay persons hold numerous positions of major responsibility.

## THE LAITY OPERATING THROUGH JURIDIC PERSONS

While sometimes the apostolate of the laity is assumed on an individual basis, more frequently it is carried out through various recognized entities, such as associations and movements of the Christian faithful, or through sponsorship structures known as "juridic persons." A juridic person generally could be understood to be the church's canonical equivalent of a corporation set up for one or more specific purposes. Each juridic person functions through legitimately designated physical persons who function as its representative according to its approved statutes. It represents the church in the same way that religious institutes did in previous times.

While we were familiar with entities such as parishes, dioceses, seminaries, religious houses and provinces, we were less familiar with other possible entities that could also be established to carry out their mission "in the name of the church" (canon 116.1). These entities are generally called "public juridic persons" (PJPs) because their ministry is formally sanctioned by church authority and is carried out publicly under its auspices. Most of the new juridic persons were organized by the religious who wished to transfer their works to a new entity that would guarantee its continuation as Catholic. The original governing body, replacing the congregational leadership, often was composed of both laity and religious.

The Holy See has seen fit to recognize this possibility in newer ways. It has sanctioned the establishment of a number of such entities in the fields of health care, education and social services. This implies profound trust and confidence in the potential for the laity to assume direct responsibility for such undertakings.

A juridic person that has been formally recognized by church authority is as "Catholic" as any other recognized entity. It functions in accordance with its statutes, just as religious institutes operate according to their approved constitutions.

More recently, in order to distinguish some of the newer juridic persons from those that had been in existence for centuries, these are now being called "ministerial juridic persons" (MJPs), with the focus being on their ministry exercised in the diocese. Some MJPs are pontifical, as are some religious institutes; others are diocesan. In the former case, those responsible for the ministry relate directly to the Holy See for matters concerning their internal governance; in the latter, they are more directly accountable to the diocesan bishop. But, when it comes to the traditional three areas — care of souls, the exercise of divine worship, and the actual Catholic identity of the apostolic works — both the pontifical and the diocesan MJPs are accountable to the diocesan bishop of the place where their ministry is being exercised.

# MINISTERIAL JURIDIC PERSONS AND
# ACCOUNTABILITY TO THE DIOCESAN BISHOP

In the case of a health care ministry, the care of souls could find its practical expression in the designation of persons called upon to serve as chaplains in the institutions (canon 565). This could become complicated at times when there is an interfaith pastoral care department. In the exercise of their ministry, chaplains belonging to other churches or ecclesial communities would not be subject to the diocesan bishop, but rather to their own religious authorities, as well, of course, as to the directors of the institution who establish its mission and values and oversee its operations. Although the *Code of Canon Law* identifies chaplains as priests, today we find many deacons and laypersons entrusted with the day-to-day responsibilities relating to the office of chaplain. The same is found in Catholic educational institutions, in prison chaplaincy and, in some countries, in the military chaplaincy. These are interesting developments and call for careful monitoring and supervision. Part Two of the *Ethical and Religious Directives for Catholic Health Care Services* provides extensive commentary on pastoral care and the authority and responsibility of the diocesan bishop.

As for divine worship, this would apply to the chapels or oratories found in the institutions and, more particularly, to the celebration of the Eucharist. The same section of the ERDs treats the celebration of the sacraments in health care institutions. In the case of an interfaith chapel, appropriate arrangements would be made with the bishop for the celebration of various liturgical functions, such as funerals or baptisms in case of necessity. Of course, priests always can visit individual patients and celebrate some of the sacraments with them, without having been designated as chaplains in the institution.

The third area of mutual cooperation concerns the identity of the apostolic work itself. In matters relating to health care, this has focused on the application of the appropriate ERDs in effect in the diocese. In the United States, these directives are generally found in the ERDs issued by the United States Conference of Catholic Bishops and applied in each diocese by the diocesan bishop, who remains the interpreter of the various norms and sees to their proper application. Statutes of MJPs regularly include, in their statement of purpose, that the ERDs are observed as interpreted or applied by the diocesan bishop where a facility is located.

Although in theory this can be rather clear, the fact that much of the U.S. health care ministry now is carried out by systems that usually are interdiocesan and function in many states, let alone in other countries as well, raises special issues. It could be very difficult for a system that directs institutions in, for instance, 10 or more dioceses to have to deal with interpretations of the ERDs that vary from place to place, depending on the outlook of the diocesan bishop or his representative.

This, obviously, calls for new and imaginative ways of promoting coordination and a relatively common approach to ecclesial communion. A good relationship between the bishop and those in charge of the institution can help avoid painful situations in which serious misunderstandings could arise. Resolution would be sought first with the administrators of the local facility; later the matter might go to the governing body of the PJP, as in the past it might have gone to a provincial or general superior.

## RECOGNITION OF THE RIGHTFUL RESPONSIBILITIES OF THE LAITY

Not everyone in the church is at ease when dealing with laypersons who are now in charge of apostolic works carried out in the name of the church, and with thousands of employees working under their guidance. There is an underlying feeling in some places that these persons in leadership positions could not possibly know enough about the church and its teachings to ensure a continued Catholic presence and identity in the ministry.

Although it often was taken for granted before that priests and religious had the appropriate background to deal with complicated ethical and pastoral matters, the same would not have been said as readily in the past regarding laypersons. But, upon closer examination, this assumption was found to be incorrect. The simple fact of being a priest or a religious did not mean that the person in question had the necessary knowledge. Indeed, in many parishes and church-related institutions today, some parishioners have deep theological and pastoral training.

## FORMATION PROGRAMS FOR LAY LEADERSHIP
## IN MINISTERIAL JURIDIC PERSONS

Nevertheless, in spite of many excellent exceptions, it must be recognized that, in a number of instances, the laypersons who represented the MJPs did not have the same background of formation, enabling them to move smoothly through the various ecclesiastical practices and policies they could meet along the way. For this reason, intense efforts have been made by the MJPs and others to ensure in-depth doctrinal and pastoral formation, not only for those with overall responsibility for the activities of the MJPs themselves, but also for those who were in charge of various levels within the systems. Formation programs, which often extend over a number of years, are probably one of the unexpected graces that have emanated from the change in leadership of our various apostolic works. What in many cases was previously seen as a "job" or simply as a form of employment, is now seen and considered to be a "ministry" and an apostolic action carried out in the name of Christ.

One area that has been developed significantly is the awareness of the need for the proper stewardship of temporal goods. Indeed, property and assets belonging to a public MJP are by definition "ecclesiastical goods," and they are subject to the church's rules relating to their acquisition, administration and alienation. In certain instances relating to administration and to alienation of temporal goods, the diocesan bishop has to give an opinion letter on the matter before these acts can be carried out.

We still are in a learning curve, but the results are now becoming more and more tangible. Laypersons who are duly qualified not only can assume responsibility for extensive ministries but also are able to represent them competently when dealing with church authorities and their representatives. The role of the diocesan bishop has not changed. What has changed is the person to whom he turns if there are questions or concerns beyond the level of the administration of the local facility.

## TOWARDS CONTINUAL BUILDING UP OF COMMUNION

Any progress, when different entities are involved, calls for continued dialogue, consultation and hard work. The church now has available an untapped wealth to be found in so many of its members who resolutely have taken the path of living their baptismal commitment in unforeseen ways. We have to learn to trust them, their judgment and their practical experience. In this way, the church will flourish, and Christ's saving message can be made more readily available to all.

### DISCUSSION QUESTIONS

1. Can you name any evidence of a relationship between your health care ministry and the local church in which it finds itself?

2. How can we help bishops see health care as an essential aspect of the church's ministry?

3. Which of the canonical requirements discussed in these articles is the most difficult to achieve?

CHAPTER SUMMARY

Too often lay leaders express the feeling they cannot do what the sisters
did. An examination of the early history of two Catholic hospitals,
St. Vincent's in New York City and St. Michael's in Newark, shows that
in those years the ministries were very collaborative in nature. Doctors
and other lay leaders such as board members, organizers of fundraising
and nurses, together with bishops and pastors, worked with sisters
in establishing these hospitals. The examples have implications for
formation: Begin with the ministry of Jesus and his mission proclaiming
and initiating the Kingdom, and demonstrate the role of the laity at
the beginning and in light of Vatican II today.

## 4.3 WHOSE MINISTRY IS IT?
## THE ROLE OF THE LAITY IN THE STORY
## OF CATHOLIC HEALTH CARE

———

Zeni Fox, Ph.D.

*Professor Emerita, Pastoral Theology*

*Seton Hall University*

I N 2011, A CONFERENCE TOOK PLACE IN SYDNEY, AUSTRALIA for leaders of Catholic institutional ministries and diocesan offices. A participant who served as chancellor in his diocese, said: "I have learned that I am not a substitute."[1] The reflections on canon law, pastoral experience and theology helped him realize that his role as a leader in the Catholic community was rightfully held, that he himself was indeed part of the mission and ministry of the church. I have pondered his comment, recognizing that it was an empowering realization and asked myself *why* this was a revelation for him. What is it in the formation of lay leaders in the church that limits their vision of the centrality of their role? What is needed to truly empower a formed laity for their full participation in the apostolate, especially as leaders of Catholic institutional ministries?

---

1   Comment at concluding session, dialogue with participants, "On Sacred Ground: Lay Leadership in Catholic Human Service and Diocesan Institutions," September 21 – 23, 2011, Sydney, Australia.

## A PRELUDE

In the Western world we live in an age when history is being re-written, not
by deleting the names of the greats — the kings and queens, popes, generals,
conquerors and reformers — but rather by lifting up the stories of the
ordinary people whose lives and work also have woven the fabric of society.
In 1942, U.S. Vice President Henry A. Wallace proclaimed the dawning
of the "Century of the Common Man." This vision was set to music by
Aaron Copland that same year when he wrote the stirring "Fanfare for the
Common Man."

This recognition of the contributions of ordinary people led to significant
archaeological excavations and reconstructions of "Mulberry Row," the
quarters for domestic slaves, artisans and workers at Thomas Jefferson's
estate, Monticello. Although his beautiful home had long been a tourist
destination, recent archaeological work and research, publications and
exhibits have expanded the story of those who lived at Monticello. In
2012 the exhibit "Landscape of Slavery: Mulberry Row at Monticello"
highlighted the cabins and workshops of slaves and freemen who provided
domestic service for the house and the crafts needed for the plantation.[2]
Thus, the story of Monticello is wider and deeper, than before, celebrating
"the common man/woman."

The story of Catholic health care also can be explored through the labor
of participants in the great work of the past that draws from the archives
of St. Vincent's Hospital in New York City and St. Michael's Hospital in
Newark, New Jersey.

## ST. VINCENT'S HOSPITAL, NEW YORK CITY

St. Vincent's Hospital was founded in 1849 when there were two hospitals
in New York City — Bellevue, for the indigent, and New York Hospital
(now NY/Cornell, Presbyterian) for the wealthy. Archbishop John Hughes
was concerned that the lack of a Catholic hospital would contribute to an

---

2   https://wwwmonticello.org/site/plantation-and-slavery; http://slavery.monticello.org/slavery-
    at-monticello/life-monticello-plantation/monticello-house, each accessed July 13, 2016.

absorption of Catholics into the Protestant culture of the city. The need was especially pressing in light of a cholera epidemic that was afflicting many immigrants in lower Manhattan. The Archbishop's sister, Mother Mary Angela Hughes, a Sister of Charity, was the first administrator of the new hospital, a 30-bed facility on 13th Street.

> The original 5-man medical staff were supported by four Sisters of Charity... including Sr. Mary Angela Hughes, sister of Archbishop Hughes and the first administrator of the Hospital. With no antiseptics beyond strong soap, water and alcohol, no aspirin or other modern drugs (morphine was the preferred pain killer), no running water, no central heating and no light beyond candles and oil lamps (the building was not set-up for gas-light which was in wide use by this time), Sr. Angela's nurses were responsible for all patient care beyond diagnosis and surgery.[3]

The book, *An Illustrated History of St. Vincent's Hospital and Medical Center*, contains pictures of four people: Dr. Valentine Mott, first president of the medical board (1849 – 1865); Dr. Wm. Holmes Van Buren, surgeon and second president of the medical board; Mother Mary Angela Hughes, first administrator of St. Vincent's Hospital, 1849 – 1855; and Mother Elizabeth Boyle, mother general of the Sisters of Charity of St. Vincent de Paul, co-founder of St. Vincent's Hospital, 1849. The photos, and the wording, "The original 5-man medical staff were supported by four Sisters of Charity...," illustrate the collaboration that characterized the early years.

Augmenting this picture is an account in a legal document from 1894 which states:

> What was the amount first contributed to its [St. Vincent's Hospital] foundation? The foundation of its funds was laid by our late Superior Very Reverend William Starrs who conjointly with the Mother House at Mount Saint Vincent advanced a sum of money to rent and furnish a three-story house.[4]

---

3   *An Illustrated History of St. Vincent's Hospital and Medical Center* [Celebrating its founding by the Sisters of Charity, Nov. 1, 1899], archives of St. Vincent's Hospital, Mount Saint Vincent, Riverdale, NY, pp. 1 – 2.

4   Archives, St. Vincent's Hospital, Mount Saint Vincent.

Significantly, this document notes that no money from the city or state was used, and adds that there were 35 sisters who were supplied by the motherhouse — without pay. However, there were about 19 salaried officers and employees with an average yearly expense of $2,627.07.[5]

Within a few years, "appeals for public philanthropy" were made to fund expansion of the hospital. Another group central to the story emerges.

> As has always been the case, the community came to the aid of the hospital. Mother Mary Jerome's appeal to the Catholic women of New York resulted in two fundraising fairs. The total funds raised, around $40,000, were enough to pay the hospital's operating expenses for several years and fueled the imagination for even more ambitious projects.[6]

In 1882, another fair raised $17,000. In 1897, overtures were made to form an Auxiliary:

> Following the familiar formula, Sr. Gonzaga appealed to Mrs. Eugene Kelly to formally organize an Auxiliary for the hospital... (I)n addition to raising funds for the building project... standing committees were formed for promoting the interests of the Training School for Nurses and a Sewing Committee engaged in cutting and sewing garments and other articles necessary for the destitute poor of the Hospital.[7]

The sisters used donations of fine china, furniture, artwork and Oriental rugs from their private patients and patrons to decorate the walls of the hospital.

The importance of the role of these women is captured in another volume which states:

---

5   A Legal Document, 1894, archives, St. Vincent's Hospital, Mount Saint Vincent.
6   A Legal Document, p. 3.
7   A Legal Document, p. 5.

Hospitals can be built more easily, either by large public or private financial grants, but our hospital was built from the meager sums derived from a generous and grateful public who were the recipients either directly or indirectly of the kind, efficient and courteous care of the Sisters.[8]

In 1941, Mrs. Edmund Borgia, a former member of the Catholic Board of Charities and Executive Board of the United Hospital Fund, "inaugurated the Volunteer Corps at St. Vincent's... (I)n 1943, 741 members helped with the staff shortage caused by the war."[9]

Support for the hospital expanded again with formation of a group of experienced business persons on an advisory board. According to its 1896 bylaws:

> The Managers of the Saint Vincent Hospital by law are the Sisters of Charity. Their sex and the religious life which they have adopted withdraw them to some extent from active participation it its external business. (I)t has seemed proper to the managers that some of the friends of the Hospital, men of experience in business matters, should be selected as Advisors in those matters the Sisters require their aid... matters appertaining to finances, contracts, erection of buildings, purchases, and other subjects of external concern.[10]

Another significant part of the story of St. Vincent's Hospital is the establishment of the St. Vincent's School of Nursing in 1892, a time marked by the opening of the first schools of nursing. (This was influenced by Florence Nightingale and was the first step in the professionalization of nursing.) The first administrator was Katherine Sanborn, a lay woman, who served from 1892 – 1934. It was said of her, "the motivation to become this trained professional nurse had to have been a motivational drive from

---

8   George R. Stuart, *A History of St. Vincent Hospital in New York City*, privately published, 1938, archives at Mount Saint Vincent, p. 12.

9   *A History of St. Vincent Hospital*, p. 12.

10   St. Vincent By-Laws of Advisory Board, 1896, in the archives of St. Vincent's Hospital at Mount Saint Vincent.

within,"[11] a comment which describes vocational call. From 1849 – 1892, nursing care was provided by the sisters; significantly, the first graduating class included eight lay women and seven vowed religious sisters.

In the yearbook for the class of 1922, one can glimpse the spirituality and link with the church which marked the life of the school. At Class Day, each woman was presented with a rosary, "as a remembrance of her days in training." For the closing ceremony, "All was so gloriously bright when we were led to the chapel by the flag bearers and junior nurses... [the] Chancellor of the Archdiocese closed the exercises... Father Barry, our chaplain, officiated at the Benediction of the Blessed Sacrament."[12]

The spirit in which the work of the hospital was done is also reflected in an entry in the *Rules and Regulations* of 1901:

> The members of the House [medical] Staff will ever bear in mind
> the Christian character of the institution, and the noble nature
> of the labor in which they are engaged, and govern their actions in
> all things in a spirit of kindness and charity for the unfortunate
> beings under their care.[13]

The picture that emerges from this history is of people with diverse skills and roles who worked with the Sisters of Charity in establishing, running and expanding St. Vincent's Hospital. These included doctors, bishops, clergy, women's groups of fundraisers and volunteers, an advisory board of businessmen, and employees. Although early records do not mention collaboration with nurses, the presence of a nursing school from its founding in 1892 is testimony to their importance as part of "a large complement of co-laborers."[14]

---

11  *History of the School of Nursing*, Part I, transcript of an interview, archives of St. Vincent's
     School of Nursing, Mount Saint Vincent, p. 17.
12  *History of the School of Nursing*, Part II, pp. 10 – 11.
13  *St. Vincent Hospital of the City of New York, Rules and Regulations Relating to the House Staff
     and Out Patient Department*, 1901, no publication information, p. 3.
14  This felicitous phrase was used by Dr. Thomas Rzeznik, Seton Hall University, in a
     communication to me on October 15, 2016. I also owe to him the idea to explore the
     important part played by the School of Nursing in the early story of health care.

Comments from Sr. Miriam Kevin Phillips, who was director of the nursing school from 1991 – 1999 and is now archivist for St. Vincent's, shed light on ways in which this pattern of cooperative work continued to influence the hospital community into the 21st century:

> A tremendous amount of humanity was exchanged in that building [Elizabeth Seton]. The doctors said that there was no place like it... it was like a family. Yes, there was hierarchical structure, and strict protocols, but there was respect on the part of all, at every level... Our nurses were almost like part of the community [the vowed religious community] — though sisters were not always easy on them. We worked as a team — and we were all crying when St. Vincent's closed.[15]

## ST. MICHAEL'S HOSPITAL, NEWARK, NJ

The story of St. Michael's Hospital began in 1867 in a small house at 69 Bleecker Street, Newark, in which five Sisters of the Poor of St. Francis served 13 patients at a time, "plus help for the out-door poor."[16] Bishop James Roosevelt Bayley had extended the invitation to Mother Frances Shervier, founder of the Sisters of the Poor of St. Francis, to come to Newark. "The St. Vincent de Paul Society, the ladies of several parishes, and the Sisters of Charity had prepared the house, linens and bandages," under the leadership of Fr. George Doane. He had asked his parishioners to provide the first meals. One sister served the poor in their homes, an outreach effort that was funded by the St. Vincent de Paul Society at an expense of $3,000 the first year. Two doctors served on the staff, including Dr. William O'Gorman who later became the medical director of the hospital. Mother Frances Shervier came to visit with Bishop Bayley and Fr. Doane, calling them "excellent souls."[17] The St. Michael's Hospital Auxiliary also began in this period which provided sewing services and prepared linens, bandages, bed jackets and towels.[18]

---

15 Conversation with Sr. Kevin Phillips at Mount Saint Vincent, Jan. 6, 2016. Sr. Kevin and one of the doctors were among the last two to exit the hospital when it closed.

16 A flyer for a new hospital, included with the papers of Bishop James Roosevelt Bayley, 1836 – 1872, "Institutions and Agencies, St. Michael's Hospital," Archives of Seton Hall University.

17 *The Healing Touch: A History of St. Michael's Medical Center, 1867 - 1992*, Joseph F. Mahoney. No publication information given, and no pagination. Papers of Bishop Bayley, Seton Hall archives.

18 *The Healing Touch.*

Expenses for the initial work were paid by the alms the sisters had collected from door to door.[19] Additional fundraising activities included a fair sponsored by the parishes, the opportunity to make monthly donations of 25 cents to $5, and solicitation of one-time donations.[20] By 1871, St. Michael's growth led to the establishment of a medical board and creation of the role of house physician. At this time, the medical and surgical staff was comprised of 10 doctors; the number of beds was 30.[21]

A significant expansion began with the purchase of property at Washington Street and Warren Street, for $16,000, with the owner donating $1,000. Five parishes participated in the collection for the hospital which would be "open to the sick no matter what their religious convictions."[22] A flyer developed by the board of trustees encouraged parishioners to donate to the Sisters.[23] The building committee sponsored five fairs, to help raise funds.[24] "Under the charge of the Sisters of the Poor of St. Francis" the new hospital was built in three years, with "all the latest and most approved ideas of sanitary architecture," with 250 beds.[25] Notably,

> The Sisters of the Poor of St. Francis, who have charge, as well as the Medical and Surgical Staff, contribute their services gratuitously. The object of the hospital is to offer the poor an institution where their sick may be received, tenderly, faithfully and intelligently nursed, and receive regular and competent medical attendance and treatment.[26]

This early history of St. Michael's Hospital was influenced more directly by the hierarchical church than was St. Vincent's. However, like St. Vincent's, St. Michael's involved businessmen and lay people, as well as doctors, in

19  *Annual Report of the Medical Board*, pamphlet, dated January 3, 1871, filed with the papers of Bishop Bayley.
20  *The Healing Touch.*
21  *Annual Report, Medical Board*, January 3, 1871, filed with the papers of Bishop Bayley.
22  *Annual Report, Medical Board.*
23  A flyer from the Board of Trustees, dated August 30, 1871, filed with the papers of Bishop Bayley.
24  Flyer developed by the Board of Trustees; a second flyer in German. Filed with the papers of Bishop Bayley.
25  *20th Regular Report of the Medical and Surgical Staff, 1892*, filed with the papers of Bishop Bayley.
26  *Regular Report of the Medical and Surgical Staff, 1894*, filed with the papers of Bishop Bayley.

its governance. In 1883, the first board of directors was comprised of 13 priests, 9 laymen and one doctor.[27] When the charter of the hospital was adopted, officers [four clergymen] were elected. At that time, "A motion to appropriate a certain number of beds for the use of each parish was also adopted."[28] This illustrates how St. Michael's was part of the ministry of the local parishes and the diocesan church. Later that year, the minutes indicate that "A layperson can be elected a member of the Board of Trustees, except the senior Trustee of each Church in the city of Newark."[29]

At St. Vincent's, the role of wealthy women was important in the funding of the hospital, while at St. Michael's the appeal for financial help was made more broadly. "A resolution was adopted to issue an appeal to the citizens of Newark requesting them to subscribe one hundred dollars each towards clearing the debt of the hospital," and a committee was appointed to decide on "the amount of assessment to be imposed upon each parish."[30] Furthermore, later that year a committee was appointed "to decide upon the amount of assessment for each parish for the life insurance of Rev. G.H. Doane." Significantly, a motion was passed to raise a mortgage of $10,000 on the hospital property.[31]

In 1880 the office of medical director was created and held by William O'Gorman. It is notable that in the list of directors given in 1883 he is not named, despite the fact that he served as medical director until his death in 1887. A news account sheds further light on the functioning of the hospital:

> [The board of directors of St. Michael's Hospital] consisting of the pastors and senior lay trustees of the Catholic churches of Newark, East Newark and vicinity, with Bishop Wigger *ex officio* chairman held a meeting to elect a successor to Dr. William O'Gorman, medical director of St. Michael's, head of the medical and surgical staff. [They commended] services he rendered when the hospital was first organized and continued so long as life and health were spared him.[32]

---

27 Board of Trustees Minutes of St. Michael's Hospital, 1883 – 1942, entry of December 19, 1883. Held in the Archives at Seton Hall University, South Orange, NJ.
28 Minutes, March 22, 1871.
29 Minutes, 1871 (month not given).
30 Minutes, February 12, 1872.
31 Minutes, April 15, 1872.
32 News clipping included in the Archives of St. Michael's Hospital, at Seton Hall University.

In addition, a hospital committee was appointed that had significant authority. "The Board of Directors may delegate their authority to a committee of three, to be styled the Hospital Committee, who shall have immediate supervision or charge of the Hospital in all its departments." At this time the physicians requested power to nominate physicians to fill vacancies, but this was declined. The authority of the board is demonstrated at a later time, when they demanded the resignation of a doctor on staff.[33] The power to appoint one of the physicians to the role of medical director was vested in the full board, or the hospital committee. The role of the director was to "specifically superintend and direct the ordinary routine duties of the medical staff." Anything out of the ordinary should be reported to the hospital committee.[34] Furthermore,

> It shall be his duty to co-operate with the Sister in charge in all matters which will tend to improve the sanitary condition of the Hospital, and which will lead to an extension of its charity.[35]

An entry from 1885 underwrites the important role of the sisters in the finances of the hospital: "A plan was submitted for a Laundry House, Boiler House and Store Room for the Hospital. It was decided to build same. The good sisters to pay for the same."[36]

Wealthy Catholics were also generous to the development of St. Michael's. The *Minutes* of 1885 mention $500 left to the hospital by Mr. M. Morrison of Paterson, and those of 1887 a bequest of property made by Mr. Augustus Pulissie.[37] The handling of the latter bequest gives further insight into the significant role played by the bishop.

> It was resolved that the Rt. Rev. Bishop and Chancellor B. Runyon should assume the whole business and definitely settle it. So ordained... And a resolution was adopted that the Bishop be empowered to sell the property thus accrued. So ordained.[38]

---

33  Minutes, Sept. 17, 1888.
34  Minutes, January 10, 1880.
35  Minutes.
36  Minutes, June 2, 1885.
37  Minutes of Jan. 5, 1885 and May 24, 1887.
38  Minutes, May 24, 1887.

People of lesser means also played a role in the financial life of the hospital. In 1890, an elderly couple was promised perpetual care for $1,500. Sr. Perpetua was "ordered to sign the agreement."[39]

By 1888, St. Michael's had again outgrown its facility, prompting the board of trustees to grant some authority to the sisters in expanding the facility.

> A suggestion of Monsignor Dorann was made to give authority to the Sisters to employ an architect to make necessary plans for buildings, a new chapel and operating room being largely needed, and that these plans be eventually submitted to the Board of Directors for authorization before any work may begin. Carried upon motion.[40]

A few months later, the issue of funding the work was again addressed. Here, the role of the board is delineated, but clearly the sisters and the wider community also have a role.

> A motion was made... to borrow $50,000... [I]t was resolved that all the rectors of Newark should assist the good Sisters in their new and most charitable undertaking... [Bids for the work are to be submitted] to a full meeting of the Board.[41]

The language here is significant: "assist the good sisters in their new and most charitable undertaking."

Later, the role of the sisters was more fully defined, and more authority was granted.

> It was then resolved that the building of the Hospital be left in the hands of the Sisters, who are authorized to receive bids, sign contracts and carry on the building in all ways. It was also resolved that the Board should acclaim what the Sisters have already done. The plans of the new building were then submitted and inspected.[42]

---

39  Minutes, April 7, 1890.
40  Minutes, January 11, 1888.
41  Minutes, April 25, 1888.
42  Minutes, July 2, 1888.

The evolution of the role of the sisters relative to the board is succinctly presented in the minutes of two meetings, one in November of 1888, the second in January of 1889. It is notable that the bishop was not present at the first, when the initial resolution was passed, but was present at the second, when the amended resolution was passed.

> [The object of the meeting is] to empower the Sisters of the Poor of St. Francis to have exclusive right and authority for the use of the Hospital properties... so long as their duties are faithfully discharged, and of that the ... Bishop of Newark is to be the judge. [And if they leave] they will sell to St. Michael's Hospital the [illegible word][43] which they bought for the price originally paid.

> [The Trustees] conveying to them [the Sisters] all their interest in the real estate and property... bind themselves by promise to allow the ... Sisters the free and continued use of the Hospital buildings and property... provided they continue to receive into said Hospital the sick and the unwanted and faithfully nurse them as they have hitherto done, and as the rules of their Institute demand. [44]

## THE EARLY STORIES: THEMES

Several themes in the history of St. Vincent Hospital and St. Michael's Hospital have significance for Catholic health care today, particularly in the context of the teachings of Vatican II.

First, is the emerging theme of health care as a ministry of the church. The range of participants illustrates the breadth of this engagement: bishops, boards/trustees (comprised of clergy and laity, medical professionals and others), doctors, donors, laymen and women, priests, professionals from various domains, sisters and volunteers engaged in diverse efforts for the good of the institutions.

---

43  Minutes, Nov. 5, 1888.
44  Minutes, Jan. 21, 1889.

A second theme is the defined structural relationship of each institution, *qua* institution, with ecclesial authority. The patterns are diverse, from one institution to another, and over time in each institution.

Third is the relationship not only with individuals in ecclesial authority, but also with the structures of the Catholic community — parish, diocese, other communities of sisters, and lay groups like the St. Vincent de Paul Society.

Fourth, lay people are significantly involved in diverse roles in these ministries from the beginning. Authority is delegated to them in various ways.

And fifth, there is a stated relationship with the Catholic spiritual tradition, especially in the mandates as to how the ministry is to be carried out. Intentional formation of lay leaders is an important part of the institutional legacy, especially the emphasis on "the extension of charity."[45]

## THE EARLY STORIES AND TEACHINGS FROM VATICAN II

### *A Vision of the Church*

The First Vatican Council from 1869 – 1870 approved a document emphasizing the role of the pope, and hence hierarchical authority in the church. Interrupted due to the outbreak of the Franco-Prussian War in 1870, the dialogue exploring the nature of the church began again during Vatican II. Over the course of three years of discussion, a new approach evolved with a broader emphasis on the whole community. First, the church is described as the People of God, all the members of the church together, in a communion. All share in the life of Christ, and the work of Christ as priest, prophet and king. All are called to holiness. This emphasizes the radical equality of all members of the People of God in the essence of who they are.

---

45   Cf. footnote 35.

In the Church not everyone marches along the same path, yet all are called to sanctity and have obtained an equal privilege of faith through the justice of God (cf. 2 Pet: 1:1).[46]

Subsequently, the council reflects on the diverse roles of the hierarchy, the laity and vowed religious.

## A Vision of the Laity

Another much discussed concept at Vatican II was the apostolate of the laity, the sharing of laypersons in the mission of the church. Some bishops contended that the apostolate was given by Christ to *the bishops*, and so the proper way to speak of the laity's role was as sharing in the bishop's apostolate, working under his authority. However, the document on the church uses the language later developed more fully in *The Decree on the Apostolate of Lay People*, indicating clearly that the apostolate does not simply belong to the hierarchy, but rather to all the baptized. Furthermore, the laity have a particular task, the renewal of all aspects of human life, in families, the larger culture, the trades and professions, the political and international communities.[47]

> The apostolate of the laity is a sharing in the salvific mission of the Church. Through Baptism and Confirmation all are appointed to this apostolate by the Lord himself.[48]

> That all people, working in harmony should renew the temporal order and make it increasingly more perfect: such is God's design for the world.

> Lay persons ought to take on themselves as their distinctive task this renewal of the temporal order. Guided by the light of the Gospel and the mind of the Church, prompted by Christian love, they should act in this domain in a direct way and in their own specific manner.[49]

46  *Dogmatic Constitution on the Church*, Art. 32.
47  *Decree on the Apostolate of the Laity*, Art. 7.
48  *Dogmatic Constitution on the Church*, Art. 33.
49  *Decree on the Apostolate of the Laity*, Art. 7.

Furthermore, the council taught that the competence of laypersons ought to be recognized, and their contributions promoted.

> By reason of the knowledge, competence or pre-eminence which they have the laity are empowered — indeed sometimes obliged — to manifest their opinion on those things which pertain to the good of the Church.

> The pastors, indeed, should recognize and promote the dignity and responsibility of the laity in the Church. They should willingly use their prudent advice and confidently assign duties to them in the service of the Church, leaving them freedom and scope for acting.[50]

Thus, we see that the history of both hospitals presents a picture of a sharing in the mission of the church by diverse members of the People of God, equal in dignity. The competence of many contributed to the growth of the hospitals, persons with different roles sharing in the common mission. The working together demonstrated by the historical record (of course, the usual struggles of people working together were surely part of the untold story) expresses the communal nature of the church, and of the exercise of her ministries. This spirit is captured in the dedication of a history of St. Michael's that was published in 1992:

> To our founders, physicians, nurses, employees, volunteers and all who have contributed to *The Healing Touch of St. Michael's Medical Center.*[51]

The same spirit is noted in a history of St. Vincent's that was published in 1938:

> This little volume is a tribute to the splendid working relationship of the Physicians, Sisters and Nurses during almost fifty years of service.[52]

---

50  *Decree on the Apostolate of the Laity*, Art. 37.
51  *The Healing Touch.*
52  Stuart, *A History of St. Vincent Hospital in New York City*, George R. Stuart, privately published, 1938, Foreword.

These early stories of Catholic health care reflect the call to sanctity (sanctity which can be fruitfully described as commitment to the loving service of others) of all who are part of the mission of the church. A telling comment appears in the *Rules and Regulations* for the house staff at St. Vincent's:

> The members of the House Staff will ever bear in mind the Christian character of the institution, and the noble nature of the labor in which they are engaged; and govern their actions in all things in a spirit of kindness and charity toward the unfortunate beings under their care.[53]

## IMPLICATIONS FOR FORMATION OF LAY LEADERS

The starting place for formation is the ministry of Jesus. Catholic health care is one way the People of God can continue the work of Jesus today. Stories of the ministry of Jesus are central. Jesus was a healer, and healing stories are often emphasized in formation. But Jesus was also a teacher and a friend of the poor and marginalized. The evolution of Catholic institutional ministries has led to an emphasis on Jesus as healer in health care ministries, of teacher in educational ministries and as friend of the poor and marginalized in charities (social service) ministries. But within each of these domains, attention to the three-fold ministry of Jesus is appropriate. Today, there is increasing recognition of this, giving added vitality to all of our institutions as they expand their focus to include broader ministries, as they strive to minister at the margins, to bring mercy to all, to address the social ills that impede the fulfillment of God's reign. Furthermore, and perhaps most important, the stories of what Jesus did provide not only a conceptual framework for ministry, but also a spiritual grounding, an inspirational invitation to follow in his footsteps. This inspiration extends beyond Christians to all persons, as the example of leaders like Gandhi have shown.

---

53  *St. Vincent Hospital of the City of New York: Rules and Regulations relating to the House Staff and Out Patient Department*, no printing information given, Archives at Mount Saint Vincent, p. 3.

A second essential theme for formation is an exploration of the mission of Jesus. Scripture scholars and other theologians today recognize that the primary proclamation of Jesus was of the kingdom of God — present, but not yet fully present. The theme of the kingdom so richly portrayed in the Hebrew Scriptures gives us powerful images of the promise that is the kingdom — a time of God's reign when there will be a fullness of peace (love, understanding, brothers and sisters living in harmony); justice (freedom, completion, swords beat into plowshares); holiness (happiness, completion, every tear wiped away); plenty (no hunger, each one with his/her own fig tree); health and well-being (the lame will dance); beauty and truth (how beautiful on the mountaintop are the feet of those who bring good news). Jesus founded the church in order to proclaim and prepare the way for such a fuller coming of the reign of God. The church prepares the way for this kingdom. And the church has created the institutional ministries which are one way that now proclaim and prepare the way for the fullness of the kingdom.

A third theme emerges when we trace the evolution of Jesus' understanding of his mission. His story shows that he gradually understood the universal embrace of his Father, his *Abba*, for all persons. From the beginning, he extended his ministry to the sick and the well, those who were outcasts in the society (lepers, tax collectors), sinners and children. But gradually he realized that his mission was also to those who were not Jewish. This is demonstrated in the healings of the daughter of the Syro-Phoenician woman and the servant of the Roman centurion, for example. The teachings of the council on religious liberty, and on the relationship of those of other faiths to the community of the church give commentary on this for our age.[54] Certainly, the history of Catholic health care demonstrates an embrace of all, even before such a vision was as fully expressed in our teachings as it is today. This perspective informs the ministry itself and embraces those serving in Catholic health care who are not part of the Roman Catholic community.

A fourth theme is the story of Catholic health care. The exploration of the mission and ministry of Jesus is the prelude to this story, both in general,

---

54  See especially, *The Dogmatic Constitution on the Church*, 15 – 16.

and in relation to individual institutional stories. These stories are, of course, stories of religious communities as founders. However, the story is incomplete if there is not due acknowledgment of the many individuals, the many roles, the varied structures (notably, parishes) which were part of the creation of the institutions of today. If only the stories of the vowed religious are told, laity may feel disempowered ("Oh, I can't do what the sisters did") or disconnected from the mission and ministry at the heart of the story. Spiritual growth will best occur when persons are deeply grounded in the why of their work, as well as the what. Laypeople will most fully embrace the mission when they see themselves as persons called to this great task.

Finally, the church's teachings about the role of the laity in "the world" are an important dimension in the formation of lay leaders. Vatican II (and papal teachings since then, notably Pope Saint John Paul II's *Christifidelis Laici* stressed that laypersons are especially charged with "the renewal of the temporal order." Our health care institutions are part of "the world" in a way that official ecclesial institutions cannot be. They have the potential to ever more fully impact the social fabric, "the temporal order," through the ways they model and advocate for practices in health care itself, but also in employee and community relations and the stewardship of resources that embody Catholic social teaching. As health care ministries are increasingly entrusted to laity, both as sponsors and as key administrators, this needs to receive increasing attention.

## CONCLUSION

When faced with the question, "Whose ministry is it?" history and theology urge us to recognize that Catholic health care is indeed a ministry of the church, precisely as church. This ministry is, and has been, the work of many persons in communion with one another, including clergy, lay leaders, vowed religious and the larger community of the people of the church. The formation of lay leaders with a deep understanding of the importance of their part in continuing the healing ministry of Jesus is central to an embodiment of this truth.

## DISCUSSION QUESTIONS

1. What stories of Jesus provide a grounding, an inspiration for you and your role in Catholic health care?

2. What is your understanding of the Kingdom of God, God's reign — a central image in Judeo-Christian theology? How does it relate to you and your ministry?

3. What do you know of the story of the founding years of your institution? How do you see yourself and your role in today's story?

========= CHAPTER SUMMARY =========

This chapter explores the theological significance of church
institutions in general, and Catholic health care in particular.
It begins by placing the topic in a broader cultural context
by considering the widespread anti-institutional bias that exists in
society and the church. It then examines the basic outlines of a
theology of church institutions that builds on the principle
of sacramentality and asks how a Catholic health care institution
can participate in the sacramentality of the church when many
of its employees are not Catholic.

## 4.4 THEOLOGY OF INSTITUTIONS

———

Richard Gaillardetz, Ph.D.

*Joseph Professor of Catholic Systematic Theology*
*Boston College*

I N THIS CHAPTER, WE WILL FOCUS ON THE *INSTITUTIONAL* character of the Catholic Church and the church's health ministry, Catholic health care. Most of us take for granted that any complex society requires institutions in order to function. Consequently, we presume that the church, at least at a pragmatic level, also requires institutions of various kinds if it is to fulfill its mission. But is there a *theological* significance to the place of institutions in the church, including those dedicated to Catholic health care? How are large Catholic institutions devoted to the work of education, health care and social services related to the church's fundamental nature and mission?

First, it might help to clarify what we mean by the term "institution." Answering this is not as easy as one might think for while modern sociology focuses considerable attention on the reality and function of institutions, there is in fact considerable disagreement regarding how precisely to define institutions. At the most basic level, institutions can be considered as sets of shared arrangements, often taking the form of shared norms and rules of conduct, that encourage patterned social behavior.[1] Institutions are

---

1  My consideration of a sociology of institutions is informed by Dave Elder-Vass, *The Causal Power of Social Structures* (Cambridge: Cambridge University Press, 2010), especially 115 – 43.

what allow us to engage in stable, cooperative action as a community. Those who participate in a given institution share a "commitment to endorse and enforce" a particular set of norms and/or rules of conduct.[2] These institutions are ubiquitous. For example, we might think of a community's arrangements regarding proper driving conduct (e.g., driving on the right side of the road, stopping at red lights) that often take the form of rules or norms regarding appropriate behavior. However, in the context of Catholic health care, when we speak of "institutions" what we generally have in mind are more complex entities, closer to what sociologists refer to as "organizations." Organizations are larger "assemblages of interacting human beings" that are structured by a complex set of interlocking roles (also referred to as "social positions"), social institutions and distinct authority relations.[3] In this chapter we will often use the word "institution" as interchangeable with "organization."

## THE CHALLENGE OF THE CONTEMPORARY ANTI-INSTITUTIONALIST IMPULSE

Today we encounter a sweeping cultural distrust of public institutions of any kind. Hugh Heclo, an American political scientist at George Mason University, wryly observes: "today's institutions have gained our distrust the old-fashioned way. They have earned it."[4] According to Heclo, this distrust takes two basic forms: culture-based distrust and performance-based distrust. Culture-based distrust proceeds from a series of shifts in Western cultural values away from a more communitarian sensibility and toward an atomistic individualism that privileges individual rights over social obligations. One thinks of the 1980s survey of young Americans that confirmed their embrace of the constitutional right to a trial by jury but also their unwillingness to serve on one.[5] This cultural distrust of institutions and civic responsibilities in American life was perceptively limned in the work of Robert Bellah and his colleagues in *Habits of the Heart* and *The Good Society*.[6]

---

2  Elder-Vass, 124.
3  Elder-Vass, 152.
4  Hugh Heclo, *On Thinking Institutionally* (New York: Oxford, 2008): 15.
5  Morris Janowitz, *The Reconstruction of Patriotism: Education for Civic Consciousness* (Chicago: University of Chicago Press, 1983): 8.
6  Robert Bellah et al., *Habits of the Heart: Individualism and Commitment in American Life* (New York: Harper and Row, 1985); *The Good Society* (New York: Random House, 1991).

A second form of institutional distrust is "performance-based." Heclo describes, in disheartening detail, numerous breaches of public trust by institutions in the private, public and non-profit sectors.[7] Heclo has no romantic pining for a happier time when all institutions worked tirelessly for the common good. However, he does argue, "in the last two generations or so, the normal range and frequency of human failings have presented themselves to the public in new ways…"[8]

This new situation is fueled by three factors. First, *the scale effect* acknowledges that modern technology dramatically magnifies the harm that can be done by public corruption. Consider the ubiquity of Internet scams and Ponzi schemes and the world of investing where electronic stock transactions occur in nanoseconds, thereby creating an unprecedented volatility in modern markets. The second factor, *the display effect*, reflects the penchant of the modern media for seeking out scandal and then obsessing over it. "Scandals and other examples of poor institutional performance are sought out, dramatically packaged, instantly communicated, and incessantly repeated for mass public consumption."[9] The display effect is particularly evident with church scandal. The tragic accounts of clerical sexual abuse have been magnified by modern media's ability to hammer into public consciousness the horrors of each instance of abuse. Lastly, Heclo considers *the PR effect*, which refers to the dramatic growth in the business of public spin. Politicians, corporate public relations representatives and even church leaders are coached by professional spin-doctors that carefully vet potential public statements by way of polling, focus groups, brand management, etc. The problem is that the public isn't stupid; it recognizes spin and consequently loses confidence in anything uttered by public officials. Combine these three performance-based factors with the broader cultural disposition toward atomistic individualism and one begins to grasp the basis for a default attitude of distrust of all things institutional, including church institutional structures.

---

7   Heclo, 15 – 32.
8   Heclo, 26.
9   Heclo, 27.

The Catholic Church has by no means been immune to this anti-institutional bias. In the decades since the Second Vatican Council we have seen a pronounced anti-institutionalism emerge in various corners of the church. This response was in part fueled by the council's decisive move away from a baroque and neo-scholastic Roman Catholicism that had reduced the church to its visible, structural dimensions: the sacraments, to be sure, but also a maze of laws, offices, jurisdictions, policies, and bureaucratic entities of one kind or another. And since at the heart of this institutional reality were the clergy — those who held most church offices, executed the church's laws and policies and to whom matters of jurisdiction applied — this way of viewing the church seemed to leave a lot out. It not only ignored the vast majority of the baptized who were not ordained, it also neglected the profoundly spiritual reality of the church, the presence and activity of the Holy Spirit through the insight ("sense of the faithful") and charisms of ordinary believers. This default bias against the institutional reality of the church was reinforced by three developments in Catholicism.

First, the growing interest in feminist theology led to a compelling criticism of the androcentric and patriarchal biases embedded in the hierarchical ordering of Catholic institutional life.[10] Feminist theologians saw in the church an interlocking system of male privilege that welcomed women's participation in the life of the church but on men's terms. In the eyes of many, Catholic institutions were little more than bastions of male, clerical power and privilege.[11] Second, many theologians and pastoral leaders began to criticize members of the church's hierarchy who had aligned themselves with oppressive military dictatorships in Spain, Latin America and elsewhere. In the eyes of these critics, many church hierarchs had become preoccupied with political privilege and ignored both the Gospel imperative to serve the poor and marginalized and the prophetic obligation to denounce all systems of social injustice. This even led some to advocate a counter proposal for a "people's church" rather than the "official" or "institutional church." Third, the many reports of clerical sexual abuse and

---

10  "Androcentrism" refers to the practice of making the experience of maleness normative for understanding what it is to be human. "Patriarchy" refers to the structuring of a society in ways that ensure that men hold power over women.

11  To be clear, this has largely *not* been true of Catholic health care institutions that were most frequently founded and initially staffed largely by women religious.

instances of ecclesiastical cover up made public in the last two
decades shattered many Catholics' trust in the sanctity and integrity
of church institutions.

It is vital that both our church and society find ways to overcome this
anti-institutional bias. Why? Because, put simply, the whole is greater
than the sum of its parts. Social institutions, organizations and structures
come into existence as humans grapple with the challenges and natural
limitations that come with engaging their world. Social institutions,
organizations and structures emerge as ways of enhancing the natural
capacities of humans while overcoming their concrete limitations. As
regards the church, this means that the church's various institutions hold
forth the possibility of extending and enhancing the call to Christian
discipleship that each person receives at baptism. This makes it all the
more important that we find a theologically compelling account of the
institutional dimension of the church.

## CHURCH INSTITUTIONS AND THE
## SACRAMENTAL PRINCIPLE

Christianity originated, as many biblical scholars have reminded us, as a
loose and fluid "Jesus movement." Yet one must remember that the founder
and locus of that movement, Jesus of Nazareth, was himself, in some sense,
"an institutional person." He participated fully in the religious institutions
of first-century Judaism. Jesus attended the synagogue regularly, according
to numerous Gospel accounts. He supported the financial upkeep of the
temple (Mt 17:24-27 and Mk 12: 41-44) even as he protested against the
Temple having become a site of religious corruption and hypocrisy (Jn 2:
13-25). Although Jesus offered a radical reinterpretation of Mosaic Law,
nowhere did he repudiate it. Donald Senior puts the matter rather bluntly,
"[i]n fact, the Church was an institution from the moment of its birth."[12]

---

12  Donald Senior, *The Gift of Administration: New Testament Foundations for the Vocation
    of Administrative Service* (Collegeville: Liturgical Press, 2016): 1 – 22, at 9. The treatment
    of the biblical testimony to the institutional elements of Christianity is drawn largely from
    Senior's work.

Gospel accounts of the life of Jesus' early community of believers reflect concerns for organizational structure. Even before Jesus' death and resurrection we find practical considerations for the financial support of early Christian communities. In one Gospel account Judas is identified as the keeper of "the common purse" (Jn 13:29), and Luke recounts women who contributed financially to the support of Jesus' ministry (Lk 8:3). Although the historicity of various accounts raises certain difficulties, there is evidence of Jesus giving a privileged role to Peter, James and John while singling out Peter for a particular leadership role (Mt 16: 16-20).[13]

This institutional dimension appears with greater frequency in the post-resurrection Christian community where the *Acts of the Apostles* provides ample testimony of organizational preoccupations of one kind or another. There we encounter deliberations on procedures for calling forth new leadership (Acts 1: 21-6; 6: 1-6) and concerns regarding the material welfare of the churches. For example, Acts offers an account of the church of Antioch's desire to send financial resources to Christians in Judea (Acts 11:29-30). As the church grew from its germinal roots in the first centuries of its existence, the process of ecclesial institutionalization continued. Larger scale institutions, including monasteries, various church leadership structures — the papacy, the episcopate, and eventually, schools, universities, hospitals, religious orders/congregations/associations — all vastly extended the church's ability to fulfill its mission in the world even as they also created a broad arena for ecclesiastical corruption.

Criticism of institutional dysfunction has been a persistent feature in the history of the church. St. Francis of Assisi, St. Bernard of Clairvaux, St. Catherine of Siena, Girolamo Savonarola, and Jan Hus all stood as prophetic voices denouncing the perils of ecclesiastical corruption and dysfunction. Many of these criticisms came to a head with the sixteenth-century Protestant reformers who leveled a series of searing attacks on the medieval church's institutional reality. Although they reluctantly granted the need for ecclesiastical structures of one kind or another, the reformers were unrelenting in their attacks on Catholicism's institutional abuses. Not

---

13  I say "possible" here only as an acknowledgement of the biblical disputes regarding whether or not Mt. 16: 16 – 20 reflects a post-resurrection account.

surprisingly, these attacks led to a predictably defensive response. Catholic apologists like the Jesuit theologian St. Robert Bellarmine defended the necessity and centrality of the church's visible, institutional reality, at times to the neglect of its spiritual reality. In his *Controversies,* he insisted:

> The church is a gathering of persons which is as visible and palpable as the gathering of the people of Rome, the kingdom of Gaul or the Republic of Venice.[14]

This Catholic reaction to the Protestant reformers set in motion a centuries-long tendency in Catholicism to focus on the church's more visible, institutional reality to the relative neglect of its spiritual dimension. It is during this period that the image of the church as a *societas perfecta*, a "perfect society," emerged. This was not an assertion of the church's moral perfection but an insistence that the church possessed all the institutional means and resources for fulfilling its mission. Convinced that uniformity in church teaching and practice was the best antidote to abuse, a thoroughly reorganized Roman curia worked to standardize church doctrine and practice, particularly regarding church liturgy. At the same time, the proliferation of men's and women's religious communities, many of which were dedicated to fulfilling the Gospel mandate to feed the hungry, clothe the naked, and educate the unlettered, furthered this institutional impulse. The sixteenth to nineteenth centuries saw an unprecedented expansion of the church's bureaucratization and institutionalization. The emergence of Catholic institutions dedicated to education and especially to health care during this period effectively channeled enormous pastoral energies toward responding to the needs of a wounded world.

One can read the achievement of the Second Vatican Council as an effort to more effectively correlate the church's institutional integrity with its spiritual vitality. The council affirmed the necessity of both institutional structure and the charismatic impulse. It posited the integral relationship between the active participation of individual believers in the church's mission through the exercise of their baptismal charisms and the ways in

---

14  Robert Bellarmine, *De Conciliis, et Ecclesia, De Controversiis: Christianae Fidei Adversus Haereticos,* (Rome: Giunchi et Menicanti, 1836), II: Book III, Chapter 2, 90.

which these charisms were often enhanced, extended and ordered through the mediation of church institutions and structures. Karl Rahner wrote:

> The Spirit has always held sway anew in the Church, in ever new ways, always unexpectedly and creatively, and bestowed his gift of new life. He has never abolished official authority and laws, which after all derive from one and the same Spirit, but again and again brings them to fulfillment in ways other than those expected by the "bureaucracy," the merely human side to office, which exists even in the Church. And he has again and again brought the hierarchy and the whole institutional element to recognize this influence of the Spirit.[15]

Since the council, Catholic theology has rightly celebrated Vatican II's reaffirmation of the importance and indispensability of the charisms of the baptized for the flourishing of the church and its mission. One way in which it balanced the institutional and charismatic dimensions of the church's life and mission was through its bold assertion that the church not only administered seven sacraments, but that it was itself a kind of sacrament.

To appreciate the significance of this claim regarding the fundamental sacramentality of the church, we need to begin by considering two fundamental Christian convictions.[16] First, Catholics believe that God has revealed God's self not through the communication of some eternal myth but in history. The Spirit of God has always been active in history, working, not in some vague, unspecified fashion, but with particular peoples in particular times and places. Thus God made known to the world God's salvific will through the story of a particular people, the assembly of Israel. In the New Testament, the specificity of God's saving work became even more dramatic. "In the fullness of time," God's unsurpassing love became concrete in a particular human being, Jesus of Nazareth (and not John the Baptist), born in a particular place, ancient Palestine (not Korea or Canada), in a particular time, approximately 2,000 years ago (not in 850, 1350 or

---

15  Karl Rahner, "The Charismatic Element in the Church," in *The Dynamic Element of the Church* (New York: Herder, 1964): 58.

16  Here I draw inspiration, in part, from a helpful essay by Michael J. Himes, "Church Institutions: A Theological Note," *New Theology Review* (May 2001): 6 – 15.

1950 CE) and as part of a particular heritage, culture and personality (Jesus was a Galilean Jew, not a Chinese mandarin or Native American shaman). That salvation of all people through all time would take place through the Incarnation — God's becoming a fully embodied human in the singular person of Jesus of Nazareth at a particular time in human history — is sometimes referred to as the scandal of particularity. It is through the particularity of human, historical existence that the saving work of God was decisively manifested. That is to say, does it shock us that God became incarnate in such a local, historically bound place, in one human person, rather than in some more general way? The doctrine of the Incarnation reminds us that our own concrete and particular bodily reality is significant; it is the site where we encounter the divine. Michael Himes sees in the Incarnation the primary example of a basic sacramental principle: "What is always and everywhere the case must be noticed, accepted, and celebrated somewhere, sometime."[17] God's universal, saving love must become concrete, sometime and somewhere; Catholics believe that this has occurred in the unique person of Jesus of Nazareth and that it continues in the life and mission of the church.

Second, Catholics believe God has created humans as fundamentally social creatures who can only realize their destiny in human relationship, that is, in community. The mediation of the saving love of God through the life and mission of Jesus was not a historical exception; God continues to make known the depth and breadth of divine love through a people. St. Paul used the image of the "body" to reflect on the life of the Christian community. For him the embodied reality of Jesus was to be extended through the embodied reality of the Christian community. We are called as a community to continue the mission of Jesus.

It is in light of our corporate, embodied reality that we can now consider the role of institutions. Church institutions function as a spatial and temporal extension of our own historical, human embodiment. Regina Bechtle writes:

---

17   Michael J. Himes, "'Finding God in All Things': A Sacramental Worldview and Its Effects," in *As Leaven in the World: Catholic Perspectives on Faith, Vocation, and the Intellectual Life,* ed. Thomas M. Landy (New York: Sheed and Ward, 2001): 91 – 103, at 91.

Institutions, much as the persons who constitute them, give and receive energy, power, and spirit. They are open to the action of grace and of evil. They act, for good or ill, with more or less freedom, to influence the world around them. By words and deeds, policies and behaviors, institutions translate their deepest dreams and desires into real time and space.[18]

Consequently, it is through church institutions that the church continues the mission and ministry of Jesus in the world. This conviction that God wishes to manifest God's work of reconciliation and healing through a people and its institutions, provides the basis for the distinctive Catholic conviction that we can see the church itself as a kind of sacrament.[19]

In the *Dogmatic Constitution on the Church, Lumen Gentium*, the council writes:

Since the church, in Christ, is a sacrament — a sign and instrument, that is, of communion with God and of the unity of the entire human race — it here proposes, for the benefit of the faithful and of the entire world to describe more clearly, and in the tradition laid down by earlier council, its own nature and universal mission (LG 1; GS 42).[20]

Later in article 48 of that same document, the council refers to the church as the "universal sacrament of salvation" (cf. AG 1, 5).

---

18  For a reflection on the spirituality of institutions that flows from this commitment to the theological significance of human embodiment, see Regina Bechtle, "Giving the Spirit a Home: Reflections on the Spirituality of Institutions," in *Called and Chosen: Toward a Spirituality for Lay Leaders*, edited by Zeni Fox and Regina Bechtle (Lanham, MD: Rowan and Littlefield, 2005): 99 – 111.

19  The council members again were influenced by the work of Karl Rahner and Otto Semmelroth. Both theologians had written of the Church as a "primordial sacrament." See Karl Rahner, *The Church and the Sacraments* (New York: Crossroad, 1963); Otto Semmelroth, *Church and Sacrament* (Notre Dame: Fides, 1965).

20  Unless otherwise indicated, all quotations from Vatican II documents are taken from Austin Flannery, ed., *Vatican Council II: Constitutions, Decrees, Declarations* (Collegeville: Liturgical Press, 1996).

This insistence on the church's own sacramentality needs to be explored further. As we saw above, the mystery of the Incarnation affirms that when God wished to manifest to us the breadth and depth of divine love, God came to us in an embodied human. The significance of human embodiment extends to the church's institutional reality. The embodiment of God's mission and ministry continues through the embodied reality of human institutions. Just as bread and wine provide the essential "matter" of the sacrament of the Eucharist and water provides the essential "matter" of the sacrament of baptism, we might ask: what is the visible, essential "matter" of the church's own sacramentality? The answer can only be, everything that comprises the church in its visible, historical existence. The church's own sacramentality begins with its members' ordinary life witness to the values of the Gospel, but also includes its sacraments, laws, offices, ecclesial practices and social institutions — all these visible manifestations of the church participate in the church's sacramental reality. Consequently, every Catholic school, every soup kitchen, every legal aid office, and every Catholic hospital shares in the sacramental character of the church.

Vatican II rejected any sense that the church existed for its own sake. It is not to hover placidly above the tumultuous vicissitudes of human history nor is it to be a safe haven for believers desiring to escape a troubled world.

> All those, who in faith look towards Jesus, the author of salvation and the source of unity and peace, God has gathered together and established as the church, that it may be for each and every one *the visible sacrament of saving unity*. In order to extend to all regions of the earth, it enters into human history, though it transcends at once all time and all boundaries between peoples (LG 9).

The church exists *for the world*; as a sacrament, it is to be a sign and instrument that makes God's saving love and action present in the world through a constructive engagement with the world. This is evident in the last-minute change in the title of the *Pastoral Constitution on the Church in the Modern World Today, Gaudium et Spes*. Where an earlier version presented this as a document on "the church *and* the modern world," the council changed the title to refer to the church *in* the modern world in order to emphasize the extent to which the church is to live *in* the world in order to evangelize and transform the world as a "leaven" (GS 40). If nineteenth-century Catholicism presented the church as a counter-society set over against a fallen world, Vatican II called for a critical yet dialogical engagement with the world.

This leads to a final question: As a sacrament, what does the church, in all its visible and institutional forms, "make present" to the world? Of what, exactly, is it to be a sign and instrument? At the council several Latin American bishops asked the council to consider making greater use of the biblical metaphor of "the reign of God" or "the kingdom of God." Although this proposal came too late to allow the theme to be comprehensively integrated into the council documents, it does appear in several key passages. For example, in article 5 of *Lumen Gentium* the council taught that the church does not exist for its own sake but rather exists in service of the coming reign or kingdom of God:

> Henceforward the church, equipped with the gifts of its founder and faithfully observing his precepts of charity, humility and self-denial, receives the mission of proclaiming and establishing among all peoples the kingdom of Christ and of God, and is, on earth, *the seed and the beginning of that kingdom* (LG 5, emphasis is mine).

Later in that same document the council refers to the church as a "messianic people" and asserts that as such the church's destiny is realized in that kingdom of God which has been begun by God himself on earth and which must be further extended until it is brought to perfection by him at the end of time when "Christ, our life, will appear" and "creation itself also will be delivered from its slavery to corruption into the freedom of the glory of the sons and daughters of God" (LG 9).

Here again the power of the biblical image of the reign or kingdom of God, an image that so dominated Jesus' own preaching, is evoked. In the teaching of the council, the kingdom of God, which was manifested in human history as Jesus Christ, continues as a force in history and will find its consummation only at the end of history. The church exists in human history as "the seed and beginning" of this kingdom.

Pope St. John Paul II, in his encyclical, *Redemptoris Missio*, gave this theme a much fuller exposition.[21] The pope stressed the inseparability of Jesus and the kingdom of God. He began by developing the biblical image of the kingdom of God in the teaching and ministry of Jesus, noting that the "proclamation and establishment of God's kingdom" constituted the essential purpose of Jesus' mission (RM 13). Jesus revealed the kingdom, not just in his teaching, but also "in his actions and his own person" (RM 14). Central to the manifestation of the kingdom of God were Jesus' ministries of healing and forgiving, ministries that result in transformed human relationships. The kingdom thereby grows "as people slowly learn to love, forgive and serve one another" (RM 15). As the pope looked to the origins of Christianity, he saw service to the kingdom of God as the very *raison d' être* of the church. In this remarkable encyclical the pope creatively developed and expanded the teaching of the council by explicitly considering the relationship between these two themes, the church as sacrament and the church as seed of the kingdom of God. He wrote:

> The many dimensions of the kingdom of God do not weaken the foundations and purposes of missionary activity, but rather strengthen and extend them. The Church is the sacrament of salvation for all humankind, and her activity is not limited only to those who accept her message. She is a dynamic force in [humankind's] journey toward the eschatological kingdom, and is the sign and promoter of gospel values (RM 20).

If we combine these two themes of the church as sacrament of salvation and the church as seed and sign of the kingdom, it is possible to speak of *the church as the sacrament of the reign or kingdom of God*. And what is the substance of the kingdom of God? It is the world as God would have it be. It is the world governed by God's *shalom*.

It follows then that Catholic institutions of all kinds, and certainly Catholic health care institutions, share in the sacramentality of the church to the

---

21  John Paul II, *Redemptoris Missio*, (1990) can be accessed online at: http://w2.vatican.va/content/john-paul-ii/en/encyclicals/documents/hf_jp-ii_enc_07121990_redemptoris-missio.html.

extent that they are oriented toward realizing the *shalom* of God and the practices and values associated with the reign of God. These certainly include practices and values associated with explicit Christian discipleship, but they also include those in which non-Christians may engage as well: education oriented toward the fuller humanization of society; advocacy on behalf of justice; accompaniment with and care for the poor, the hungry, those with special needs, the sick and dying. Insofar as Catholic hospitals — in all their practices, policies and values — extend the healing ministry of Jesus to all who are ill, affirm the intrinsic goodness and value of human bodily existence, manifest the radical inclusivity of God's reign by providing care to all, and offer compassionate palliative care for the suffering and dying, they participate in the sacramentality of the church as a sign and instrument of God's reign.

## CAN A CATHOLIC INSTITUTION BE STAFFED AND LED BY NON-CATHOLICS IF IT IS TO SHARE IN THE CHURCH'S SACRAMENTALITY?

This conviction that church institutions, including Catholic health care institutions, participate in the sacramentality of the church as a sign and instrument of God's kingdom raises a fundamental question. Can these institutions share in the sacramentality of the church when they are staffed and even led by many non-Catholic employees? Given the large numbers of non-Catholics currently employed in Catholic health care institutions, the question cannot be avoided.

Charles Curran contends that the presence of large numbers of non-Catholics in Catholic health care institutions need not compromise the participation of those institutions in the sacramentality of the church. These institutions "make it possible for the characteristic Catholic values of the dignity of the individual, the importance of the common good, and special concern for the poor to become more present in our institutional structures and contemporary ethos."[22] Curran contends that non-Catholic employees can participate in the mission of these institutions, and by extension I

---

22  Charles E. Curran, "The Catholic Identity of Catholic Institutions," *Theological Studies* 58 (1997): 90 – 108, at 93.

would argue, in the sacramental character of the church itself, because it is possible for non-Catholics to affirm the central values and fundamental orientation of Catholic health care. This position proceeds from a Catholic natural law framework in which much of what constitutes the substance of Catholic ethical teaching can be accepted by many who do not share specific Catholic faith commitments.

A complement to Curran's recourse to natural law would be a more explicitly theological commitment to the universality of God's grace. As the theologian Karl Rahner often reminded us, the grace of God is not limited to those who possess explicit Christian faith:

> It is quite conceivable that wherever a human being really affirms moral values as absolutely binding, whether expressly or merely in the actual unreflecting accomplishment of his nature, intrinsically oriented as this is beyond and above itself toward the absolute mystery of God, he possesses that attitude of authentic faith (even if only virtually).[23]

Rahner's theology further supports the claim that a non-believer who participates in the work of a Catholic institution, affirming the fundamental moral values and practices that guide that institution, can in fact share in the sacramentality of that institution as an instrument in service to God's coming reign. The arguments of Curran and Rahner support the claim here that there are many who are not Catholic but who nevertheless subscribe to a Catholic institution's values and practices and, in subscribing to those values and practices, can be said to participate in the sacramental character of these institutions.

To conclude, we can affirm that a Catholic health care organization can be said to participate in the church's mission as a sacrament of God's reign even when many who work in that organization are not Catholic. This holds insofar as the organization has as its primary orientation the furtherance of those practices and values we identify with God's reign, which are deeply human practices and values. This generally will require, however, that there

---

23 Rahner, "The Charismatic Element in the Church," 64.

be specific institutional offices and mechanisms in place that insure that the
mission of the institution remains oriented toward the realization of these
practices and values. I have in mind here the situation in Catholic health
care where consecrated religious communities play a distinctive "sponsoring"
role in collaboration with independent lay boards that may have significant
non-Catholic representation. In this situation, according to Curran, the
sponsoring community's primary purpose "is to integrate values and mission
into the organization's daily operations. They see themselves as catalysts,
tone and direction setters, facilitators, resource persons, and educators."[24]
Still another model concerns the establishment, according to the norms of
Catholic canon law, of a "public juridic person."[25] In this situation the role
of Catholic sponsorship is formally transferred to an independent governing
body comprised of consecrated religious and/or laypersons who are charged
with ensuring the institution's continued commitment to participate in the
service of God's reign through its healing mission. Action to ensure the
continued commitment of the health care institution to the values of God's
reign is undertaken by "mission integration leaders." This can take various
forms. It will mean working to see that fundamental principles in Catholic
medical ethics remain at the forefront of policy decisions. It will mean
encouraging direct caregivers to understand their work in the light of Jesus'
accompaniment with the broken and sick of this world and the Catholic
call to a deep solidarity with all who suffer.

There is, however, a flip side to this commitment to the sacramentality of
Catholic health care institutions. It is possible for sin, in both its personal
and structural forms, to impede an institution's participation in the
church's sacramentality. When individual employees and/or institutional
policies and organizational structures run counter to the values and
practices appropriate to God's reign, the sacramentality of the church and
its institutions is compromised. When the human dignity of those whom
Catholic institutions were created to serve is obscured or effaced by the
profit motive, the sacramentality of the church is attenuated. When the
employees in Catholic institutions are treated as mere instrumental cogs
in a larger, dehumanizing system, the efficacy of the church as sign of the
saving and healing love of God is threatened. When care of the sick and

24  Curran, 96.
25  See the *1983 Code of Canon Law*, canons 116 – 23.

infirm is reduced to the status of a commodity subject to a crass cost-benefit analysis, the church, as manifested by that institution, no longer appears before the world as an effective sign and instrument of the reign of God. In the end, the sacramentality of any Catholic institution will depend on more than the number of Catholics it employs or the name that appears on the institutional logo and stationery. It will depend on that institution's transparent commitment to the values and practices of God's reign.

## DISCUSSION QUESTIONS

1. What are some concrete ways in which the larger anti-institutional bias in our culture has spread to people's attitudes toward Catholic institutions?

2. What are some concrete obstacles that a Catholic health care institution faces in trying to be a sacrament for the reign of God?

3. How does Pope Francis' image of the church as a field hospital shed light on how we might think of Catholic health care's participation in the mission of the church?

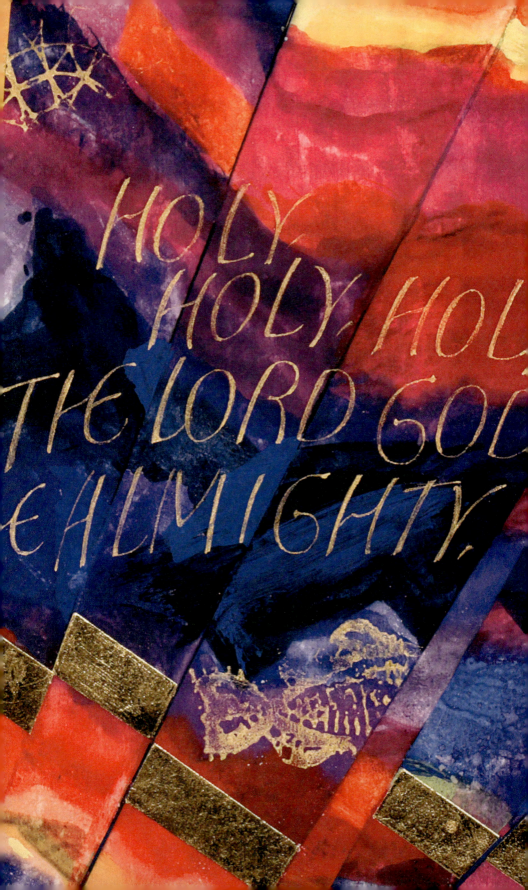

# CONCLUSION

CHAPTER SUMMARY

While formation for health care ministry leaders has become
accepted practice throughout Catholic health care, the question of
whether and to what degree Catholic theology should and can be
incorporated into formation programs is still a matter of debate.
This chapter proposes three essential theological concepts —
reign of God, nature of the human person and health care as a
ministry of the church — that can serve as a core to formation
programs at all levels, and it offers examples of how these concepts
can be meaningfully engaged with diverse groups of participants.
Building on this foundation, a more extensive curriculum of
theological and spiritual concepts and practices is presented that can
prepare senior executives to fulfill their responsibility to assure that
Catholic identity is embedded and evident in all strategic, operational
and clinical policies and practices.

## FORMATION: CATHOLIC THEOLOGY ALIVE
## IN CATHOLIC HEALTH CARE

<hr>

Celeste DeSchryver Mueller, D.Min
*Vice President, Spiritual and Theological Formation*
*Ascension*

### BACKGROUND

IN THE LAST 30 YEARS, CATHOLIC HEALTH CARE organizations have moved from a wary acceptance of formation for lay leaders to an expectation that formation is essential to sustaining Catholic identity and advancing the mission. Those who facilitate formation face a series of challenges for their work. First, although many persons in Catholic health care have heard the word "formation," they have widely different understandings of what it means. Second, those who join Catholic health care from secular and for-profit corporations often are perplexed by the invitation to participate in formation. Third, formation participants have broadly diverse backgrounds and faith commitments. Fourth, executives, board members, physicians and front-line associates who are invited to formation have limited time for it in light of extensive responsibilities and busy schedules. In addition, the growing number of partnerships between Catholic institutions and secular entities creates questions about the role of formation, Catholic identity and the meaning of health care as a ministry of the church.

These challenges, coupled with increasing demand for formation, have created a laboratory within Catholic health care for experimenting with design and facilitation of formation. As these programs have multiplied within Catholic health care, definitions, desired outcomes and methods have evolved as well. Presently, there is not a uniform approach or methodology for formation.

One of the open questions in formation is the degree to which it engages theology and spirituality. Refinement of our formation efforts at Ascension has led to a simple description of formation: *reflective practice in community.* The purpose is *personal flourishing in community and organizational integrity as a ministry of the church.* To achieve these outcomes, we create opportunities for reflection on individual and organizational practices, and the reflection is consistently grounded in theology, both implicitly and explicitly.

## THREE FUNDAMENTAL AFFIRMATIONS

Three theological concepts are core to the ministry of Catholic health care and to formation: the reign of God, the call to ministry and the nature of the human person. These foundational concepts come up often as we ask participants to reflect on their experience in leadership.

## 1. THE REIGN OF GOD AS THE WIDE HORIZON OF CATHOLIC HEALTH CARE

> The spirit of the Lord God is upon me, because the Lord
>     has anointed me!
>
> God has sent me to bring good news to the afflicted, to bind up the
>     brokenhearted,
> To proclaim liberty to the captives, release to the prisoners,
> To announce a year of favor from the LORD and a day of
>     vindication by our God;
> To comfort all who mourn; to place on those who mourn
>     in Zion a garland instead of ashes,
> To give them oil of gladness instead of mourning, a glorious
>     mantle instead of a faint spirit.

> They will be called oaks of justice, the planting of the LORD
> to show God's glory. (Is 61:1-3)

These words from the prophet Isaiah trace the vision and promises of God's reign and are echoed by Jesus in the Gospel scene that begins his public ministry (Lk 4:16-21). They situate Catholic health care within Jesus' mission and the mission of the church. As Richard Gaillardetz notes elsewhere in this volume, "Catholic institutions of all kinds, and certainly Catholic health care institutions, share in the sacramentality of the church to the extent that they are oriented toward. . .the practices and values associated with the reign of God." (263) Catholic health care does not exist solely to care for the sick or even to preserve health and restore relationships, but to be a sign and instrument of God's reign on earth. Jesus' proclamation, "Today this scripture passage is fulfilled in your hearing" (Lk 4:21), invites Catholic health care to serve this vision with confidence that God's reign is already alive in our midst and in faith that our organizational efforts contribute to the realization of God's reign in its fullness.

One might argue that the idea of the reign of God is too theologically complex and too explicitly Christian to be meaningful to diverse audiences. Examples from our formation settings tell a different story. In formation sessions with boards which regularly include persons of other or no faith traditions, we have found the reign of God to be an effective way to ground the identity of Catholic health care by connecting three dot points: 1) the "substance of the kingdom of God. . .[that is,] the world as God would have it be. . .the world governed by God's *shalom*" (Gaillardetz, 263); 2) notions of human dignity; and 3) the common good.[1]

These important connections lead from structures, policies and practices that are familiar to board members to the less familiar "reign of God" in such a way that promotes understanding of the theological concept. The idea that the whole organization in all its diversity contributes to a vision for all of creation and is oriented to an end beyond its own corporate good

---

1     This is expressed in our Ascension mission as *"we commit ourselves to serving all persons with special attention to those who are poor and vulnerable. . . . We are advocates for a compassionate and just society through our actions and our words"* and the diverse ways that Board members enable organizational structures, policies and practices that honor human dignity and advance the common good.

provides an opportunity for deeper discussion of organizational identity about who we are and who we can become. A participant in a recent board formation session said:

> "I have spent my life running a for-profit company. I have operated on this board on the principle that we must build our margin so that our mission could have impact. That is entirely the wrong approach. I see now that the mission exists with or without us. We are part of something much bigger. The mission has to come first. Then we must find every way possible to advance it."

Introducing people to the concept of the reign of God also makes language that is core to our Catholic identity part of the accepted vernacular for leadership and governance.

We introduce our mid-level leaders to the concept of the reign of God in the context of the mission that motivated our founders and as an integral part of understanding of Catholic identity. One dimension of the reign of God that is highlighted in our Foundations of Ministry Leadership program is the tension between the in-breaking, or initial human experience, of the reign and its ultimate fulfillment. Participants in the program include executives, front-line clinical staff, leaders in other areas of our organization and individuals among entities partnering with us — all of whom recognize that our mission is realized in ways beyond what we can see or even imagine. The dynamic tension between the initial awareness of the reign of God and its final fulfillment offers a way for participants to reflect on their personal journey to discover and grow into their true selves. It also enables them to reflect candidly on their actions as leaders. These actions impact right relationships with colleagues and contribute to a fuller realization of our identity and mission. Comments about the formation experience include:

> "I was burdened by the desire to live in the ideal world and my lived experience in real world left me unhappy. When I feel the stress of living in the tension, I spend time in reflection and remind myself that I am not in control. I do my best and let it go. Personally, I have been most impacted by God's love for me ... unconditionally. When I allowed myself to believe this truth it changed me."

"... reading, hearing and clearly understanding about the reign of God and our founding sisters' journey, their struggles, unknowns and yet the perseverance to continue on their journey to serve has helped me to understand that I do not have a job to fulfill but I have a mission to continue what God and sisters started, [and helped me] to understand the reasons why we try and retry on our journey to carry on God's mission."

"No matter what your faith practice is, this formation experience will help you to better understand yourself and others to be a more effective leader in Catholic healthcare, and in life. My management formation journey helped me to better define my mission and work towards fulfilling the template that God created for me. I am now able to connect to the deeper meaning of who I am and my work. For me it is the understanding of all of these connections that has helped me make intentional changes to be a better leader/manager."

Engaging the idea of the reign of God in a variety of settings is an attempt to situate the work of formation (and mission integration in general) against the horizon of God's plan. This enables formation to serve an end beyond the corporate good of any particular organization and invites those who serve in Catholic health care to participate in a mission that is deeper than shifting political and economic forces. The vision of the reign of God is a standard by which we consider every facet of how we understand our work in formation; it is both the starting point and the destination of our efforts.

## 2. UNDERSTANDING HEALTH CARE AS A MINISTRY OF THE CHURCH

The notion that Catholic health care serves the reign of God as a ministry of the church informs how we understand our identity and our organizational accountabilities. By asking what it means to be a ministry of the church, Bouchard notes elsewhere in this volume that we are forging a path into the theologically uncharted territory. One way we introduce the idea of health care as a ministry is our *Orientation to Ministry Leadership* program designed for executive leaders new to Catholic health care. These participants lead our hospital systems, supporting functions, or subsidiaries that may function as for-profit entities.

The key question is identity. Who is Ascension? What is Catholic health care in its DNA? Our identity as a ministry begins with the vision of God's reign which has been…

+ Entrusted to, proclaimed by, and embodied in Jesus as witnessed in the Gospel portrayal of his ministry of healing, teaching and care for the poor, his total gift of self, and the mystery of his suffering, death and resurrection
+ Entrusted to the community called church, which strives, despite failures, to embody the reign of God, especially through its ministries of healing, teaching, social service, preaching/sacraments, carried out in specific ways at specific times in history by clergy, religious men and women and laypersons
+ Entrusted to Catholic health care, which is called to embody this vision by expressing it through every policy, process, decision and action.

Ministry is presented as a call *to be certain kinds of persons* and to *act in certain ways* that are rooted in our tradition. This description resonates with those who are unfamiliar with Christian history and establishes a lived sense that Catholic health care is part of a living tradition. Through sponsorship, which rests with a religious community, a public juridic person or in a few cases, with a bishop, there is a legal connection to the universal church. This canonical connection strengthens a leader's sense of the accountability that comes with being entrusted with the identity of the ministry. We describe this reality in our mission statement by adapting O'Meara's classic definition of ministry:

> We are a ministry of the church. We are a community called and animated by the Spirit to serve the good of all persons — with special attention to those who are poor and vulnerable — on behalf of the Catholic Church, through our witness to the Gospel, in order to bring about a more just and compassionate society.[2]

---

2    Ascension theological perspective paper, "Being a Ministry of the Church" February 2015.

Recognizing that Ascension is a sponsored ministry of the church drives home the point that all parts of Ascension — clinical as well as non-clinical functions, hospitals as well as subsidiaries — together constitute the ministry, the proclamation of God's saving work.

While we await the evolution of a fuller theology of corporate or institutional ministry in response to Bouchard's question, "In what sense can institutions be considered as ministries?" (199), we believe that we do *minister* as a corporation. Seeing ministry as a corporate activity avoids the temptation to restrict ministry only to the direct delivery of medical care or to those individuals whose work is ministerial in the narrow sense, e.g., those who work in spiritual care.

Bouchard notes that our use of the word ministry is still confused, but we can provide some clarity by focusing on outcomes and functions such as those suggested by Caroll Watkins Ali, viz., *Sustaining, Guiding, Reconciling, Nurturing, Empowering, Liberating.*[3] These are a useful framework for executives to reflect on the meaning of ministry and they give rise to important questions: How does Ascension offer guidance, nurturing, reconciliation and sustenance? Do we function as an agent of empowerment and liberation to the individuals and communities we serve? Using the best image of minister that one can conjure, could Ascension, as a whole organization, be seen as a minister in the community? Can this corporation be recognizable as a sign and instrument of the reign of God?

These functions and the questions they raise are reflected in the Catholic Health Association's "Shared Statement of Identity," which calls us to

+ Promote and Defend Human Dignity
+ Attend to the Whole Person
+ Care for Poor and Vulnerable Persons
+ Promote the Common Good

---

3   Carroll Watkins Ali, "A Womanist Search for Sources" in *Feminist and Womanist Pastoral Theology*, 51-64. Ali recalls the evolution of understanding of the functions of ministry through the works of Seward Hiltner, *Preface to Pastoral Theology: The Ministry and Theory of Shepherding*; W.A. Clebsch and C.R. Jaekle, *Pastoral Care in Historical Perspective*; A.S. Wimberly, *Pastoral Care in the Black Church.*

+ Act on Behalf of Justice
+ Steward Resources
+ Act in Communion with the Church"[4]

Executives in the *Orientation to Ministry Leadership* program realize that a living tradition reaching back to Jesus has been entrusted to them. They come to realize they are responsible for assuring that the whole organization is faithful to the specific values that the principles of Catholic identity represent.

Statements from participants illustrate how they integrate these ideas:

> "Being a secular guy, "ministry" scared me — past tense; no longer. Ministry is something that is inherent in me and my past — bringing this to my daily work will be very satisfying."

> "This explained the thread. The thread is our Ascension mission. The thread is also God-Jesus-Church-Catholic health care-Ascension-me."

> "Ministry – Church (lead with direction); alignment of inner aspiration with spirit to shine and overflow; to align with the ministry and look forward."

## 3. THE PERSON AT THE CENTER

The principles of Catholic identity are rooted in the distinctive understanding of the human person. Common secular views of personhood, one of which is described by Dan Daly elsewhere in this volume, contrast sharply with Catholic views. I have never encountered the extreme view he describes among any of our formation participants, but some approaches to productivity measures and performance management practices suggest an implicitly "performance-based" notion of personhood (85 – 86). More often I have observed operative theologies of persons that

---

4    Available on the CHA website at www.chausa.org/mission/a-shared-statement-of-identity.

are utilitarian (people are good only if they are useful) or pessimistic (people are inherently unworthy or evil). Participants are generally unaware of the presuppositions they hold or of the practical implications of their views. For example, in a recent gathering of a new group in our Executive Ministry Leadership Formation program, I asked participants if they thought human beings were intrinsically good or intrinsically evil. The moment was revealing. The group split in half on that question, which startled everyone, and it enabled them to recognize some of their unexamined assumptions. The central importance of a Catholic theology of persons demands that it be embedded in all our formation curricula, and it has shaped the rationale for our formation efforts as well as our formation methods.

We try to summarize the Catholic understanding of the human person in language that is meaningful and clear. How we understand the person is of primary importance. We want everyone throughout our organization to be able to give voice to this view of the human person as the "why" behind individual behaviors and organizational practices. In all formation experiences, participants reflect on the idea that every person is:

+ A unique being created in love in the image of God
+ Social by nature and made for community
+ An integrated whole: both spiritual and embodied
+ Endowed with gifts by the Holy Spirit to be given in service
+ Free and responsible, creative and created
+ Transcendent yet limited and finite
+ Destined for the reign of God in which God's mercy, justice and forgiveness prevail.

Fig. 1

A three dimensional figure of the Mobius strip (Fig. 1) helps to stimulate reflection on the paradoxes of human experience and on human person as a unique and integrated whole of body, mind and spirit in which every dimension of a person is imbued with and expresses spirit — one's unique human spirit and God's spirit which sustains us in being. It helps to avoid portraying the "spirit" as a separate compartment of the human person, an increasing tendency in both secularism, which denies spirit, and in some New-Age movements, which can tend toward a spiritualism that neglects the physical. This image has provided an avenue to a theological consideration of three calls of the human vocation: the call to full humanity, or true self, the call to community, and the call to service.[5]

Like other Catholic ministries that seek the good of the human person "fully and adequately considered"[6] we are committed to the flourishing of the individual in community, and we are intentional in cultivating a working environment in which each person can experience "spiritually centered holistic care" and have the opportunity to develop mentally, physically, emotionally and spiritually. In other words, we are called to create the conditions in which individuals in community can become who they are called to be as human persons.

---

5   Michael Naughton and Jeffrey Cornwall, *Bringing Your Business to Life* (Ventura, CA: Regal, 2008).

6   This phrase emphasizes how central the idea of the person is to Catholic theology and ethics. In our tradition, the person, "fully and adequately understood" is the norm for virtually all of our ethical positions because we believe that we can know something of God's plan for us by careful reflection on human experience. The phrase itself is commonly understood to be rooted in the official commentary on *Gaudium et Spes 51* ("The Pastoral Constitution on the Church in the Modern World" from Vatican II) and is fully explained by Louis Janssens in his article "Artificial Insemination: Ethical Considerations" *Louvain Studies 8* (1980): 3-15.

A description of formation we sometimes use acknowledges that formation "invites persons to an ongoing transformative process that opens them to God's action and connects them more deeply with self, God, others, and the world."[7] Formation does not end with our programs and offerings; individuals are "in formation" throughout their lives.

Fig. 2

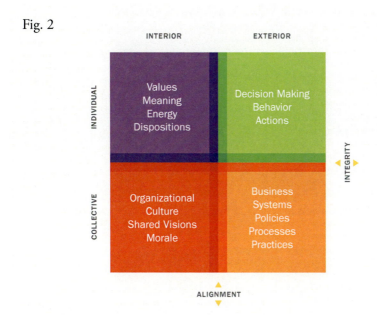

## INTERIOR VALUES, EXTERNAL ACTIONS

The formation "integration map" (Fig. 2), adapted from the work of Ken Wilber,[8] is a primary tool used in all our formation activities to focus attention on four interrelated dimensions of human experience. The upper tier of the grid illuminates the reality of the individual, while the lower tier addresses our experience as persons in community. The right side of the grid shows the more familiar territory of external actions and behavior of individuals and the visible processes, policies, structures and practices of our common life. The left side concerns the less familiar territory of the

7   Ascension Theological Update, "Defining Formation," 2014.

8   Ken Wilber, *A Theory of Everything*, (Boston: Shambhala, 2001): 43. This is just one of the many works in which Wilber explores his integral vision.

inner life of individuals and the elusive inner life of an organization, most often referred to as culture. Each quadrant of the map provides an avenue for deeper awareness of our human experience and invites reflection on the inner life of the self and of the community or organization.

Personal flourishing in community entails growth in human wholeness. The individual interior dimension is the locus of personal values and meaning which ultimately drives behavior. In other words, it accounts for why one does (interior) what one does (exterior). Reflection on one's personal decisions, behaviors and actions facilitates deeper awareness of the more *and less* desirable dispositions, attitudes and personal values. These can be challenging to discover as they reveal the influence of the inner life on decisions and behavior.

Similarly, by reflection on the lower quadrants, we become more attentive to the often hidden dimensions of organizational culture, our desired culture and the policies, practices and systems that either support or hinder a mission-focused culture.

## SPIRITUAL PRACTICES

Parker Palmer says, "The soul is like a wild animal - tough, resilient, savvy, self-sufficient, and yet exceedingly shy,"[9] and for many of our associates, the inner life is a foreign territory. We use various spiritual practices to help our associates become more familiar with their souls and to help them listen more attentively to the action of the Holy Spirit within them. Some practices are common to all formation activities — the use of silence, prayerful reflection and personal storytelling.[10] Other practices require sufficient time for both the practice itself and some explanation and reflection on the experience — journaling, meditation, reflection on scripture and other spiritual texts, ritual, art, music, spiritual assessments, soliciting personal feedback, spiritual direction, and a formal communal

---

9   Parker Palmer, *Let Your Life Speak,* (San Francisco: Jossey-Bass, 2000): 9.
10  See Celeste DeSchryver Mueller, "Create Sacred Space with Stories," *Health Progress* (November – December 2010): 17 – 21.

leadership reflection process.[11] The practice that has been most widely used and enthusiastically received is *Lection Divina* (a slow, meditative reading of Scripture) done in community. We invite associates to be attentive to more than their behaviors and actions by emphasizing the inner life, fostering what classically would be called the spiritual life and spiritual development.

## WHAT ABOUT THEOLOGICAL FOUNDATIONS OF TRINITY, CHRISTOLOGY, ECCLESIOLOGY AND MORAL THEOLOGY?

Bouchard notes "Whatever shape . . .formation takes…it is clear, that there can be no meaningful appropriation of the term 'ministry' to describe Catholic health care unless it is nourished with serious theology and spirituality at a number of levels. Senior leaders, board members and sponsors must acquire fluency in theological questions that impact health care just as they have fluency in organizational development, finance and strategic planning" (205). The three theological concepts mentioned above — the reign of God, Catholic health care as a ministry of the church and a Catholic understanding of persons — are a theological foundation for Catholic health care and essential components of our formation programs. The responsibility for integrating these concepts into the life and culture of Catholic health care rests first and foremost with sponsors, followed by leaders who create a vision, set strategy, establish structures, policies and practices, and make decisions.

Catholic health care will become a more authentic sign of the reign of God as a ministry of the church to the degree that its leaders function not simply as *leaders* but as *ministry* leaders. Leaders have the responsibility to "steward and integrate ministry identity for the sake of realizing our Mission." Three leadership competencies in our leaders' performance reviews highlight distinctive dimensions of that role. We ask them if they:

---

11  See Celeste DeSchryver Mueller, "Servant Leadership, The Way Forward," *Health Progress* (September – October, 2011): 21 – 25.

✦ Integrate the key elements of Catholic identity in shaping
  organizational culture
✦ See leadership as a spiritual practice and a service of persons
✦ Ensure ongoing personal formation to grow in virtue and
  servant leadership

Richard Gula affirms that "The capability and practice of theological
reflection is a *distinguishing* characteristic of ministry leaders."[12] Effective
ministry leadership requires the ability to engage experience from both
personal and communal perspectives, within a context of the complex
circumstances, challenges and opportunities facing Catholic health care, all
in light of our Catholic spiritual and theological tradition. Our Executive
Ministry Leadership Formation (EML) program is designed to provide
our health care executives with this important proficiency in theological
reflection. The EML program expects that all executives will:

✦ Be personally committed to practices and habits of spiritual reflection
  that foster deeper relationship with self, God, others, community and
  the world as part of their ongoing formation journey

✦ Be professionally committed to the healing ministry and mission of
  Jesus, with special attention to those who are poor and vulnerable

✦ Consistently integrate and practice virtuous servant leadership while
  being and building community

✦ Articulate foundational principles from the Catholic theological,
  moral and spiritual tradition in order to communicate Catholic
  health care's ministry identity and mission

✦ Interpret and lead our integrated strategic, operational, financial,
  clinical and organizational processes through the lens of Ascension's
  identity as a ministry of the church.

Retreats held at the beginning and end of each class weave together personal
spiritual reflection, individual and organizational theological reflection
on health care leadership, five courses of online theological study, and the

---

12   Richard Gula, *Ethics in Pastoral Ministry,* (New York: Paulist, 1996): 54.

development and execution of a practicum that demonstrates the program objectives through a project within participants' area of work in Ascension. This helps participants bring their work home, and make it relevant to what they do every day.

There are challenges in such a program. It demands a lot of women and men who are not theologians. It asks leaders with faith commitments as Jews, Muslims, Hindus or mainline and Evangelical Protestants to learn Catholic theology. It requires a significant commitment from executives that have many other responsibilities.

In 14 years we have never encountered resistance from participants, nor are we aware that anyone has been offended by the invitation to theological study. An important element of formation is creating an environment that is hospitable to questions and dialogue and that encourages participants to bring perspectives from their own traditions, beliefs, perspectives and questions into the conversation. We believe this approach allows learning but alleviates worries about proselytization.

## INTEGRATION THROUGH BASIC THEOLOGICAL AFFIRMATIONS

To address the challenges of providing meaningful access to serious theological concepts within limited timeframes, we built a series of eight-week courses.[13] Each course is rooted in a set of theological claims or affirmations that provide continuity and reinforcement.

The affirmations deepen leaders' understanding of the reign of God, ministry, and theology of persons. Each affirmation has a direct connection to the decisions health care leaders make every day. The affirmations provide creative approaches for engagement and offer participants insights into important theological concepts. For instance, Course One: The Mystery of God who Calls, explores the following affirmations:

---

13   See Celeste DeSchryver Mueller, "Connect the Practical to the Theological," *Health Progress* (March – April 2011): 52 – 55 for the logic of the course sequence.

1. God is known and knowable; revealed through experience
2. God is mystery: transcendent and immanent
3. God is a community of persons
4. God is Good; God is Love
5. God is creator who invites co-creation; we are made in image of God
6. God is just and merciful
7. God acts on behalf of the poor and vulnerable
8. God wills the wholeness of all creation

Each session incorporates readings, brief videos and group discussions. Faculty members meet face-to-face with the participants at the beginning and end of the course. Each course begins with an introduction to uncover the participants' experiences and current knowledge of the topic and ends with an activity for participants to demonstrate and apply what they have learned.

Retreats between courses offer opportunities for participants to engage in theological and spiritual reflection on their individual leadership and organizational practices. The program concludes with an integration retreat in which participants create their ongoing personal formation plan and develop an integration project that serves a particular need within the ministry.

Two concluding comments from participants show the kinds of outcomes we hope for:

> "During this time of formation I have discovered some different ways of thinking about God, church and ministry. I believe the shift in my perspective- though subtle- will have profound effects on my leadership. It already has. . . Very specifically the ethics exercises challenged my thinking and were emotionally challenging. Having spent a professional lifetime practicing obstetrics and gynecology I find that objectivity still eludes me when it comes to reproductive issues. The mechanisms of discernment and the language of different forms of dialogue and discernment remain frustrating and opaque. That being said - this experience has given me an opportunity to learn to listen and engage in healthy dialogue about issues that have been

closed books to me for many years. The practices required for ethical discernment have further shown me how difficult true listening, dialogue, forgiveness and acceptance are. I understand that formation is a lifelong pursuit. This formation time provides me a community through which to pursue it." (A chief medical officer)

Overall, I was surprised at how well all of these teachings integrated with and even enhanced my own spiritual development, despite not being Catholic. The program has helped me to see that spirituality is a lifelong journey that is shaped by the Divine Mystery and not limited on one particular doctrine or set of beliefs." (An executive in quality/risk and safety)

Fig. 3

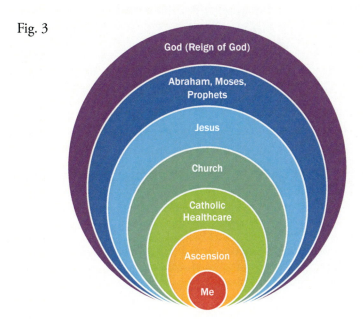

## MY STORY, OUR STORY, GOD'S STORY

The theological framework we have discussed here is represented in Fig. 3, which is used in formation programs and reflections with groups at all levels of responsibility within Ascension. When invited to "describe what you see and what it means to you," participants can articulate personal connections to the unfolding story and pose their own questions about our theological foundations. The successive layers of history evoke a sense of responsibility for being entrusted with a sacred legacy. When invited to picture it in three dimensions, like a wedding cake, the figure suggests the firm foundations, support and resources upon which our associates can rely. It invites reflection on how one's individual story and our common story as Catholic health care is connected to a much wider story: Serving the mission and ministry of the church, carrying out the mission and ministry of Jesus, heeding the vision of the patriarchs and prophets, and realizing the reality and hope of the reign of God.

The following quote from Richard Rohr suggests both the intimate and cosmic dimensions of formation. Perhaps it is an appropriate conclusion to this chapter as we continue the conversation about the nature and methods of theological and spiritual formation:

> Human history is one giant wave of unearned grace, and you are now another wave crashing onto the sands of time, edged forward by the many waves behind you. . . .It is the best and deepest understanding of how God spreads God's forgiving heart through history. It is not a role or office that we are passing on, we are passing on the very love of God from age to age. Apostle means one who is "sent," and we are all sent to advance the history of divine love through space and time.

> Saints and mystics such as Francis and Clare of Assisi, Lady Julian of Norwich, and so many others [with the founders of Catholic health care] have passed this baton on to those who would receive it. They would not be honored or even interested in us pulling them out of their single place in the eternal Divine Flow and making an exception or idol of them. They joined the "great cloud of witnesses" (Hebrews 12:1) and are most honored by you now getting in line with everybody else, just as they did in their time. We are saved by simply remaining in the one circle of life and love, and not by standing separate or superior.

Life is not about being correct but about being connected. At all costs, stay connected! Our only holiness is by participation and surrender to the Body of Love, not by any private performance contest. This is the joining of hands from generation to generation that can and will change the world. Love is One, and this Love is either shared and passed on or it is not the Great Love at all.[14]

---

14  Adapted from Richard Rohr, *Eager to Love: The Alternative Way of Francis of Assisi* (Franciscan Media: 2014): 206 – 207.

### ACKNOWLEDGMENTS

This book began several years ago as I became aware that there were more theological issues in health care than ethics. If health care is a ministry, then it should be informed by the whole breadth of the church's theological tradition. I had to put my work on hold for a few years, but its completion is due to the generous cooperation of many people starting with the authors, who participated in many phone calls and teleconferences to achieve cohesion among the chapters. Their names and biographies follow. To them, my deepest gratitude.

Let me also acknowledge the work of many CHA staff members including my assistant Linda Raney, Ellen Schlanker and Mary Ann Steiner in our communications department and Ken Schanuel in production. Their faithful attention to detail compensated for many of my own limitations.

Sr. Patricia Talone, RSM and Sr. Mary Haddad, RSM, both encouraged this work and provided the time for me to produce it.

Finally, let me thank the fine design folks, especially Liz Mohl and Laura McCarthy at Toky Branding + Design. This is just the latest example of their long and fruitful association with CHA.

Finally, let me acknowledge Jim Triggs and the St. John's Bible in Collegeville, Minnesota. Their magnificent artwork brings our scholarship to life and helps us remember that the beauty of our tradition is not found only in theological propositions.

**FR. CHARLES BOUCHARD, OP**
**EDITOR**

## AUTHOR BIOGRAPHIES

**FR. CHARLES BOUCHARD, OP, S.T.D.,** is senior director, theology and ethics for the Catholic Health Association of the United States, St. Louis. He educates and advises the Catholic health ministry nationwide on the church's theological and ethical teaching, and is executive editor of *Health Care Ethics USA*. Previously, he was vice president for theological education at Ascension Health, St. Louis, from 2008 – 2011 and served as president and professor of moral theology at Aquinas Institute of Theology, St. Louis, for 18 years. He has a doctorate in theology from The Catholic University of America, Washington, D.C.

**BARBARA ANNE CUSACK, J.C.D,** is chancellor for the Archdiocese of Milwaukee and previously served as a judge for the Archdiocese of Chicago. She has been a consultant for a variety of dioceses and committees of the United States Conference of Catholic Bishops. She earned a doctorate in canon law from The Catholic University of America, Washington, D.C., and has been an active member of the Canon Law Society of America since 1983.

**DANIEL J. DALY, PH.D.,** is associate professor, theology at Saint Anselm College in Manchester, New Hampshire. He received his Ph.D. in theological ethics from Boston College. Dr. Daly's research and publications have focused on end of life ethics, virtue ethics, and the morality of social structures. He also serves on the ethics boards of Catholic Medical Center and the Eliot Hospital in Manchester.

**ZENI FOX, PH.D.,** is professor emerita, pastoral theology, Immaculate Conception Seminary at Seton Hall University, South Orange, New Jersey. She received her Ph.D. from Fordham University. She is co-editor of *Called and Chosen: Toward a Spirituality for Lay Leaders* and the author of books and articles on lay ministry and laity in Catholic health care. She presently serves as a member of the Sponsor for Ascension, St. Louis.

**RICHARD GAILLARDETZ, PH.D.,** is the Joseph Professor of Catholic Systematic Theology at Boston College and chair of the theology department. He received his Ph.D. in systematic theology from the University of Notre Dame, Notre Dame, Indiana. Dr. Gaillardetz has published numerous articles and has authored or edited 13 books. He served as president of the Catholic Theological Society of America from 2013 – 2014.

**FR. DAVID GENTRY-AKIN, S.T.D.,** is professor of theology at Saint Mary's College of California, Moraga, California, where he is currently serving as chair of the department. He earned his M. Div. from the University of Notre Dame, Notre Dame, Indiana, and his pontifical licentiate and doctorate in sacred theology (S.T.L., S.T.D.) from the Catholic University of Louvain in Leuven, Belgium. He is a Roman Catholic priest of the diocese of Stockton, California.

**DARREN M. HENSON, PH.D.,** is system vice president, mission and discernment, at Presence Health in Chicago. He earned a Ph.D. in religious studies with a specialization in Catholic health care from Marquette University, Milwaukee. He also earned the pontifical degree of a licentiate in sacred theology and a master of divinity from the University of St. Mary of the Lake, Mundelein, Illinois.

**SR. SHARON HOLLAND, IHM, J.C.D,** is vice president, General Leadership Council, of the Sisters, Servants of the Immaculate Heart of Mary in Monroe, Michigan. She served as a consultant to religious congregations and sponsored ministries in health care and higher education and was president of the U.S. Leadership Conference of Women Religious (LCWR) for three years. From 1988 – 2009, Sr. Sharon served at the Vatican Congregation for Institutes of Consecrated Life and Societies of Apostolic Life (CICLSAL) working with canonical matters regarding religious institutes, constitutions, public juridic persons and ecclesiastical property. She earned her doctorate in canon law from the Gregorian University in Rome.

**CONOR M. KELLY, PH.D.,** is assistant professor in the department of theology at Marquette University, Milwaukee. He earned his Ph.D. in theological ethics from Boston College and holds master's and bachelor's degrees in theology from the University of Notre Dame, Notre Dame, Indiana. His research focuses on the connections between theology, ethics and everyday life.

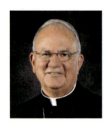

**MOST REVEREND ROBERT N. LYNCH, D.D.,** is bishop emeritus of the St. Petersburg Diocese in St. Petersburg, Florida. He served as bishop of the diocese from 1996 until his retirement in 2016. He serves on the board of the Catholic Relief Services Foundation as well as the Catholic Foundation. From 2002 – 2007, Bishop Lynch was board chair of Catholic Relief Services and was a board member of the Catholic Health Association from 2007 – 2012. He has a master of divinity from Pope John XXIII National Seminary, Weston, Massachusetts.

**M. THERESE LYSAUGHT, PH.D.,** is associate dean and professor of moral theology and health care ethics at the Institute of Pastoral Studies at Loyola University Chicago. She also has a secondary appointment at Loyola's Neiswanger Institute for Bioethics at the Stritch School of Medicine. In addition to consulting with health care systems regarding mission, theology and ethics, she is the co-editor and author of numerous publications, including *Caritas in Communion: Theological Foundations of Catholic Health Care* published by the Catholic Health Association in 2014. She received her Ph.D. in religion from Duke University, Durham, North Carolina.

**FR. SEÁN CHARLES MARTIN, S.T.D.,** is president of Aquinas Institute of Theology in St. Louis. A priest of the Catholic Diocese of Dallas since 1981, he is a biblical scholar and holds a doctorate in biblical theology from the Pontifical Gregorian University in Rome.

**FR. FRANCIS MORRISEY, OMI, PH.D., J.C.D,** is professor emeritus of canon law at Saint Paul University, Ottawa, Ontario, Canada. He is a member of the special Papal Commission for the simplification of marriage nullity procedures and is a consultant for religious institutes and health systems (MJPs) in the U.S., Canada, Ireland, England and Australia. Formerly he was a consultant for the Congregation for Institutes of Consecrated Life and Societies of Apostolic Life and the Pontifical Council for Legislative Texts. He earned a J.C.D. from Saint Paul University.

**CELESTE MUELLER, D. MIN.,** is vice president, theological and spiritual formation, for Ascension where she provides formation programs, services and resources for Ascension's ministries and subsidiaries. She holds a doctor of ministry in practical theology from Eden Theological Seminary in St. Louis as well as degrees in theology from the University of Notre Dame, Notre Dame, Indiana, and Aquinas Institute of Theology, St. Louis.

**FR. THOMAS O'MEARA, OP, PH.D.,** is the William K. Warren Professor of Theology Emeritus at the University of Notre Dame, Notre Dame, Indiana. Fr. O'Meara is the author of 15 books including, *Theology of Ministry*; *Thomas Aquinas, Theologian*; and *Vast Universe: Extraterrestrials and Christian Revelation*. He earned a Ph.D. at the University of Munich and is a past president of the Catholic Theological Society of America.

**NEIL ORMEROD, D.THEOL,** is professor of theology in the Institute for Religion and Critical Inquiry at Australian Catholic University, Sydney, Australia. He is widely published with expertise in Trinity, ecclesiology and foundational theology. He received his doctorate in theology from Melbourne College of Divinity. He draws inspiration from the work of Bernard Lonergan. His writings regularly appear in *Theological Studies* and *Irish Theological Quarterly*.

**FR. ROBIN RYAN, CP, PH.D.,** is associate professor of systematic theology and director of the Master of Arts in Theology Program at Catholic Theological Union in Chicago. He is the author of *God and the Mystery of Human Suffering: A Theological Conversation Across the Ages* (Paulist Press, 2011) and Jesus and Salvation: Soundings in the Christian Tradition and Contemporary Theology (Liturgical Press, 2015). He earned a Ph.D. in systematic theology from The Catholic University of America, Washington, D.C.

**JAMES M. SCHELLMAN, M.A.,** is vice president for mission integration at Our Lady of Lourdes Regional Medical Center in Lafayette, Louisiana. He previously served as director of the North American Forum on the Catechumenate and as associate director of the International Commission on English in the Liturgy (ICEL). He has a master's degree in theology from the University of Notre Dame, Notre Dame, Indiana.

**SR. CATHERINE VINCIE, RSHM, PH.D.,** is provincial councilor for the Religious of the Sacred Heart of Mary. She served on the faculty of the Aquinas Institute of Theology from 1995 – 2015 and earned a Ph.D. in liturgical studies from The Catholic University of America, Washington, D.C.